A GREEK CRITIC:
DEMETRIUS ON STYLE

THE PHOENIX
SUPPLEMENTARY VOLUMES

A GREEK CRITIC:
DEMETRIUS ON STYLE

BY

G. M. A. GRUBE

THE PHOENIX

JOURNAL OF THE CLASSICAL
ASSOCIATION OF CANADA
SUPPLEMENTARY VOLUME IV

UNIVERSITY OF TORONTO PRESS: 1961

EDITORIAL COMMITTEE

MARY E. WHITE
CHAIRMAN

W. P. WALLACE

L. E. WOODBURY

University of Toronto Press

Diamond Anniversary 1961

PREFACE

EVERYONE knows the *Poetics* and the *Rhetoric* of Aristotle, and that Plato banished the poets, or most of them, from his ideal republic, but the remaining texts of later Greek critics are to-day very little read, and, indeed, have been much neglected since the eighteenth century. This is probably due in part to the rhetorical slant of ancient literary criticism. Yet the works of Dionysius of Halicarnassus in the first century B.C., the treatise *On the Sublime*, and Demetrius' *On Style* are "rhetorical" only in the Greek sense, for they concern themselves with all literature and with rhetoric as only one of the literary genres. These men were, it is true, all trained in rhetoric, but they were men of letters, not rhetoricians. Their approach was objective: with the exception of Longinus they analysed the finished product and not the mind of the writer and in this they adopted the analytic method of Aristotle and others. Their works embody and preserve for us, within those limits, much of the conventional Greek wisdom on the art of expression through words, while each of them added something of his own. And since the Greeks discovered literature and developed it almost to perfection in nearly all its genres, it is not surprising that all these works are, or should be, of considerable interest to literary students, as to all would-be writers, and that they can still illuminate our own literary taste in an age that is much less concerned with language as an art—a τέχνη.

The treatise *On Style* was traditionally attributed to Demetrius of Phalerum, the contemporary of Theophrastus. This authorship is at least very doubtful, indeed improbable if not impossible, and two generations ago it was the contention of most scholars that the work itself should be dated in the first century B.C., if not A.D., or later. Contemporary scholarship, however, is veering back to a date much closer to the traditional. I have myself argued for a date around 270 B.C., or not much later, but in any case there can now be little doubt that the treatise belongs to Hellenistic times, and is the only extant critical text between Aristotle on the one hand and, on the other, the writers of the first century B.C. in Rome, whose works we possess. This alone would make *On Style* a work of unique interest to students of Greek literature as well as to students of criticism, whether they study the ancient texts in the original Greek or in translations.

This translation is addressed to students of both kinds, and, indeed, to a wider circle also, for our author should have a much wider appeal to all those interested in using their own language effectively and with some artistic skill. Both the introduction and the notes, which are printed *pari passu* with the translation, aim to give such information as may be helpful to general readers, as well as to convince the specialist of the soundness of my contentions; the appendixes are especially directed to the latter, but it is my hope that even these may be of interest to those with little or no Greek. I have tried to write a translation in the true sense, not a mere exegesis of the Greek text.

For indeed there is much in our Demetrius which has a direct and immediate appeal to anyone interested in style, whether of writing or speaking. His discussion of the proper style of letter-writing is justly celebrated, and unique. We have no other such discussion till centuries later, and then nothing as good. And as we write our sloppy and hasty letters of today, we might do well to remember that "everyone draws, in his letters, an image of his personality" and that "a letter is a piece of writing and is sent to someone as a kind of gift." Demetrius may not be an original genius like Longinus, and we shall see that he has his weaknesses, but his literary judgments are nearly always sound and obviously based on his own reading and study, even though he often uses what were already stock examples, as every teacher and critic does, and as the ancients never hesitated to do. Their attitude is quite obvious from the fact that the same, usually excellent, examples—like Demosthenes' use of *klimax* quoted in section 270—recur in critics and rhetoricians centuries apart: once a perfect example of a certain figure or quality of speech is found, why look for another, probably less good? In any case, Demetrius uses plenty of illustrations not found in other extant texts, and to regard him as a mere excerpter from other (unknown) writers is, in my opinion, quite unwarranted.

On the contrary, as we read the text, a definite personality seems to emerge, one with the gift of the striking phrase ("Every master is monosyllabic to his slaves"), a discerning eye ("Pretence and frigidity are alike. One who deals with a trivial subject in weighty language is like a man who pretends to qualities he does not possess..."), with a dry humour of his own, and, indeed, with some independence of mind, which I believe he shows in his treatment of Aristotle and elsewhere. Moreover, his analysis of the four "styles" or manners of writing is far more pliable, more useful, and more realistic than the later rigid formula of "the three styles." The best way to appreciate Demetrius is to read a play of Shakespeare or any great modern speech—be it the Gettysburg address, a fireside chat, or a piece of Churchillian oratory—with Demetrius' figures and qualities in mind. His relevance will then be obvious.

I wish to acknowledge my indebtedness to the editions of L. Radermacher and Rhys Roberts. Both published at the turn of the century, they are still the standard editions.

It has been my privilege to read Demetrius with graduate students on several occasions in the last few years, and all teachers know how useful that can be. Among these the Rev. Angus Macdougall, with whom I read the text while this book was being prepared, was particularly helpful.

I also owe much to a number of colleagues, and particularly to members of the *Phoenix* editorial committee: Professors R. J. Getty, Walter Graham, Mary White, W. P. Wallace, and L. E. Woodbury—all of whom read the manuscript as a whole or in part, and made many helpful suggestions. Professor Woodbury and Professor A. Dalzell also read through the proofs and have my special thanks. Needless to say, whatever inaccuracies, mistakes, or wrong theories are still found in what follows are my sole responsibility.

G.M.A.G.

Trinity College, University of Toronto

CONTENTS

INTRODUCTION

INTRODUCTION

THE BACKGROUND

GREEK criticism of literature was derived from two distinct and independent sources, the philosophical and the rhetorical. The philosophers were first in the field. As early as 500 B.C. we find Xenophanes and Heraclitus vigorously censuring Homer for his immoral and untrue stories about the gods.[1] Thus started what Plato was to call the ancient quarrel between poetry and philosophy, in which the philosophers stressed the social responsibility of the poet, and the importance they attached to this reflects the vital place of poetry in the life of Classical Greece. Formal education consisted, as is well known, mainly of physical training, music, and poetry, especially Homer. The Olympian gods cared little for the conduct of their worshippers; except for a very few traditional requirements such as the sanctity of an oath, respect for parents, and the laws of hospitality, they insisted only on the performance of due ritual. There was no preaching in the temples, and men turned to the poets for guidance in the art of living. Hence the deep-rooted feeling that the poets were the teachers of men; we find this point of view first clearly formulated in Aristophanes, but it is, as a feeling if not a theory, very much older. This moral responsibility might well have surprised Homer, but Hesiod would have accepted it, so would most of the lyric poets, and by the time of the great tragedians it was well established. In any case, where poetry is a vital force in society, it cannot live in an ivory tower. Art for art's sake is a theory which does not arise until poetry has retired to the study and music to the studio. It was therefore very natural that criticism of literature—and this up to the third quarter of the fifth century meant criticism of poetry exclusively—should, particularly in Greece, have begun as moral criticism, as criticism of content rather than of form, and this philosophical approach was rarely absent in the better critics of antiquity.

From the middle of the fifth century, however, a quite different approach to literature was being developed by the teachers of rhetoric.

[1]H. Diels, *Die Fragmente der Vorsokratiker*⁶ (Berlin 1951), Xenophanes fragments 1 and 11, also 14, 15, 32, and 34. Heraclitus fragments 40 and 42.

3

First in Sicily, then in Athens, with the growth of democracy, the art of swaying assemblies and juries was the road to political power, and this was clearly recognized by the ambitious. Teachers of rhetoric were in great demand, and the Sophistic movement arose to fill this demand, for, in spite of their individual differences, the Sophists all had an interest in language in common.

When Gorgias of Leontini came to Athens in 427 B.C. and brought with him from Sicily all the tricks of his rhetorical trade, he is said to have taken Athens by storm. Certainly, the Athenians were predisposed to appreciate the new art of speech: their education had endowed them with a sensitive appreciation of poetry; they eagerly discussed the works of the great dramatists; they had applauded Pericles and other orators in the assembly. Indeed it may well be argued that they were already thoroughly familiar, in practice, with Gorgias' antitheses, homoioteleuta, balanced clauses, and so forth, and it is probable that the direct influence of Gorgias on the style of the great writers of the time, Euripides and Thucydides for example, has been exaggerated by both ancient and modern critics. Nevertheless, as the first *theorists* of the art of language, the Sophists did have a very great influence on the development of Greek style.

When Gorgias praised the power of Logos, the spoken word, he was claiming for prose a place by the side of poetry as a sister art and he clearly wakened the Athenians to a new awareness of the art of speech. Indeed, when Aristotle speaks of the old simple style of writing,[2] he means writers before the time of Gorgias, including Herodotus. As a theoretical innovator, however, Gorgias went too far, and it was easy for Aristotle and later critics to ridicule his poetic diction, his far-fetched metaphors, his too neatly-balanced clauses, his word-jingles, rhymes, and the rest. Indeed his fragments fully deserve their censures.

Gorgias and the other teachers of rhetoric were interested only in the art of persuasion, in rhetorical tricks to arouse the emotions of an audience, and Plato was no doubt right when he maintained that they felt no moral responsibility whatever. "The word" said Gorgias "is a mighty power;... it can end fear, remove pain, bring joy, and increase pity." He went on to extol the power of words to play upon human emotions, and to show how a speech (*logos*) can delight and persuade a great crowd "not because it is spoken with truth but because it is skilfully composed." Gorgias may be regarded as the first conscious technician of the art of speech in continental Greece; he brought with him an already well-developed technical vocabulary. From him ultimately derives that

[2]*Rhetoric* 3.9.1–2. For Gorgias' praise of Logos see Diels, 2. 290.

tendency to analyze figures of speech and thought which, in the rhetorical works of later criticism, often looks upon literature, from Homer down, as a mere treasure-house of rhetorical devices.

This emphasis on the means of persuasion and on rousing the emotions, fear and pity in particular, without regard for morality or truth, naturally went hand in hand with scepticism, with a questioning of all accepted values. The new teachers undoubtedly helped to undermine the traditional education of Athens and the traditional social morality. Because of this they aroused the anger and resentment of conservative Athenians, whose spokesman was Aristophanes, the great comic poet (ca. 450–385 B.C.).

The comedies of Aristophanes bear convincing witness to the important place which poetry—tragedy in particular but not tragedy only—held in Athenian life. They are full of literary allusions, parodies, and criticisms which he expected his audience, the people of Athens, to appreciate and enjoy. His hatred of the new education and the new scepticism is especially clear in the *Clouds* (423 B.C.), where Socrates is his chief butt. For twenty years he attacked Euripides as the exponent of the modern spirit. But Aristophanes' greatest contribution to literary criticism is the famous contest in the *Frogs* between Euripides and Aeschylus for the Chair of Tragedy in Hades. The comedy was produced in 405 B.C., soon after Euripides' death. Aeschylus had been in his grave for fifty years, and he stands here as the defender of tradition. Euripides is attacked for his immoral subjects and evil influence, but there is also much criticism that is purely aesthetic, where the younger poet is censured for his realism, his innovations in metre and music, his use of a narrative prologue, his excessive use of lyric monodies, his prosaic everyday language. The whole debate puts before us two different views of drama, and of literature generally, which are perennial and irreconcilable. The differences can in part be explained historically: the tempo of Aeschylean tragedy was already archaic in 405 B.C. and so was a good deal of its language; the more "sophistic" techniques of Euripides are also partly due to his date. Essentially, however, the conflict goes very much deeper, for it is the conflict between the romantic and the realist, the former believing that many true things are better ignored, the latter that truth, the whole truth, will make men free. The grand manner of Aeschylus requires the grand style and impressive language; the realism of Euripides inevitably requires a simpler diction. Aristophanes' sympathies were all with Aeschylus, but the criticisms of him which he puts in the mouth of Euripides also neatly hit the mark, and in the end he refuses to judge between them as dramatists or as poets. The contest is one of the most vivid pieces of literary criticism in ancient literature, as well as the most amusing. For all his dislike of the new techniques, Aristophanes was clearly thoroughly familiar with them.

So was Plato (who was growing to manhood at this time) in spite of all the bitter things he said against the Sophists and rhetoricians in his dialogues. In practice he was a most careful stylist, and one likes to remember the story told by Dionysius of Halicarnassus that, when Plato died, tablets found among his belongings showed how he had tried many different word-orders for that simple, easy-flowing sentence with which he begins his *Republic*.[3] His style takes its place in the history of fourth-century Greek prose as the superb culmination of that process of development which Gorgias and the rhetoricians had started about the time of Plato's birth. But Plato was a philosopher, the disciple of Socrates. He knew, better than Aristophanes, that Socrates had laboured for a much deeper, more philosophic education than that of the Sophists, an education which aimed at philosophic inquiry into the nature of reality by way of painful self-knowledge and self-criticism. When, a teacher himself and the spiritual heir of Socrates, Plato opened his Academy in the eighties of the fourth century, it was natural that he should examine critically the claims of those other teachers old and new, the poets and the rhetoricians. It is thus that he approaches rhetoric in the *Gorgias*, and poetry in the *Republic*. What are their claims to knowledge and what is it they can claim to teach? The world of literature has never forgiven Plato for banishing the poets, or at any rate most of them, from his ideal republic, but that banishment is essentially a challenge to the poets to recognize their social responsibility, a challenge which has never been completely answered. Every civilized state except ancient Athens has adopted Plato's theory of censorship—the subordination of the artist to the legislator, in some form or other. Nor have they waited, before doing so, for the establishment of the ideal republic or the rule of the philosopher-king! Plato was deeply convinced that poetry, music, and the arts had a tremendous influence upon the formation of character, and he was terribly afraid of an uncritical emotional response to that influence, especially in drama where impersonation makes the response more immediate and more complete, both for the actor and for the audience. Hence the vigour of his attack, and his forbidding the impersonation of any evil at all upon the stage.

His theory of art as imitation of life does not mean, of course, that the best painting is a coloured photograph or the best drama a mere record

[3]*On Composition*, ch. 25.   Diogenes Laertius (3.37) tells the same story and attributes it to Euphorion and Panaetius.

of actual conversations, though it must be confessed that his ironically emphatic language almost seems to say so at times. It does mean, however, that the artist, and especially the dramatist, must draw his material from life and be true to life. This is, to him, an accepted truism[4] rather than an original theory, and, after it had been more calmly stated and more fully worked out by Aristotle, it was never challenged in antiquity. Moreover, when he insisted that the poet could not directly imitate or represent the eternal verities that are the Platonic Forms, but could do so only indirectly as they are mirrored in actual life, was he not right at least to the extent that drama must be represented through individuals, and that a drama of pure ideas is not drama, or indeed poetry, at all?

The *Phaedrus* is a corrective of the too intellectual and social approach of the *Republic* with its apparent attack upon passion and emotion. The myth of the *Phaedrus* is a superb vindication of passion and inspiration, but the inspiration must come from the gods. This, translated into philosophical terms, means that the passion of the poet must be directed towards beauty and truth, and directed by reason.

The second part of the *Phaedrus* is written in a calmer mood. It sets out to discover how to write well, whether in prose or verse, and it contains a statement of basic critical principles. Plato states clearly, for the first time, the difference between criticism of form and of content.[5] He insists that the writer must know his subject and adds ironically that he will find this useful even if his aim is only to deceive. He must define his subject. Every *logos*, every work of prose or poetry, should have a definite structure, with a place and function for each part, like a living organism ($\zeta\hat{\omega}o\nu$), with a beginning, middle, and end, and with every part in its proper place, in its proper relation to the whole. The techniques of writing or speaking are a preliminary requirement, but technique is not art. Plato dwells on this last point at some length: the man who knows the notes of the musical scale but cannot relate them to each other is no musician; the man who knows the effects of drugs but not when to use them is no doctor; the man who can make speeches, long or short, to arouse pity or fear, but knows not *when* to make them, is no tragic poet. Sophocles and Euripides would laugh at his pretensions "knowing well that the art of tragedy is no other than the interrelating of these elements in a manner fitting to each other and to the whole work." And Plato goes on to pour ridicule upon the rhetoricians' boast that they can arouse and calm emotions at will, as also upon their ever more complex technical

[4]*Laws* 2. 668b-c.
[5]At 236a he formulates it as a difference between $\delta\iota\acute{a}\theta\epsilon\sigma\iota\varsigma$ and $\epsilon\check{\upsilon}\rho\epsilon\sigma\iota\varsigma$.

vocabulary and their neglect of the fundamentals of their own craft.[6]

Plato discussed poetry and music once more, in the second book of the *Laws*, the work of his old age. *Mousikê*, which includes both, is a gift of the gods with two functions: the training of the emotions in youth and the recreation of emotional stability at all ages. Poetry and music have their roots in primary human needs and instincts, in the natural need for motion and utterance. As the random movements of the infant, gradually brought to orderly control by the human sense of harmony and rhythm, culminate in the dance, so the same sense of rhythm and meaning brings under control the infant's random cries until this process culminates in reasoned speech and ultimately in poetry. We all speak and move; we are all to some extent poets and musicians.

There are, in the *Laws*, three criteria by which art must be judged: one of these is still the moral criterion; the second is pleasure, even though Plato insists that it must be the pleasure of the educated and that art must not be judged, as we might put it, by box-office receipts. The third criterion is artistic or aesthetic, even though the formulation of it is rather rudimentary, that is, the "correctness" of the imitation. Both pleasure and artistic perfection are thus recognized as criteria. We are further told that the poet need not be the judge of the moral values of his work but he must, in that case, accept the judgment of the legislator who in turn must, in order to give an adequate judgment, understand the aim of the artist.[7]

The *Poetics* of Aristotle continues the philosophic approach to literature and at many points tries to answer Plato. It is important to realize that Aristotle accepts, in the main, the moral approach of Plato and his philosophic predecessors. This is quite clear from the *Politics*, the only place where he discusses the function of *mousikê* in society. Even in the

---

[6]*Phaedrus* 255–267. Plato selects a few technical terms for mention: προοίμιον (proem or exordium), διήγησις (statement or narrative), μαρτυρία (witnesses' evidence), τεκμήριον (proof), τὰ εἰκότα (probability), πίστωσις (proof or confirmation), ἐπιπίστωσις (further proof), ἔλεγχος (refutation), ἐπεξέλεγχος (further refutation), ὑποδήλωσις (insinuation), παρέπαινος (indirect praise), παράψογος (indirect censure), διπλασολογία (repetition), εἰκονολογία (figurative language), ὀρθοέπεια (correct diction), ἐπάνοδος (recapitulation). This casual selection of technical terms, some of which do not recur elsewhere, obviously from a far larger number, is a salutary reminder of how little we know of the rhetorical vocabulary of the fourth century. Some of these elaborate compounds are of the kind we often consider as "later" because we do not come across them again till Roman times.

[7]*Laws* 2.653–673. For full references and a discussion of Plato's views on poetry and rhetoric see my *Plato's Thought* (London 1935 and Boston 1958) 179–215.

Poetics tragedy is "the imitation of a morally good action."[8] He accepts the principle of censorship, and the place of poetry and music in both education and recreation. He accepts, too, Plato's theory of art as "imitation," *mimêsis*, though he adds that the poet may imitate or represent things as they are, as they were, as they were thought to be, or as they ought to be, thus making it clear that the Greek *mimêsis* does not mean copying. He modifies the moral criterion to the extent that any evil act or speech in a play must be judged not in itself but in relation to the effect of the play as a whole, and in relation to the character concerned. His theory of catharsis: "tragedy . . . by means of pity and fear achieves the purgation (catharsis) of such emotions" is now generally accepted as a medical metaphor. The effect, as he explains in the *Politics*, is the same as that of orgiastic music which through exciting emotions to a crisis has an ultimately calming effect. And he answers Plato by suggesting that "the more vulgar parts of an audience, mechanics and general labourers . . . whose souls are perverted from their natural state" and in a state of over-excitement, need this catharsis to recreate emotional stability and that this kind of dramatic performance should therefore be allowed. The passage makes it abundantly clear that the cathartic effect of drama is mainly restricted to these weaker types. The Aristotelian philosopher, who has perfect emotional control, presumably remains unaffected. Even Aristotle's theory of the tragic hero as neither villain nor saint, but a man with some flaw in his character and therefore more "like ourselves," recognizes the need at least for weaker men, if not for himself, of that emotional identification which Plato so greatly feared. Moreover, where he insists upon the unity of plot (the only kind of unity he does insist on) and explains how one incident should follow the other as inevitable or at least probable, with the end emerging from the plot itself, he is elaborating upon the Platonic conception of the unity of a work of art as an organism. He adds important suggestions of his own: the preference for an unhappy ending, the importance of *peripeteia* or the sudden change of direction toward misfortune, and of recognition and discovery. The *Poetics* is a triumph of unemotional analysis; it is extraordinarily suggestive in detail; some of its limitations are due, however, precisely to the fact that the author's emotions are nowhere engaged.

[8]The πρᾶξις σπουδαία in Aristotle's definition of tragedy at least includes the notion of moral goodness. See my *Aristotle on Poetry and Style* (New York 1958) xxi–xxii and xiv–xvii for *mousikê* in the last chapters of the *Politics*. For another view see S. H. Butcher, *Aristotle's Theory of Poetry and Fine Art* (republ. Dover Publications 1951) 198–214.

What we have called the philosophic, as against the rhetorical, approach to literature thus began with moral criticism and continued to insist upon the writer's responsibility to society, but in Plato and Aristotle it also developed a considerable body of literary theory. Of this approach in its purer form the *Poetics* is our last extant example.

During the century between the famous visit of Gorgias to Athens and the publication of Aristotle's *Rhetoric*, textbooks on rhetoric multiplied, and it is these which both Plato and Aristotle regard with contempt. Most of them, undoubtedly, were purely technical and amoral. Of this considerable literature very little remains. We know that Thrasymachus of Chalcedon, a contemporary of Gorgias, was an adept at arousing and again calming the passions of his audiences, that he paid some attention to rhythm, wrote in short rhythmical clauses, and affected the use of paeonic feet. He seems to have been able to arrange his material clearly, to express his thoughts with succinct compactness, and to have developed a kind of prose diction that was neither too poetical, like that of Gorgias, nor lacking in distinction.[9] We have a short essay of another rhetorician, Alcidamas, on the necessity for an orator to speak extempore.

But if rhetoric finally established itself as *the* higher education from the fourth century B.C. onward—and to this place of rhetoric in education the rhetorical nature of our later critical texts is largely due—the credit or discredit for this should be given mainly to Isocrates (436–338 B.C.). Several years older than Plato, he died at the time of the battle of

[9]For Thrasymachus' capacity to rouse the emotions see Plato, *Phaedrus* 267c and Aristotle, *Rhetoric* 3.1.7. Also *Rhet.* 3.8.4 for his use of paeonic rhythms. His short rhythmic clauses are mentioned by Cicero, who contrasts them with the rounded periods of Isocrates (*Orator* 39–40). Dionysius of Halicarnassus, in *Lysias* ch. 6, credits him and Lysias with a virtue of style which he defines as ἡ συστρέφουσα τὰ νοήματα καὶ στρογγύλως ἐκφέρουσα, λέξις οἰκεία πάνυ καὶ ἀναγκαία τοῖς δικανικοῖς λόγοις καὶ πάνυ ἀληθεῖ ἀγῶνι. . . . This I believe to mean the capacity to express thoughts succinctly and compactly. That the usual interpretation of this "virtue" as the periodic style is mistaken, seems to be proved conclusively by the fact that in ch. 8 Dionysius specifically tells us that Lysias' ἠθοποιΐα made him use a simple and *not* a periodic word-arrangement, ὁρῶν ὅτι οὐκ ἐν τῇ περιόδῳ καὶ τοῖς ῥυθμοῖς, ἀλλ' ἐν τῇ διαλελυμένῃ λέξει γίγνεται τὸ ἦθος. In his *Demosthenes* ch. 3 the same author speaks of Thrasymachus as the originator of a τρίτη λέξις. What he has in mind, I believe, is a third type of diction or ἐκλογή, neither the poetic diction of Gorgias nor the language of conversation, and not a third style including both diction and word-arrangement, so that diction is the subject of the first part of the *Demosthenes* and word-arrangement of the second part. For a full discussion of these interpretations see my "Thrasymachus, Theophrastus and Dionysius of Halicarnassus" *AJP* 73 (1952) 251–267. See also G. A. Kennedy's "Theophrastus and Stylistic Distinctions" in *Harvard Studies in Classical Philology* 72 (1957). He agrees that "the stylistic distinctions of Dionysius of Halicarnassus (i.e., in the first seven sections of the *Demosthenes*) are made on the basis of diction" (p. 101).

Chaeronea which established Philip's supremacy over Greece. He was the teacher of most of the great Athenians of his day. He called himself a philosopher, though neither Plato nor Aristotle would have conceded him the title. He had little respect for "useless" knowledge; he was the apostle of general education, which for him consisted in being able to speak well on great subjects—and this also meant to be able to write. He rejected, however, the amorality of the rhetorical technicians; he insisted that you cannot speak well on noble subjects without practical knowledge of them, and, furthermore, since an orator (or writer) must make a good impression on his audience, he will desire to be a good man: "To speak well is the greatest sign of intelligence; a truthful, lawful, just speech is the outward image of a good and loyal soul."[10] The later theory of Cicero and Quintilian, that the good orator is a good man— *vir bonus dicendi peritus*, as old Cato put it[11]—ultimately derives from Isocrates' theories of education, superficial as these obviously were.

It may be added that Isocrates, though included in the later canon of the Ten Attic Orators, was prevented from public speaking by a physical handicap; he published his speeches as pamphlets, and *logos* obviously means, to him, both the written and the spoken word. Of poetry he says very little. He was a pupil of Gorgias and a very careful stylist: antitheses and balanced clauses follow one another in carefully constructed periods, and he avoids any hiatus like the plague. His patriotism was sincere, but it never caused him to write an inelegant sentence, and the total effect— we have a considerable number of his "speeches"—is one of deadly monotony. His contemporary influence however was very great (greater than that of the Academy or the Lyceum); his posthumous influence was no less—we can trace it clearly in the texts we possess, in Cicero, Dionysius, and Quintilian.

Although Isocrates was a teacher of the art of speech, he was hardly a rhetorician in the strict sense; he did try to communicate to his pupils a general philosophic outlook. For an example of the more strictly rhetorical approach at this time we have to go to a treatise preserved for us among the works of Aristotle, the *Rhetorica ad Alexandrum*. The dedication, a letter from Aristotle to Alexander the Great, is an obvious forgery. The work itself, however, is definitely dated in the fourth century B.C. and often thought to be the work of a contemporary of Aristotle, the rhetorician and historian Anaximenes. It is, at any rate, our sole remaining example of the more sophistical treatises of the period. It displays the completely cynical, amoral attitude which was so repugnant

---

[10]*Nicocles* 7. See also *Antidosis* 184, 207, 271–272, 344.

[11]Seneca Rhetor, *Controversiae* 1. Praef. 9; cp. Quintilian 1. Praef. 9.

to Plato; it is concerned exclusively with the question: what kind of arguments will, in particular kinds of cases, be convincing? These are listed, named, and described at considerable length and with great precision. Even if this particular work was not written before Aristotle's *Rhetoric*, there can be no doubt that many works of the type were in existence, and it is against this kind of background that the *Rhetoric* of Aristotle must be judged.

Unlike the *Poetics*, the *Rhetoric* had an immediate and lasting influence in antiquity. It is a very different kind of book, for here Aristotle meets the rhetoricians on their own ground. He writes the kind of book which should be written about their craft. Indeed, it might well be said that he establishes the art, and even Isocrates' theory of education, on a much more solid philosophic foundation. Aristotle himself, in the *Poetics*, refers us to the *Rhetoric* for all that concerns the expression of thought in words, be it in poetry or prose. For we should never forget that *rhêtorikê* was the art of expression as a whole, even if oratory was the art of expression par excellence. And in part Aristotle is still, as so often, answering Plato: he sets forth in the first two books the kind of knowledge of politics and psychology which an orator should have, and which can suffice, the kinds of arguments and proofs, based on probability, which he should employ. The first twelve chapters of the third book then deal with style, and concern us closely; we shall see that the author of our treatise *On Style* is thoroughly familiar with them, and much indebted to them. Many of the later critical and rhetorical formulae of the schools appear here for the first time, at least for us.

Among these are the statement that the diction of poetry is necessarily different from that of prose; the division of rhetoric into three kinds : the forensic, the deliberative, and the epideictic; the division of style into diction (or the choice of words) and the arrangement of the words thus chosen; the further division of word-arrangement into the running or strung-along style of the "ancient" writers and the periodic structure. Here too are the divisions of a speech into proem or introduction, narrative, proofs, and epilogue. Aristotle will allow only these four; he would prefer two only, statement and proof, and he mentions with Platonic contempt the over-subtle subdivisions affected by contemporary rhetoricians. Prose must have rhythm but not metre, a statement repeated for centuries by Greek and Roman critics.

Aristotle recognizes only one "virtue" (ἀρετή) of style, lucidity. This is most easily attained by the use of current, everyday language, but men like the strange and the new, so we must introduce a certain number of unusual words and a degree of ornamentation, in order to strike a happy mean, always making our style suitable and fitting (πρέπον, the Latin *decorum*) to the occasion, the audience, and the speaker. Aristotle deals at length with metaphor, the chief ornament he allows in prose; it is also the one thing that cannot be learned from others for it involves a capacity to see similarities in things. Like every Greek, Aristotle is well aware of the importance of semantics, of whether, as he puts it, you call Orestes his mother's murderer or the avenger of his father. The discussion of style ends with an attempt to analyze the reasons for successful sayings:[12] their success is related to man's delight in learning something new—a delight that can be derived from a good metaphor, a particularly apt word, a clever antithesis or argument. All these gain from brevity, for example, Pericles' famous remark after many young Athenians had been lost in battle that "the year had lost its spring." Vividness, riddles or half-riddles, similes, proverbs, hyperboles, all these can contribute to success. Moreover, there is not one perfect style suited to all occasions; each kind of rhetoric has its own appropriate style. The style of written work is not that of debate; it is more precise, less histrionic. Nor will Aristotle accept brevity as necessarily a good thing: one should be neither too concise nor too verbose, but seek the right mean.

The rest of the book is more definitely concerned with rhetoric in the more restricted sense: it deals in turn with the aim and purpose of each of the four parts of a discourse and how the speaker should deal with each part (13–17). This section is also much drier and more technical in style. If Aristotle shared Plato's contempt for the technicalities of the rhetoricians, he had a good deal more patience in dealing with them.[13]

From the time of Aristotle to the first century B.C. we have no extant critical texts, unless indeed it be our treatise *On Style*. We know that Theophrastus, the disciple and successor of Aristotle, wrote a book on style, the περὶ λέξεως. The references to this work in later writers, who

[12]Ch. 10. It is obvious from the illustrations in this chapter that ἀστεῖα does not refer to witticisms only (the later meaning of the word) but to "happy" or "felicitous" sayings. See the word ἀστεῖος in App. I, A under ἀστεϊσμός.

[13]Aristotle (*Rhet.* 3.13) would, as a philosopher, prefer to recognize only two necessary parts of a speech, the statement (πρόθεσις) and the proofs (πίστεις). However, he compromises by accepting four: the introduction (προοίμιον), the statement or narrative (πρόθεσις or διήγησις), the proofs, and the epilogue or peroration (ἐπίλογος). He notes and discards as ridiculous further subdivisions such as ἀντιπαραβολή (contrast), ἐπάνοδος (recapitulation). From Theodorus of Byzantium, he quotes ἐπιδιήγησις (supplementary narrative), προδιήγησις (preliminary narrative), ἔλεγχος (refutation), ἐπεξέλεγχος (supplementary refutation), and, from Licymnius ἐπούρησις (improving one's case, lit. wafting along), ἀποπλάνησις (digressions, lit. wanderings) and ὄζοι (ramifications).

usually mention him along with Aristotle, are scrappy and tantalizing. Scholars have attempted to reconstruct his critical theories, but the evidence is insufficient. On the whole it would seem that he did not depart very far from his master's theories which he expanded and explained.[14]

During the third and second centuries B.C., Alexandria developed a school of literary scholarship rather than of rhetoric or literary criticism. The scholars of the Museum edited, with commentary, all the great classical writers. The catalogues of the great library formed the basis of the first histories of literature, while the commentaries did evolve some critical principles, notably those of Aristarchus (*ca.* 217–143 B.C.). He stated that Homer must be interpreted in the light of the social customs of his day and not those of a later age; that any statement must be judged by reference to the character who makes it or, as he put it, "all that is said in Homer is not said by Homer"; that poets must be given some licence in dealing with historical facts: they need not tell us every detail of what happens but may leave certain things to the reader's imagination. Aristarchus championed the unity of Homer and he may have defended the artistic unity of the *Iliad* and the *Odyssey*.[15]

We know that the so-called Asiatic style developed rapidly as the Greek language spread over Asia Minor and that Hegesias of Magnesia (*fl.* 250 B.C.) was criticized by Dionysius and Cicero as the great exponent of that florid, over-rhythmical, artificial manner. In the next century Hermagoras revived rhetorical studies and seems to have written a great work in which he classified all the possible kinds of court cases, the different kinds of issues and how each should be dealt with. It must have been during this period too that the various formulae which we find in the Roman rhetorical writers of the first century B.C. were developed: that of the three main styles, for example, or that of a specific number of rhetorical virtues, but we cannot trace the origin of either for lack of evidence. Nor did the philosophers, as far as we can make out, make any further

[14]In particular, scholars have attempted to trace back to Theophrastus the formula of three styles and that of four virtues (ἀρεταί) of style. See H. Rabe, *De Theophrasti libris περὶ λέξεως* (Bonn 1890); A. Mayer, *Theophrasti περὶ λέξεως Fragmenta* (Leipzig 1910); and J. Stroux, *De Theophrasti Virtutibus Dicendi* (Leipzig 1912). See also G. L. Hendrickson, "The Peripatetic Mean of Style and The Three Stylistic Characters," in *AJP* 25 (1904) 125–146, and my "Theophrastus as a Literary Critic," in *TAPA* 83 (1952) 172–183. The controversy is in any case somewhat academic, as most of the ideas involved, apart from the actual formulae, were doubtless discussed by Theophrastus, as they were by Aristotle.

[15]See A. Roemer, *Aristarchs Athetezen in der Homerkritik* (Leipzig 1912) and *Die Homerexegese Aristarchs* (Paderborn 1924); A. Severyns, *Le Cycle épique dans l'école d'Aristarque* (Liège 1928).

substantial contribution. While the Peripatetics probably continued in the tradition of the *Rhetoric* to analyze style and to use both prose and poetry to illustrate the points they made, the Stoics seem to have concentrated on allegorizing Homer so as to make a Stoic of him, and on pure linguistics. Their main contribution seems to have been to add "brevity" to whatever list of rhetorical "virtues" then came into fashion, and though brevity is often to be commended it is not in itself, as Aristotle knew, necessarily a virtue.[16] But the Stoics seem to have despised all conscious stylistic effort, and the Epicureans, by and large, seem to have taken little interest in literature of any kind.

When we come to the first century B.C., however, we again have a large number of texts, partly Latin and partly Greek. As we are here primarily concerned with a Greek treatise, it will not be necessary to follow, in any detail, the development of Roman rhetoric or criticism, for the Greek rhetoricians hardly ever mention a Latin writer or a Latin theorist. This is not primarily due to arrogance, or to discretion, but to the simple fact that they had no need to mention them. They were concerned with Greek literature and with Greek style; they took their illustrations from the Greek authors of the classical age and, to a lesser extent, from those of Alexandria. Nor could they be required to mention Roman critics or rhetoricians, for the Romans took their theories from the Greeks. There were, to be sure, specifically Latin or Roman problems such as, for example, the quarrel between the champions of the ancient Latin writers and those "moderns" who took the Greek classics as their models, but these were of no concern to a Greek writer.

Suffice it to say, therefore, that in the Roman tradition there is nothing to correspond to what we have called the purely philosophical approach. The ancient quarrel between poetry and philosophy was long forgotten, and in any case Rome produced no original philosophers. The approach was therefore rhetorical, but of two kinds: the strictly rhetorical on the one hand, and on the other what may well be called the Isocratean, that more general approach which, though still rooted in rhetorical training, nevertheless stood for a more cultivated outlook and a general interest in human affairs. Our first Latin text, the *Rhetorica ad Herennium*, is of the first, more professionally rhetorical kind. It is preserved among the works of Cicero; it was most probably not written by him, but was in any case written at the time when he was a very young man, probably between 86 and 82 B.C.[17]

[16]*Rhet.* 3.16.4. For the Stoics see Karl Barwick, *Probleme der stoischen Sprachlehre und Rhetorik* (Berlin 1957).
[17]See H. Caplan's edition in the Loeb Library (1954), especially the introduction.

The *Ad Herennium* is of considerable interest as the first extant attempt to Latinize the Greek rhetorical vocabulary, and, although the author is impatient of the over-elaborate subtleties of the Greek rhetoricians, all the formulae are carefully set down: the three kinds of rhetoric which we saw in Aristotle; the main formula, also used by Cicero, of the capacities the orator must possess: he must be able to think of what he should say (*inventio* = εὕρεσις), to order his material (*dispositio* = τάξις), he must have style (*elocutio* = λέξις or ἑρμηνεία), memory, and a good delivery (*actio* = ὑπόκρισις). Each part of a speech, of which the author recognizes six,[18] is discussed; we then proceed to *inventio* in relation to the types of argument to be used in each type of case, and so with the other parts of the main formula. The fourth and last book discusses the three styles, the plain, the grand, and the intermediate, all of which the good orator should be able to use at the right moment, and various kinds of qualities, ornaments, and figures (sixty-four of these altogether).

The more technical of Cicero's rhetorical works are of much the same type—the *De Inventione*, the *Topica*, the *Partitiones Oratoriae*. He shows the same impatience with Greek subtleties and the same inability to shake them off, a greater virtuosity in the translation of technical terms, and an occasional purple patch, usually the introduction. His more general works, however, take a broader, more Isocratean view; in them the technical formulae take second place. The *Brutus* is largely a history of Roman oratory introduced by a brief sketch of Greek oratory. It also, however, contains many passages of more general interest. Cicero wrote very quickly and he is extremely careless in the use of technical terms, but his main concern, as in the three books of the *De Oratore* and in the *Orator*, is to rescue rhetoric from the study of mere techniques, to insist that oratory is an art which must be solidly rooted in a general education in philosophy, history, and jurisprudence, an education in the liberal arts which will ensure a moral education as well. He goes into a good deal of detail but he never forgets his main purpose: the general education of the orator. In spite of his own predilection for the grand manner, he recognizes that the orator must instruct (*docere*) and entertain (*delectare*) as well as rouse the emotions (*movere*) and he must therefore be able to use each of the three styles at the right time (*apte*). His lists of "virtues" of style vary from one work to the other but purity of language (*Latinitas*), lucidity (*dilucide*), appropriateness (*decorum*) and stylistic ornament (*ornatum*) are the most frequent.

When we turn from Cicero to Dionysius of Halicarnassus, who settled

---

[18]The six parts of a speech are (1.3 (4)) *exordium, narratio, divisio, confirmatio, confutatio,* and *conclusio.*

in Rome about twelve years after Cicero's death, we find ourselves in a world still dominated by the rhetorical education but definitely more literary than oratorical. Dionysius never mentions Cicero, nor Horace whose contemporary he was; yet, as we know from his history and from the introduction to his work on the orators, he was extremely well-disposed to the Romans. It was to the cultured Romans of his day that he gave the credit for stamping out, as he thought, the plague of Asianism in style. We have a considerable bulk of his critical writings. One of them, the περὶ συνθέσεως, *On Composition* or *Word-Arrangement*, is a master-piece. It deals with the collocation of words from the point of view of sound, the music of language which results from the sound of letters in combination, from rhythm and pitch and stress. The Greeks were extremely sensitive to this music of language even in prose; Dionysius pursues its aesthetic appeal to its very elements and discusses the sound of each letter and its contribution to the total effect, incidentally giving us a good deal of information about the correct pronunciation of Greek. When dealing with rhythm he tries to prove too much, for he reduces his examples to metrical feet whereas, in prose, it is the total effect that matters, as Theophrastus seems to have realised.[19] Dionysius insists that there must be variety, and that the language-music must be appropriate to the matter, the occasion, and the emotions which the speaker or writer wishes to arouse.

Dionysius recognizes three main styles of word-arrangement, the dry or austere (αὐστηρόν), the flowery (ἀνθηρόν), and the intermediate. The first is the severe style of Thucydides: the words stand apart and cannot be run together, harsh collocations are deliberately used, with an abundance of broad syllables; the rhythms are impressive, the clauses not balanced equally. Sense and sentence-structure do not correspond, smoothness of every kind is avoided and even grammatical sequence at times disregarded. The other extreme is the flowery, elegant word-arrangement of Isocrates, and there the words are run together in flowing continuity, and only the periods come to a definite and distinct end. The clauses are carefully balanced, the rhythms neither too heavy nor too light, all harsh collocations are avoided, as is any hiatus between words. The general effect is like that of a painting where light and shade everywhere merge into one another. The intermediate type, which uses the effects of both extremes at the appropriate time, is the composition or word-arrangement which we find in Homer, Sophocles, Plato, and Demosthenes.[20]

[19] See Demetrius 41, below.
[20] The three styles of word-arrangement are described by Dionysius in his *Composition*, chs. 22–24.

Dionysius' other extant works include fragments of a work on *mimêsis* or emulation, separate studies on the style of Lysias, Isocrates, Demosthenes, and Thucydides, and three short treatises known as the Three Literary Letters. The work on Emulation consisted of brief critical valuations of classical authors much in the manner of Quintilian's historical sketch of Greek and Roman writers in the tenth book of his *Institutio Oratoria*; indeed Dionysius may have been one of Quintilian's sources, but of course only for the Greeks. Dionysius' enthusiasm for Isocrates is for a practitioner of the true practical philosophy, an educator who made his pupils "not only clever speakers but men of good moral character, men who served their house, their city, and the whole of Greece."[21] This is akin to the liberal education of the orator as understood by Cicero and Quintilian, but with more emphasis on rhetoric and less on general education.

Dionysius is unique among our extant critics in that he uses his critical-rhetorical formulae as a means of evaluating the style of an author, and not his authors merely to illustrate the formulae. He quotes freely from their writings and discusses certain passages at considerable length; he compares them with passages from others. This method of comparative criticism seems to have been characteristic of Greek criticism, at least in Rome, in his day, for we know that his contemporary and friend Caecilius of Calacte wrote critical essays on Lysias, whom he preferred to Plato, and attempted comparative valuations of Cicero and Demosthenes, of Demosthenes and Aeschines.[22]

Dionysius has certain weaknesses: he is somewhat naïve and lacking in imagination, as in his strictures on Plato's diction; his moral earnestness betrays him into an unbounded admiration for Isocrates and condemnation of Thucydides as unpatriotic, or as inferior to Herodotus in his choice of subject: "one war, which was neither noble nor fortunate, which had much better not have happened, and, when it had, should have been left to silence and oblivion, and ignored by posterity."[23] It is only fair to add that this kind of nonsense is quietly dropped in his later essay on the historian. The moral earnestness itself, however, shows him to be more a man of letters than a rhetorician in the stricter sense, even though Demosthenes, for him as for Cicero, is the greatest of all writers.

Horace's letter to the Pisos on the *Art of Poetry* is, as already

[21] *Isocrates* 4–7 (543).

[22] See J. W. H. Atkins, *Literary Criticism in Antiquity* (London 1952) 2. 106–108 for references.

[23] *Letter to Pompey*, ch. 3. For a full account of Dionysius' criticism of Thucydides see my "Dionysius of Halicarnassus on Thucydides," in *Phoenix* 4 (1950) 95–110.

mentioned, contemporary with Dionysius. There is little in this informal, delightfully phrased advice that is original. We may note, however, that Horace is, in a sense, trying to do for poetry what Cicero attempted to do for prose: he insists that his poet must understand life and man, and that his work must be true to that knowledge. He emphasizes the need for unity and appropriateness, the need for talent and training, the importance of the choice of subject, of the choice of words, of structure, and so on; behind the deliberate informality of the epistle we can easily trace a thorough knowledge of the critical-rhetorical formulae of the day. But Horace is also concerned with specifically Roman problems, as for example, the controversy between the "ancients" and the "moderns."

After Horace we find ourselves in the world of the rhetorical schools, where the practice of *declamatio* was becoming increasingly fashionable and almost superseding every other method of teaching. Declamations were of two kinds: the *suasoria* in which the pupil had to imagine himself in some historical dilemma—should Alexander, for example, cross the Indus?—and devise a speech appropriate to the occasion; and the *controversia*, where he had to speak in an imaginary, often highly artificial and improbable, law-suit. The masters of rhetoric themselves gave display declamations of both kinds before an admiring public. The elder Seneca published a curious collection of such *suasoriae* and *controversiae* for the benefit of his sons, in which he records the adroit and clever things said by the rhetoricians of the Principate. His book is extant, and from it we gain a better understanding of how this practice, which put all the emphasis on ingenuity and clever epigram—for the same subjects were dealt with again and again—affected silver Latin style. The dangers of declamations and of their increasing artificiality are vigorously denounced throughout the first century by the elder Seneca himself, by Petronius, by Persius, by Tacitus, and at the close of the century by the great Quintilian, but they flourished in spite of them all.[24] It was in the last years of the century that Quintilian published his massive work in twelve books on the education of the orator, the *Institutio Oratoria*. Quintilian was Professor of Rhetoric by imperial appointment, and his book, complete, authoritative, lucid, sensible, not too original and at times more than a little dull, is an almost perfect pattern of what a professorial work should be. We find in it, in proper historical perspective, all the best thought of Rome on education, literature, criticism, and rhetoric.

We have no critical or rhetorical texts in Greek for this period, though

[24]See S. F. Bonner, *Roman Declamation in the Late Republic and Early Empire* (Liverpool 1949) and H. Bornecque, *Les Déclamations et les déclamateurs d'après Sénèque le Père* (Lille 1902).

it is fashionable among scholars today to assign to the first century A.D. both our Demetrius' treatise *On Style*, about the date of which more will be said later, and the famous short treatise *On the Sublime* which tradition attributed to Longinus in the third century A.D. In the second century A.D., however, we have the considerable works of Hermogenes on various qualities of style and forms of argument. They are purely rhetorical text books, dry and over-subtle in distinctions and classifications. We note that the theory of styles is now quite abandoned, and that Demosthenes is solidly established as the one supreme model for the young. The works of Hermogenes continued to be edited, commented on, and studied for the next ten centuries, but no really original mind appears in the vast collection of rhetorical writings which we still possess from that millennium.

Something more needs to be said, however, about the short and fragmentary treatise known as "Longinus on the Sublime."[25] Whatever its date it is a work of original genius. The author knows and uses many of the usual rhetorical formulae, but he remains their master, they never master him. It is not a work on the grand style or any other particular style, indeed the theory of particular styles is completely absent. Rather the author seeks to find the secret of the kind of great writing which suddenly sweeps one off one's feet. He traces it to five sources: vigour of mental conception, strong and inspired emotion, the skilful use of figures, noble diction or the proper choice of words, and dignified and spirited word-arrangement. The first, vigour of mental conception, implies nobility of mind, the power of grasping great ideas, and undoubtedly a certain grandeur. This, however, does not mean grand words; indeed it sometimes requires no words at all, as when Homer makes Ajax stride away in silence when Odysseus addresses him in the underworld, or the simplest of words, as in Ajax' famous prayer to Zeus to clear away the mist from the battlefield "that we may die in daylight." It does imply, however, the capacity to select the significant details and to weld them into a meaningful picture, and of this quality Longinus gives as an example the famous ode of Sappho, preserved here only, which begins "φαίνεταί μοι κεῖνος ἴσος θεοῖσι. . . ."

The treatment of passion is lost. To illustrate the proper use of figures—a favourite subject in rhetorical critics who usually discuss it with great care and dullness—"Longinus" first gives a full and brilliant analysis of one sentence of Demosthenes, the famous Marathon oath in his speech *On the Crown*, and then gives examples of other figures to show how "as

[25]See my translation *Longinus on Great Writing* (New York 1957) and Rhys Roberts' *Longinus On The Sublime* (Cambridge 1907).

dimmer lights are lost in the surrounding sunshine, so pervading greatness all around hides the presence of rhetorical devices." Of the treatment of diction much is lost; what remains shows Longinus to be fully aware of the importance of the choice of words which "endows the subject matter with a speaking soul." He very properly allows vulgarisms in the right places, and insists that there is no limit to the number of metaphors that may be used in a passage provided that successfully conveyed passion can make them convincing.

As for composition, that is, word-arrangement and sentence structure, he glorifies the music of language in poetry and prose, a music allied with meaning and thus making a powerful appeal to the soul and mind of man. Like all the critics, he rejects both metrical, as against rhythmical, prose, and also broken, hurried, or monotonous rhythms. He insists that the anatomy of the sentence must be such that each part fits into the whole like the parts of a living organism.

"Longinus" sees the dangers of attempting greatness, and he names four vices into which the attempt may fall: turgidity, puerility ("the thinking of the schools which ends in frigidity through over-elaboration"), misplaced or artificial passion which leaves the reader unaffected, and frigidity which is often due to strange conceits. Faults and virtues are both illustrated from the greatest writers, and not even Homer is spared criticism. Indeed one of the most striking passages is where he argues that greatness is always accompanied by faults, for genius is careless, but it is always to be preferred to flawless mediocrity. The whole work is full of quotable passages such as the famous comparison of Cicero and Demosthenes: "The greatness of Demosthenes is for the most part abrupt, that of Cicero is like a flood. Our man is violent, swift, strong, intense; he may be compared to a lightning-bolt which burns and ravages. Cicero is like a spreading conflagration which rolls and ranges far and wide. . . ."

With "Longinus"—whether we place him before or after Hermogenes in time—the living stream of Greek criticism reaches its end. We saw that the philosophers of the fifth and fourth centuries posed the problem of literature's social function and responsibility, and built up the beginnings of literary theory. The contemporary development of rhetoric led to a study of style and stylistic devices as such, and it is this approach which triumphs after Aristotle. A continuous output of rhetorical textbooks was published throughout the centuries, but the more responsibly-minded men of letters, while they remain in the stylistic tradition of the rhetoricians, yet have absorbed from Isocrates and the philosophers a sense of the social function of literature, and it is upon literature as a whole, of which oratory is only a part, that they direct their attention. That the Roman rhetorical and literary theories remain derivative, while the Greeks still retained some originality, is proved by Dionysius and, gloriously so, by "Longinus" at the very end. Where, in this general line of development should we place the work known as "Demetrius on Style"?

THE TREATISE ON STYLE

The author of our treatise obviously belongs to the rhetorical, not the philosophic tradition. Moreover, the moral concern for the character and education of the orator—the good man skilled in speech—which we have traced from Isocrates through Cicero to Quintilian, is totally absent. "Demetrius" is concerned with style exclusively. There is in his work no comparative criticism such as we have noted in Dionysius. His approach is quite objective: the theoretical framework is stated and illustrated from great and less great writers. On the other hand, he seems to be a man of letters rather than a professional rhetorician: he says nothing about types of cases, arguments, or issues, about ways of convincing a jury, or about methods of handling the different parts of a speech. His interests are obviously literary rather than rhetorical in the strict sense: the orators are frequently quoted, but only as practitioners of one kind of literature among many. We have here an example of literary criticism from a cultured man with a very good knowledge of Classical and early Alexandrian Greek literature, a man rhetorically trained, but not a mere rhetorician. The work is in many ways unique, the more so if it belongs to Hellenistic times, as it was traditionally thought to do, for we have no other extant critical text from this period.

The date of the work is, however, uncertain, and modern scholars have argued for various dates from the late third century B.C. to the middle of the second century A.D., but they have all but unanimously rejected the manuscript tradition which gives the author as Demetrius of Phalerum.[26] This Demetrius was the pupil and friend of Theophrastus, a distinguished man of letters and a voluminous writer. He ruled Athens

[26]The two standard editions of our treatise were published almost simultaneously: L. Radermacher's *Demetrii Phalerei qui dicitur de elocutione libellus* (Leipzig 1901) and W. Rhys Roberts' *Demetrius on Style* (Cambridge 1902). Roberts' text and translation were reissued, with a brief introduction in the Loeb Library in 1927, reprinted in 1953.

Both editors agree in rejecting the manuscript tradition which attributes the treatise to Demetrius of Phalerum, and would date the work between Dionysius of Halicarnassus and Hermogenes, that is, in the first century A.D. or early in the second. This was the generally accepted view at the end of the last century; see in particular the monographs of R. Altschul, *De Demetrii rhetoris aetate* (Leipzig 1889), F. Beheim-Schwarzbach,

from 317 to 307 B.C. on behalf of Cassander, the king of Macedon. He then fled from Athens to Thebes and later, after the death of Cassander, to Alexandria, where he enjoyed the patronage and friendship of Ptolemy Soter. Nothing is known of his later life or the time of his death except what we are told by Diogenes Laertius (5.78):

Hermippus says that, after the death of Cassander, in fear of Antigonus, he made his way to Ptolemy Soter. There he stayed a considerable time, and advised Ptolemy, among other things, to hand on the kingly power to his children by Eurydice. The king did not take his advice but passed on the diadem to his son by Berenice (Ptolemy Philadelphus) who, after the death of his father, decided to have Demetrius kept under guard in the country, until he decided what to do with him. There Demetrius lived in discouragement. He was somehow bitten in the hand by an asp while he was asleep, and died . . . .

Diogenes (or Hermippus?) does not directly connect the death of Demetrius with the king's displeasure, though he may seem to imply it, but Cicero, in his speech against Rabirius Postumus (9.23) quotes the case of Demetrius as one of those who owed their death to the enmity of a despot, and clearly suggests that he was murdered (*aspide ad corpus admota*). Ptolemy Soter died in 283/2 B.C.

Before we consider the evidence, internal and external, for both date and author, however, let us first consider the content and nature of our treatise, and, to avoid awkward circumlocutions, we may as well call the author Demetrius without assuming him to be Demetrius of Phalerum.

Nature and Structure of the Work

It falls into five sections. The first, which is also the shortest (1–35), is introductory and deals with different kinds of sentence structure, while

Libellus περὶ ἑρμηνείας *qui Demetrii nomine inscriptus est* (Kiel 1890), and K. Dahl, whose *Demetrius* περὶ ἑρμηνείας (Zweibrücken 1894) contains the fullest study of the language of the treatise. Some, like Dahl, and Hugo Rabe in *De Theophrasti libris* περὶ λέξεως (Bonn 1890) 19, favoured the second century A.D. because they thought that the language was that of the period of strict Atticism, while others favoured the first century. The last defender of the Phalerean authorship was Hugo Liers in his *De aetate et scriptore libri qui fertur Demetrii Phalerei* περὶ ἑρμηνείας (Bratislava 1881), while some, notably C. Hammer in his *Demetrius* περὶ ἑρμηνείας (Landshut 1883), continued to favour an earlier date, about 100 B.C.

This last opinion has more recently been supported by F. Boll in *Hermes* 72 (1917) 25–33; more recently still, F. Kroll in his article on rhetoric in *RE*, Suppl. 7 (Stuttgart 1940) 1078–9, has argued for an earlier date, namely the end of the third century B.C. It is clear that the arguments, based on both language and content, which were thought to have settled the matter at the beginning of this century are not as definitive as they then appeared.

the other four discuss four different "styles" or manners of writing, the grand, the plain, the elegant, and the forceful.

It is natural enough that the treatment of sentence structure should form a general introduction, since, with some exceptions to be mentioned later, different kinds of sentences can be used in all four "styles," and Demetrius begins with the general advice that the structure of the sentence must correspond to the structure of the thought. This correspondence must apply also to the clauses (the *kôla*, the basic units in prose as the verses are in poetry) and even to the shorter phrases or *kommata*. After he has repeated, but in his own terms, the Aristotelian distinction between the periodic style and the looser, non-periodic sentence structure, he differentiates three kinds of periods (a formula not found elsewhere).

At one extreme is the involved, Demosthenic period which he calls rhetorical; at the other extreme the looser, simpler, apparently effortless period of dialogue or conversation, which approaches the loose, non-periodic style; intermediate between these is the period he calls historical. There are some further remarks on different kinds of clauses, on the relation of sentence to sense, and a correction of Aristotle's definition of a clause (34).

After these general remarks, Demetrius proceeds to a description of what he considers the four main manners or styles of writing. This is his notorious theory of four "styles." But the word "style" is misleading, first because we think of style as something peculiar to the individual writer whereas the ancients thought of it more objectively, but mainly because, in ancient criticism, we associate the word χαρακτήρ mostly with the formula of the "three styles" which is found in later and mostly Latin writers.[27] There we find three separate styles rigidly differentiated, and while an orator is supposed to be able to use each of the three as the occasion demands, only one style can be used at a particular time.[28] But the Greek term χαρακτήρ is very general in meaning, and Demetrius' use of it is much less rigid. His "styles" can, with the exception of the plain and the grand, be mixed, that is, used at the same time. One can be elegant and forcible, plain and elegant, forcible and plain. The same word χαρακτήρ, which is applied to these four "styles," is also applied to the faults to which each of them is prone; and Demetrius speaks of the

[27]Dionysius of Halicarnassus does indeed have three styles of composition in his *Composition*, and he classes authors in accordance with these; he also has three styles or types of diction, but the two formulae cannot be telescoped. Isocrates, for example, whose composition is flowery (ἄνθηρος, an extreme) uses the mean or mixed type of diction. See note 9 (above).

[28]See, for example, *Ad Herennium* 4.16 (ch. 11) and Cicero, *Orator* 69.

"frigid style," "the affected style," and so on. He also speaks of the "epistolary style." The point is of some importance if we are to understand his intention: he is not drawing up a list of four styles by which you may judge this author or that, or different writings. He believes that there are four main elements of style, four qualities or manners of writing or speaking, and he examines how these are to be practised.

Each "style" is analyzed under three aspects: diction or the choice of words, composition or the arrangement of words, and subject-matter. On this last he has least to say.[29] And, somewhat irregularly under one heading or the other, he also brings in the figures of speech or thought that are most appropriate to each style.

The distinction between content and style is, as we have seen, found in Plato, and may be older. The subdivision of style into diction and word-arrangement is, if not explicitly formulated, certainly implicit in Aristotle, for chapters 2–7 of the third book of his *Rhetoric* deal with diction, while 8–9 deal with word-arrangement. The formula may have been clarified by Theophrastus.

It is important to realize that these subdivisions do not quite correspond to modern categories. Diction, which was later more precisely termed the choice of words, includes not only the choice of current or unusual terms, of rare or newly-coined words, but also words which express passion and character (an angry man uses different words from those he uses when sorrowful), different forms of the same roots, and so on. Further, diction also includes the use of loaded words, of metaphors and similes.[30] It includes all this in Aristotle as well as in later critics. We have already seen that the Greeks were shrewdly aware of the importance of semantics, illustrated in Aristotle by the story of Simonides who refused to write an ode on the victors in a mule race, "half-asses" as he contemptuously called them, but when the fee was increased he wrote the poem beginning: "Hail, ye daughters of storm-footed steeds, ..." but, the philosopher comments, they were still the daughters of asses.[31] Diction then includes

---

[29]Radermacher (p. xii) suggests that the poverty of the treatment of subject-matter is due to the fact that this heading was not dealt with in the books περὶ λέξεως which our author had before him, and in particular in that of Theophrastus. As we have no knowledge of these "sources" the suggestion cannot be disproved. The poorer treatment may also be due, however, to the fact that the category is not a very sound one, even though it might be traced to Aristotle's dictum that different genres of imitation imitate different objects (*Poetics* ch. 3.5).

[30]For the weakness of this approach to metaphor, which is common to all Greek critics, see W. B. Stanford's stimulating little book, *Greek Metaphor* (Oxford 1936), especially pp. 6–9.

[31]*Rhet.* 3.2.14.

in part the expression of emotion as well as the writing in character, in so far as these follow from the use of certain words.

Synthesis, or the arrangement of words once chosen, ("composition" though etymologically correct, is a misleading translation) has three things in view: the structure of the sentence, the sound of the words in collocation, and rhythm. The first of these Demetrius has already discussed in the introductory section. The second (much neglected today) is part of that music of language to which we have seen that the Greeks were extraordinarily sensitive. It too has a part to play in the expression of emotion, for, though we are less aware of this, an angry man uses harsh, guttural sounds where a lover or a suppliant quite unconsciously will use mutes and labials. It is still true that words that can be run into one another, without pauses between, are softer than those that willy-nilly make us stop. No one, however hard he tries, can (meaning apart) put the same emotional tone into two phrases such as "You accursed crooked cur" on the one hand and "My lovely angel sweetheart" on the other. The third point, closely connected with the other two, is rhythm, and this, in Greek prose as in Greek poetry (except when it was set to music) has nothing to do with stress or pitch, but only with the length or shortness of syllables. Here Demetrius, like all ancient critics, repeats the Aristotelian dictum that prose must be rhythmical but not metrical, that is, its rhythms must be more varied and never repeated regularly. It is then with these three things in view—word-arrangement, diction, and content —that Demetrius discusses each "style."

"Neighbouring" each successful style or manner is a particular vice or faulty style into which an unsuccessful attempt will fall. An unsuccessful attempt at grandeur or impressiveness is apt to fall into frigidity, attempted elegance into affectation, simplicity into dryness or aridity, and forcefulness will become bad taste. This theory of the "neighbouring vice" is found in other critics too—we know it best in Horace and Longinus[32]—but whether Demetrius was the first to put it forward we cannot tell. As in so many things, our opinion will depend upon our view of his date. He does not claim to be original at this point.

Structure of the Work

This general plan is quite simple and clear. It is also carried out more systematically than is often alleged, and what appears at first sight to be a digression or repetition seems to be reasonably well placed in the work as a whole. Demetrius does, however, seek variety, and he deliberately

[32]*On the Sublime* ch. 3; Horace, *On the Art of Poetry* 25–31; also *Ad Herennium* 4.15 (ch. 10).

begins one section with subject-matter, another with diction, and so on. Certainly there are repetitions: a figure of speech may in one place be said to contribute to elegance, for example, while later we find it contributing to forcefulness. There are many such cases, and this seems at first sight confusing, but is Demetrius not essentially right? Is it not true that the same way of putting things has, in different contexts, a different effect? We will take one example which is found in the discussions of three of our "styles," namely *anaphora* or the repetition of words at the beginning of consecutive clauses.

In 61 we have the passage on Nireus in the Homeric catalogue of ships. Demetrius says that Homer makes this one mention of Nireus, who led only three ships to Troy and is never heard of again, much more impressive by the use of anaphora. This is the passage (*Iliad* 2.671–674):

> Nireus from Syma brought three curved ships,
> Nireus, son of Aglaïa and of Charopus,
> Nireus, most beautiful of all the Greeks
> Who came to Ilium, save Achilles only.

Here, surely, Demetrius is right. In 141 he is discussing the elegant charm of a poem of Sappho, of which he quotes:

> O Evening Star, all things you bring;
> You bring the sheep, you bring the goat,
> You bring the child to its mother.

Dimly through this inadequate translation, and much more clearly in the Greek of Sappho (see note on 141), we can see that the same figure of speech has a quite different effect from that in the Nireus passage, that the effect here is one of charm, not of grandeur or impressiveness. Then we find anaphora once again in 268, from the great speech of Aeschines against Demosthenes: "You call him as a witness, a witness against yourself, a witness against the laws, a witness against the democracy."[33]

Here again Demetrius is right. The effect of the repetition in this passage is like a series of blows, it is forceful, certainly not charming! The fact that these effects are so different may raise doubts as to the soundness of Demetrius' basic categories but, given these, the discussion of the same figure in different sections is justified, and Demetrius is the better critic for having seen that figures of speech depend for their effect on other

---

[33]The translation given here is different from that in the text because there are other figures involved in the Greek passage, which must also be rendered. Here, however, it seemed better to translate the *anaphora* only, as the other figures are not relevant.

factors. Not all his repetitions can be justified in this way, and we shall note them as we read the text, but some of them can be, and the point should be kept in mind.

Demetrius has also been criticized for digressions. Rhys Roberts (pp. 28–31) listed no less than fifteen "subsidiary topics" of this kind, in fact every passage where Demetrius ventures upon some general description or explanation which is perhaps not immediately required by his present purpose. Of the nine so listed in the discussion of the grand style, only one is of any length and worth mentioning here; all the others seem perfectly natural where they occur. It is the discussion of metaphors and similes (78–90), a subject which Aristotle had discussed at some length and regarded as the main ornament allowed in prose. Now metaphor is appropriate in a discussion of impressiveness, but not only there, and it is a general discussion of the subject which we find at this point. It is an extremely interesting passage, in which Demetrius discusses, where it first comes up in a natural way (there are several references to impressiveness in the passage), the whole subject of metaphor. And he does not discuss it again, although, obviously, a metaphor can be elegant or forcible!

The digressions found under the plain style are clearly due to a change of plan in this section. Demetrius deals mainly with the *qualities* which the plain style should have, namely lucidity, persuasiveness, and vividness, and he tells us how to achieve these by means which may concern both diction and word-arrangement. Hence, after a very brief statement (190–191) on simple subject-matter and diction, he says that lucidity is here the chief aim, and proceeds to tell us how this lucidity is to be attained (192–203). He then goes on to word-arrangement (200–208); we are told that vividness and persuasiveness are most acceptable to the plain style and we proceed to deal with these two qualities (209–220 and 221–222). After this comes one of his best passages, on the style of letter-writing: this too should be in the plain style (222–235).

Thus the treatment of the plain style follows a different plan. Perhaps Demetrius felt that all that could be said about plain diction and composition was that they should be plain, and that it would be both more profitable and more interesting to discuss the main qualities which this style strove to attain. He may also have welcomed the opportunity for a variation in his approach. It is true that these qualities are not the exclusive possession of the plain style; and it is true that in the discussion of these three qualities, lucidity, vividness, and persuasiveness (especially the last two), he goes beyond the bounds of the plain style. He does not deal with them again.

The discussion of the proper style for writing letters (223–235) can hardly be called a digression since it is a particular application of the simple style and is discussed under that heading. Demetrius may at first sight seem to contradict himself when, after saying that letters require the simple style, he concludes the discussion by saying that it needs to be a mixture of the simple and the elegant. This, however, is not really the case. He begins by disagreeing with Artemon who said that a letter should be regarded as one side of a dialogue. Dialogue as a literary genre tries to reproduce the style of actual conversation, but Demetrius feels that a letter is something more than that. While it is true that the subject and the style should both be simple, a letter is also an expression of friendship, a "gift" from the writer to the recipient; hence it deserves more care (though not too obvious care) on the part of the writer, whose character it inevitably reflects; it must not, on the other hand, become a treatise. Such treatises, it is true, are often addressed to a correspondent, but they are essentially quite another genre. The proper epistolary style, then, is basically simple, but there should be a certain admixture of elegance, and the letter may be said to require a mixture of the simple and the elegant styles.

This is the first discussion of letter-writing in ancient texts and as such of considerable historical importance. The principles it expresses are found reflected in all later theorists on epistolography.[34]

Finally, in the section on the forceful style, there are two alleged digressions, the treatment of "figured language" (287–298) and that of the hiatus (299–300). The second of these is very brief and, since hiatus is said to contribute to forcefulness, it is no digression at all but a further reference to a subject already more fully discussed under impressiveness (68–74).

The first is more important and more interesting for the light it throws

[34]See on this point H. Koskennieni's "Studien zur Idee und Phraseologie des griechischen Briefes bis 400 n. Chr." in *Annales Academiae Scientiarum Fennicae*, B 102 (Helsinki 1956) 18–47. On the general subject of ancient letter-writing see J. Sykutris, "Epistolographie" in *RE* Suppl. 5 (1931) 185–220. Neither the references to Aristotle's letters nor to one of Thucydides in section 264 (which latter is not likely to have been genuine) should be used as evidence for a later date. The writing of letters in the person of famous men became a literary genre which is often said to have begun in the second century B.C., but for this date there is no evidence. Sykutris suggests that the practice began in the fourth century and points out that there may have been many motives for such writing, quite apart from any intention to deceive. One may add that this would be especially true at a time when the introduction of historical and nearly contemporary personages into dialogues was a well-accepted literary convention. See also, on this point, Ernst Howald's *Die Briefe Platons* (Zürich 1923) 14–15; J. Harward, *The Platonic Epistles* (Cambridge 1932) 65–78.

upon our author's method. After treating of the peculiar force of Demades, he is led to mention a figure, much misused (presumably to attain force-fulness) by contemporary orators (287), which he calls τὸ ἐσχηματισμένον, not so much "figured language" as allusiveness or innuendo. This can properly be used for reasons of good taste or discretion. In the first case it is forceful, as is shown by an example from Plato (288–289); then the cases of discretion are explained: the figure is used when addressing a despot, an all-powerful populace, and the like (292–295). The subject of this figure arises naturally in a discussion of forcefulness, to which it often contributes, and, as it is of some interest, its other uses are then added, even though they are not strictly relevant. At this point comes a true digression (296–298) on the different forms in which a thought may be expressed—statement, advice, question, and so on. This arises very natur-ally from the different effect of allusiveness and bluntness, but it is irrelevant to the subject under discussion, to which we then quickly return.[35]

From this brief survey of supposed digressions we may conclude that Demetrius does here and there allow himself to pursue for a moment a particular point which has come up naturally, and to do so at greater length than strict relevance would demand. He also varies his method, particularly in the section on plain style where he deals more with the qualities at which it aims than with the means of attaining it, but he does not seriously transgress the scheme he has set himself. Whether we blame or praise him for these near-digressions will depend upon the rigidity of our own minds.

Elegance or Wit?

A much more serious flaw in our treatise, one of ideas rather than of structure, seems to have escaped attention. It is a basic confusion in Demetrius' account of τὸ γλαφυρόν—the elegant or polished manner (128–189). This "style" does not, like the others, express one clear basic idea, and the confusion is reflected in the terminology. The word γλαφυρός, by which it is described in contrast to the others, is almost immediately replaced by χάρις, charm or grace, and is thereafter little used in the discussion.[36]

[35]Demetrius passes, we might say, from the use of the particular figure of innuendo for a particular purpose (forcefulness) to other uses of it which are not strictly relevant in a discussion of forcefulness, and then from the use of a particular form or figure of speech to different forms in which the same thought may be cast (the more general meaning of σχῆμα). A modern writer would avoid the charge of irrelevance by using footnotes.

[36]From 128 to 185 the generic term γλαφυρός is used only 11 times; of these 7 are in

At the very beginning (128) we are told that elegant language may be described as a gay playfulness of expression.[37] The charm is then said to be of two kinds: on the one hand the graceful poetic charm of such passages as Homer's description of Nausicaa playing among her handmaidens; and, on the other hand, witticisms. The difficulty is that too much is included under the second: the witticisms quoted at the very beginning (e.g. the old woman's teeth are sooner counted than her fingers) have no trace of charm, or indeed of elegance or grace. Moreover, this is true of many other jests quoted; for example, the grim humour of the Cyclops (130) and Xenophon's jest (134) about the hard-headed Persian from whom it would be easier to strike fire than laughter.[38] When Demetrius calls this the most effective charm—ἡ δυνατωτάτη χάρις— (135) he is straining the meaning of that word beyond all bearing. He seems to have included all witticisms, whether gracious or crude, under his second kind of χάρις, and to believe that, because they could all be called χαριεντισμός, a word that could be applied to any kind of witticism, he could use the root word χάρις to apply to them also, although in all its usages elsewhere the word implies what we would call charm or grace or graciousness. Even if it could be so used—and no doubt it is presumptuous to challenge the Greek usages of a Greek—the ideas he deals with have nothing in common with each other except a certain cleverness in the handling of words, which is not enough to class them together under one and the same manner of writing. Homer's description of Nausicaa has grace and charm in plenty, but no wit; Sophron's remark about the rascal who made as many drachmas as he deserved strokes of the lash is very witty but by no stretch of imagination can it be called charming or gracious. It is a χαριεντισμός but it has no χάρις. It seems more than a matter of taste, which notoriously varies in different places and ages.

connection with rhythm (178, 179 twice, 183, 184, 186), and two more, also in 186, are to describe γλαφυρὸς χαρακτήρ generally, corresponding to the first mention in 128. The remaining usage, in 138, as equivalent to χαριέν, seems almost accidental. The word χάρις (usually in the plural) and its derivatives, on the other hand, occur very frequently indeed. This is unlike the descriptions of the other styles where the main descriptive term used in 36 occurs frequently and regularly.

[37]ὁ γλαφυρὸς λόγος χαριεντισμὸς καὶ ἵλαρος λόγος ἐστιν. The use of λόγος instead of χαρακτήρ is interesting. Probably unconscious, it seems to imply an emphasis on actual language, even though λόγος can be used of content as well as the expression of it. χαριεντισμός, which means jest, often a mild kind of playfulness, seems to cover both kinds of χάρις better than any other term used, from the charming scene of Nausicaa to the brutal jibes of Lysias and Sophron. The other word is ἵλαρος, "bright."

[38]It is significant that Demetrius himself, perhaps unconsciously, uses the terms δεινός, "forceful" and δεινότης, "forcefulness," in describing the effect of such witticisms at 130 and 131.

Demetrius may well have considered the cruder witticisms he quotes as in good taste—and here lies another verbal confusion for he later uses the word ἄχαρι, bad taste, for the vice neighbouring on forcefulness (302). He might therefore have considered these witticisms as εὔχαρι (he uses that term as nearly equivalent to χαρίεις in 156), but witticisms can be in good taste without having grace or charm. The confusion of words implies a confusion of thought.

Demetrius seems to have realized something of this when he, at a later stage in this discussion (163), draws a definite distinction between the charming (εὔχαρι) and the ridiculous (γελοῖον), but only for a moment, for we find that this becomes only a repetition of his former distinction between poetic grace and jest. The section is confused (163–169) both in thought and language since up to this point he had called *both* divisions χάριτες and χαρίεις, that is, charming.

This confusion is a serious flaw in the discussion of the elegant style. True, elegant playfulness of language can be divided into charming grace on the one hand and gracious wit on the other. The mistake is to include all witticisms, even the grimmest and the merely witty, under the second head, and not to have excluded here, as he should have done, those grim and satiric jests which he himself later includes under the peculiar forcefulness of Demades (282–286). He does not there draw attention to their wit; yet a comparison with 130–131 will show that they are essentially of the same kind, and that he was aware that a relationship existed between wit and forcefulness.

However, where he is dealing with the elegant and charming properly so-called, he has a great deal to say that is worthy of our attention.

Demetrius and Aristotle

Another feature of our treatise is its peculiar, indeed in many ways unique, relationship to Aristotle. It is obvious, and universally admitted, that much of what Demetrius says can be traced back to the *Rhetoric* of Aristotle. It is also clear that this dependence is far more pronounced in certain sections of the book than in others. But there is more than that: our author seems to use Aristotle in a manner unparalleled in other critical texts. Sometimes he corrects what Aristotle says and improves on him; at other times he changes the Aristotelian terms in what seems a deliberate manner, now and again making them simpler and clearer. In a word, he uses Aristotle for his own ends. The question is whether such changes as he makes should be attributed to unknown intermediate sources or whether they argue personal knowledge of the *Rhetoric* and, further, whether his attitude to Aristotle is more likely at an early date such as the early third century. Certainly no parallel can be adduced from Roman times.

The introductory section makes use of Aristotle at every turn; that on the grand manner makes use of him on particular subjects such as rhythm (38–43), metaphor (78–90), and frigidity (116), and there are frequent Aristotelian echoes, particularly at 58, 77, and 93–115. The discussion of the elegant style has very little that is Aristotelian, though his writings are three times used in illustration (144, 154, 157). On the simple style there are a few Aristotelian echoes (190–194) and references to his letters in the section on letter-writing. The section on forcefulness has practically nothing that recalls him. Demetrius' scheme of four styles is of course quite un-Aristotelian, for to Aristotle there was only one right way of saying a particular thing at a particular time; moreover he recognized only one virtue or *aretê* of speech, namely lucidity.

As the greatest use of Aristotle is made in the discussion of sentence structure the peculiar nature of the relationship will emerge most clearly if we deal with it first (1–35). We may note at the outset that the very title περὶ ἑρμηνείας instead of the more usual περὶ λέξεως (Theophrastus had already written a work of that name and there were others) already seems to betray a careful use of words. Aristotle had used λέξις in many senses, for style in general, for diction in particular, and in other senses as well. Demetrius, however, uses ἑρμηνεία in the more general sense, and reserves λέξις for diction.[39] He seems to be the only Greek critic who thus restricts the word.

Any reader who will glance at the first five sections of the ninth chapter of the third book of Aristotle's *Rhetoric* will see at once how much Demetrius' discussion of sentence structure derives from it. All the main ideas are there, but they are mostly applied with a difference. Aristotle says the period limits the sense, should end with it, and that this is the main difference between the periodic and the loose or un-

---

[39]λέξις is used of style in all its aspects at the beginning of *Rhetoric* 3, as against πράγματα and τάξις, and under this generic word Aristotle discusses diction (including the use of metaphors and similes) to the end of ch. 7, while in chs. 8 and 9 λέξις refers to word-arrangement. This is in no way surprising, since λέξις is the generic term which can refer to style as a whole or any department thereof. Demetrius uses ἑρμηνεία as the generic term, which can then also refer to any aspect of style, but he restricts λέξις to diction, a restricted use which does not seem to recur elsewhere. Once or twice, however, where he follows Aristotle closely, he is betrayed into using λέξις as Aristotle does; so in 193 he speaks of διαλελυμένη λέξις which refers to word-arrangement and is contrasted with γραφικὴ λέξις in the general sense of "written style" (cp. *Rhet.* 3.12.2, quoted in note 45). For the confusion which may follow a loose use of λέξις see *AJP* 73 (1952) 257–258 and note 11 there.

periodic structure. A period should also be capable of being uttered in one breath. All this is in Demetrius, but he goes further: he applies the correspondence with the thought also to clauses (1–3) which to him are the basic unit; they too must be of reasonable length (4–7, cp. *Rhet.* 3.9.6). He associates brief clauses—and here he brings in the even smaller division, the phrase or *komma*—with maxims and laconisms (cp. *Rhet.* 2.21.13). He then quotes Aristotle's definition of the period, but he quotes it only in part, and expands this with the image of runners who have their goal in view (11, cp. *Rhet.* 3.9.2–3), using his own words and adding the etymology of the word περίοδος which Aristotle does not mention.

There are interesting changes in terminology. Aristotle's term for the periodic style is λέξις κατεστραμμένη, Demetrius keeps the adjective but changes the noun to ἑρμηνεία; Aristotle's term for the looser, non-periodic style is λέξις εἰρομένη, a rather difficult phrase—the "strung-along" style. This Demetrius changes to the simpler διῃρημένη ἑρμηνεία —"the disconnected style"—an adjective which Aristotle used for a period of which the clauses are not in antithesis (3.9.7). Both writers note the loose style of the older writers (*Rhet.* 3.9.1 ἀρχαία) but Demetrius quotes Hecataeus instead of Herodotus. He ignores at this point Aristotle's division of periods into those with one and those with more clauses, but later (19) replaces it by a tripartite division of his own into rhetorical, historical, and conversational periods. When he does mention the one-clause period (17) he does not apply Aristotle's adjective ἀφελής to it (this is a word he seems to avoid, though it is common in later critics), and again uses a simpler term, ἁπλῆ. He then uses as an example of this single-clause *period* the sentence of Herodotus which Aristotle used as an example of the *non*-periodic, and which Demetrius there replaced by an example from Hecataeus.

In 15 Demetrius says, with emphasis on the first person singular, "I consider" that a discourse should not consist of a series of periods. There is no such statement in Aristotle, but it is a commonplace in Dionysius of Halicarnassus and in Cicero. The advice to avoid monotony is Aristotelian in other contexts (e.g. on rhythm, 3.8.1). Nor is there anything in Aristotle to correspond to the requirement (18) that the final clause of the period should be the longest.

At 22–24 we come to antithesis, also discussed by Aristotle (3.9.7) who does not distinguish between antithesis of thought and of words (a doubtful distinction). He does, however, also condemn the fake verbal antithesis (3.9.10) and Demetrius uses his example of it, adding a comment of his own.

At 25 there is another change of terminology. Where Aristotle (3.9.9) restricts *paromoiôsis* to similarities of words or sounds at the beginning or the end of consecutive clauses, and uses *parisôsis* for balanced clauses of equal length, Demetrius uses the adjective παρόμοιος to cover both—a more natural use since the word simply means similar—but he uses ἰσόκωλον, a much more expressive word, to refer to balanced clauses. Of his three examples, the first comes directly from Aristotle in this passage, the second is used by the philosopher in another connection (3.9.7); the third is not found in the *Rhetoric*. Neither is Demetrius' comment that the use of these studied devices is inadvisable in forceful or emotional passages, but he illustrates his point by examples from a lost work of Aristotle.

The definition of the enthymeme (30–33) is Aristotelian (*Rhet.* 1.2.8) and Demetrius' insistence on the difference between it and the period is in accord with that meaning.[40]

The last references in this section are the most interesting. Demetrius quotes (in his own words) the Aristotelian definition of a clause as "one of the two parts of a period" and naturally complains that this contradicts the existence of the one-clause period. He then quotes and accepts the correction of one Archedemus into: "a clause is either a simple period or a part of a composite period" and he ends his discussion of sentence structure by another statement (35) about Archedemus: that he *seems* to imply that a period may consist not only of one or two, but of three or more clauses. Demetrius had already stated (16) that he considered four clauses the advisable limit. Let us be quite clear that Archedemus (whoever he was) is quoted only for his definition, with a comment that this definition *appears to imply* that Archedemus established no limit to the number of clauses.[41] I am at a loss to understand

[40]See note on section 30 of the translation and Appendix I, A, *s.v.* ἐνθύμημα.

[41]Demetrius seems to have misunderstood Aristotle. The reference is *Rhet.* 3.9.5. Aristotle has been criticizing a period he attributes to Sophocles as improperly divided (he seems to take the lines as equivalent to *kôla*):

Καλυδὼν μὲν ἥδε γαῖα Πελοπίας χθονὸς
ἐν ἀντιπόρθμοις πέδι' ἔχουσ' εὐδαίμονα . . .

(This country, Calydon, of Pelops' land,
The opposite shore, fertile and happy plains.)

Aristotle's criticism is that if we stop at the end of the first line, the division is haphazard, and does not correspond to sense. He tells us that a complex period must not be divided in this manner and he continues: κῶλον δ' ἐστι τὸ ἕτερον μόριον ταύτης. The difficulty is the reference of ταύτης of which the κῶλον is "one of the two parts"—if it refers to the correct period, then as Demetrius says, Aristotle commits himself to

the position taken by Roberts (and others), when he says (p. 218) that this reference to Archedemus "is of such a nature as to suggest that the author of the π.ἑρμ. may have drawn a good deal of his doctrine from him."

In the other sections the dependence on Aristotle is less constant. When Demetrius begins his discussion of the impressive style with a discussion of rhythm, he is obviously making use of *Rhet.* 3.8.4–6. But the way he uses it should warn us to be cautious in the use we make of such alleged quotations where we do not have the original text before us. Demetrius' words are: "A paeonic arrangement is, *as Aristotle says* (φησί),[42] impressive" (38). Occurring as this does in a discussion of the grand manner, it might be thought to imply that Aristotle said that the paeonic rhythm was appropriate to the impressive style, and one might well deduce from this that the theory of several styles goes back to Aristotle. Fortunately we have Aristotle's text, and he says nothing of the kind. His discussion of rhythm has nothing whatever to do with any theory of styles, nor does he use the adjective μεγαλοπρεπής, grand or impressive. What he does say in his discussion of rhythm is that one should aim at dignity and take the hearer out of himself (δεῖ δὲ σεμνότητα γενέσθαι καὶ ἐκστῆσαι), and he then goes on to advise the use of the paeonic metre at the beginning and end of clauses, presumably as having this effect. Since both dignity and passion belong, for Demetrius, to the impressive style, he is quite justified in saying that, as Aristotle says, the paeonic is impressive, for what Aristotle says does fit in with the description of the grand manner. There is no intention to deceive, only to use Aristotle for his own purposes. He then goes on (41) to use Theophrastus to improve on Aristotle. Even if we cannot have paeons exactly at the beginning and the end of a clause, we can still have a general paeonic effect, "*and this is what Aristotle, it would seem, recommends,*" and he gives an example of his general paeonic rhythm from

---

periods of two κῶλα only. On the other hand, if it refers to the sentence quoted in part, that is, "a colon is either part of *this* sentence" (which is grammatically preferable), we hardly have the general definition which we should expect. Modern editors seem to gloss over this difficulty (see Frese's Loeb translation p. 289, Cope and Sandys, 3. 97–98, Voilquin and Capelle's Budé edition, p. 343) and generally agree with Demetrius who boldly replaces ταύτης by περιόδου. It is not certain whether Archedemus interpreted the passage as Demetrius does. Even if he did, this does not prove that Demetrius did not have the *Rhetoric* before him. Modern editors certainly do.

[42]It may be worth noting that φησί does not introduce a direct quotation. As we have the controlling text of Aristotle, no harm is done. But we do not have the text of Theophrastus, for example, and this kind of semi-quotation only too often has been built on excessively.

Theophrastus. But Aristotle did not say so, and probably did *not* mean this.

Sometimes our author obviously has a passage of Aristotle in mind, but does not mention him. Aristotle said that connectives such as μέν and δέ should correspond exactly (*Rhet.* 3.5.2) but Demetrius says they should not, at least in the grand style (53), and gives an example from Antiphon.

The discussion of metaphors and similes (78–90) is full of Aristotelian echoes. A number of the same examples are used. There are also several things which Aristotle does not say: that a metaphor is sometimes more lucid and precise than the specific term (82), and that the transference should, at least in the grand style, be from the greater to the less, not *vice versa* (83), that in metaphors from one species to another, the transference does not always work both ways, so that you can say the foot of a mountain but not the slope of a man (79). These are good points, not in Aristotle.

The treatment of similes in the two authors is perhaps the most interesting of all. Demetrius says that when the metaphor is too bold we should convert it into a simile, and similes are safer in prose (80); the examples he gives conform to Aristotle's classic distinction between the two (*Rhet.* 3.4.1), namely that "Achilles leapt *like* a lion" is a simile, while "A lion, he leapt" is a metaphor. But when Aristotle goes on to say that "the simile is useful in prose, but rarely, for it is poetical" while he allows metaphor as *the* ornament in prose (3.2.8–15), we are confused, for it is simply not true that "Achilles, a lion, leapt" is less poetical than "Achilles leapt like a lion." This strange advice is almost certainly due to Aristotle's having the extended Homeric simile in mind, but the confusion remains. Demetrius clarifies all this: to him the simile, as stated above, is safer, but he adds that the simile must be brief (89); if it is extended it becomes a "poetic comparison" (παραβολὴ ποιητική, i.e., a Homeric simile) and this can only be used in prose with the greatest caution (90). There can be no doubt that Demetrius is improving on Aristotle.

Enough has been said to show that our author's relation to Aristotle is unique in extant critical texts. It might be described as respect falling short of veneration, and he does not hesitate to improve upon the master. He is quite ready to give credit to others, as when he quotes Theophrastus, always very aptly, but he does seem to be himself quite familiar with Aristotle. He may be quoting from memory, and this may account for some inaccuracies, but it would not seem to account for his changes in terminology which impress one as purposeful. The use he makes of

Aristotle is everywhere subordinated to his own categories.[43] This way of using Aristotle cannot be paralleled in any other critic whether Greek or Roman, in the first century B.C. or later, and it seems unlikely that it derives from one or more intermediate sources.[44] I am again at a loss to understand Rhys Roberts' view (p. 249) that "the relation . . . of the περὶ ἑρμηνείας to Aristotle suggests a follower far removed in time." As far as it goes, it suggests to me the exact opposite.

We cannot prove, of course, that this or that point was not derived from an intermediate source, but we must not automatically assume that this applied to everything Demetrius says where no sign of such sources is found in our text and we have no evidence elsewhere that the opinions found here were held by anyone else. Our author's attitude as a whole seems to be far more easily explained as that of a man who had read Aristotle himself, and used him independently. Such a man is much more likely to have lived in the late fourth or early third century than at a much later date.

Theophrastus

Next in importance to Aristotle himself comes Theophrastus. He is quoted four times in all, each time on a specific topic, and each time he was well worth quoting. Curiously enough, the particular theories attributed to him here are not found elsewhere. At 41, Theophrastus' example of a paeonic clause which does not begin or end with a paeon

---

[43]There is an excellent article by Alfred Kappelmacher in *Wiener Studien* 24 (1902) 452–456, on "Die Aristotelzitate im der Schrift der Pseudo-Demetrius" which shows how Demetrius reproduces the sense rather than the words of Aristotle. In 116 on frigidity, as Kappelmacher points out, the parallel with *Rhet.* 3.3 is so close that we can with certainty fill in the sense of the lacuna; and yet Demetrius gives the four causes of frigidity in a different order with only one example of each (Aristotle gives many) and one of his examples is not in Aristotle. Kappelmacher also deals with Demetrius 11 and 34 (see note 41) and the "misleading" quotation in 38 (see above pp. 36–37). Even from such an incomplete survey the conclusion is convincingly established.

[44]As is supposed by F. Solmsen in "Demetrios περὶ ἑρμηνείας und sein peripatetisches Quellenmaterial," in *Hermes* 66 (1931) 241–267. Solmsen tries to link the four "styles" of Demetrius with the four virtues of style attributed to Theophrastus, but this too is a conjectural reconstruction of modern scholars, and based on doubtful evidence. See *TAPA* 83 (1952) 179–181. Solmsen's article, however, contains a useful discussion of Demetrius' indebtedness to Aristotle. Solmsen is right when he says that the four styles of Demetrius are more like qualities than "styles."

We know of course that a number of works on style were written by Peripatetics, but the insistence on intermediate "sources" at all costs seems to assume that no Greek or Roman critic can ever have quoted directly from Aristotle, and that known parallels are always due to some unknown intermediate source. These persistent attempts to explain the known by the unknown seem to me in the present case quite unnecessary.

leads to the improvement already noted on Aristotle's conception of prose-rhythm, and for this improvement Theophrastus was probably responsible, though the improvement may have been implicit rather than explicitly stated in Theophrastus. At 114 a general definition of frigidity from Theophrastus precedes quotation of Aristotle's analysis of frigidity of *diction* into four kinds (116). At 173–174, Theophrastus' analysis of the causes of beauty in words is quoted in preference to Aristotle's remarks on the subject (*Rhet.* 3.2.13, in the discussion of metaphors, of which Demetrius makes use elsewhere), probably because his terminology was clearer and because he dealt with the subject specifically. Finally, at 222 we have Theophrastus' suggestion that some things should be left to the imagination of the reader; to this there is no parallel in Aristotle.

This seems to imply that Demetrius knew his Theophrastus as well as his Aristotle. If he were quoting from an (unknown) intermediate source, it is unlikely that he would have restricted himself to these four cases or that, in each case, the reference would have been so apt; it seems very much simpler to conclude that Demetrius made his own selection. Nor do I see any supporting evidence for the suggestion that "Theophrastus is probably followed in many other places." It may be so, but it is at least as likely that Demetrius took Aristotle as his primary guide in certain sections, and quoted Theophrastus when he found something particularly good in his works.

The Question of Date

References to Aristotle and Theophrastus do not, in themselves, affect the question of date, though the manner of them may, if we believe it to indicate considerable familiarity and a freer use of them than is found in writings of Graeco-Roman times. References to later writers, however, may well affect the date of our treatise. We will now examine further references which have been considered incompatible not only with the authorship of the Phalerean Demetrius but also with an early Hellenistic date.

1. *References to persons.* One unusual feature of our treatise is the large number of references to, and quotations from, persons who are known to have lived in the late fourth and early third centuries. These are interesting in themselves; moreover, they would seem at least as compatible with an earlier as with a later date.

There is, first of all, Demetrius of Phalerum himself. Words spoken by him about Craterus are quoted as an example of innuendo at 289. As long ago as 1594 Victorius took this as a proof of the authorship of that Demetrius, which it obviously is not. On the other hand, Rhys Roberts expresses the view now generally accepted when he says: "No literary reference throughout the *De Elocutione* is so damaging to the traditional view as this," presumably on the assumption that such a self-revelation is in impossibly bad taste. But that is not true either. Plato and Xenophon, for example, do mention themselves in their works. All we can be sure of is that if our author did tell a story about himself, he would certainly have told it, as it is told, in the third person. The story itself is no evidence one way or the other. One interesting point about it, however, is that it is a late fourth-century anecdote told by no one else.

At 193 where Demetrius has been speaking of disconnected sentences as more appropriate for oral delivery, he continues: "That is why Menander, whose style lacks connectives, is mostly acted, while Philemon is read." Menander's date is 342–291, and Philemon's 361–262. This way of referring to them, we are told, "seems to be the judgment of *posterity*" (Rhys Roberts, p. 53). But is it? There is a parallel in Aristotle where he too is discussing the difference between oral and written style, a passage which our author most probably had in mind.[45] Aristotle says: "Poets who write to be read are in everybody's hands, like Chaeremon . . . or Licymnius. . . ." Licymnius lived a generation or two before Aristotle, but Chaeremon, the tragic poet, was certainly his contemporary. Aristotle never hesitates to mention contemporaries where appropriate. Our author need not avoid doing so. His reference to Menander and Philemon does not prove them contemporaries, of course, but neither is there any reason to consider this "the judgment of posterity." In fact the passage proves nothing at all, except that the treatise cannot have been written *before* Menander and Philemon were well known to their contemporaries, but then they both were well known before the end of the fourth century!

The lengthy reference to Ctesias (212–216), whom others criticized for prolixity while Demetrius defends him as being vivid, offers no difficulty of dating, since he was writing at the end of the *fifth* century, and it is difficult to see the point of Roberts' remark that he was "not yet a classic" in the time of Demetrius of Phalerum. He had been dead over a hundred years by the early third century and could, whether a "classic" or not, be the subject of literary controversy.

[45]*Rhet.* 3.12.2. And there are interesting verbal parallels. Aristotle says: ἔστι δὲ λέξις γραφικὴ μὲν ἡ ἀκριβεστάτη, ἀγωνιστικὴ δὲ ἡ ὑποκριτικωτάτη . . . βαστάζονται δὲ οἱ ἀγωνιστικοί, οἷον Χαιρήμων . . . καὶ Λικύμνιος . . . and Demetrius has: ἐναγώνιος . . . ἡ διαλελυμένη λέξις, ἡ δ' αὐτὴ καὶ ὑποκριτικὴ καλεῖται . . . γραφικὴ δὲ λέξις ἡ εὐανάγνωστος . . . . This is one of the few passages using λέξις in the general sense as Aristotle did (see note 39 above).

A sentence is quoted at 182 from Dicaearchus, a contemporary of Theophrastus, and Nicias, the painter, is quoted at 76: (*fl.* 340 to after 306). We cannot build much on the tense of these various references, though "Nicias *used to say* (ἔλεγεν) that the choice of subject was no smaller part of the art of the painter" is at least as compatible with personal knowledge or oral tradition as with quotation from another intermediate source.[46]

The three references latest in time seem to be Clitarchus who is criticized for bad taste in 304; Praxiphanes, who is quoted in 57 as a literary critic, and Sotades referred to in 189. Clitarchus' exact date is uncertain. Roberts puts his *floruit* at 300 B.C., the *Oxford Classical Dictionary* speaks of him as writing some time after 280 B.C. Praxiphanes cannot be dated exactly; he is said to have been a pupil of Theophrastus, and Callimachus (305–240 B.C.) wrote a book against him. Sotades was a contemporary of Ptolemy Philadelphus and seems to have been old enough to object to that king's marriage in 289.[47] All three seem to have belonged to the first half of the third century, and indeed to have been active in the first quarter. Sotades was notorious later for his broken and soft verses, known as Sotadeans. Roberts says: "the use of the term 'Sotadean' for feeble and affected rhythms is probably of still later date." We might reply that the term need not have been in general use when it was used for the first time, but it is more profitable to reflect that the Alexandria of, say, the second quarter of the third century was a highly sophisticated literary society where reputations were quickly made (and unmade). We know that there was a great deal of literary controversy among contemporaries. The literary war between Callimachus and Apollonius of Rhodes is famous enough; the book of Callimachus *Against Praxiphanes* has already been mentioned. In that kind of atmosphere references to contemporaries (in a work like ours) would be very natural, and even the term "Sotadeans" might well be current during the lifetime of Sotades.

This does not prove that our author was writing in Alexandria at that time, but not one of these references is incompatible with this assumption, nor are they evidence of a "later" date. And if we ask at what time these unusually frequent references to writers of the later fourth and early

[46]It is interesting to note a close parallel to this use of the imperfect in the treatise *On the Sublime* 3.5, where the author discusses the vice of false enthusiasm "which Theodorus used to call parenthyrsos"—ὅπερ ὁ Θεόδωρος παρένθυρσον ἐκάλει, and that scholars have *there* argued from the imperfect that "Longinus" must have heard Theodorus and was indeed a younger disciple. See for references my "Theodorus of Gadara" in *AJP* 80 (1959) 360.

[47]See *OCD, s.v.* Sotades and Ptolemy Philadelphus.

third centuries are most likely, we may well answer that they would be much more likely in the first half of the third century than at the "later date," such as the first century B.C. or A.D., to which our treatise is now commonly assigned. Indeed it would be hard to find any author in those centuries as familiar with the late fourth century and early third as our Demetrius seems to be.

The references to the orator Demades (*fl.* 350–319 B.C.) as an exponent of forcefulness where he gets a brief section all to himself (282–286) is also significant. The works of Demades were, according to Quintilian (2.17.13), not committed to writing, so that they were not extant in Roman times. We may, if we wish, suppose that the examples given here were taken from a "collection" of his sayings, which would then have to have been made shortly after his death and survived. We have no evidence of such a collection, nor is he often quoted by later writers. It is at least as likely that these very striking sayings were remembered in oral tradition at the time of our treatise; they would certainly live on for some time. And we are reminded that Theophrastus valued Demades more highly than he did Demosthenes.[48]

I have not so far mentioned the unknown three, Archedemus (34–5), Artemon (233) and the mysterious Gadereus (237), because we know nothing about them. Archedemus corrected Aristotle's definition of a *kôlon* or clause: there is no reason whatsoever to connect him with a Stoic philosopher of that name who *may* have lived as late as 130 B.C., except that they have the same name. Nor do we know anything about Artemon except what we are told here; true, we know of several other men of that name, one of whom also *may* have been living in 130 B.C., but there is no reason to identify him with our Artemon.[49] However, the real display of ingenuity is in connection with ὁ Γαδηρεύς of 237: "as Gadêreus wrote (in trivial fashion) about the battle of Salamis." This improbable name is likely to be a corruption, and editors have amended it to ὁ Γαδαρεύς, that is, "the man from Gadara." This Gadarene is then identified with Theodorus of Gadara, the famous rhetorician and tutor of Tiberius, but if he wrote on the battle of Salamis, trivially or otherwise, we have no record of it. The identification is then used as evidence for a later date, and so is the manner of referring to him by the

[48]Plutarch, *Demosthenes* 10. See below, p. 54–55.

[49]See H. Koskenniemi's "Studien zur Idee und Phraseologie des griechischen Briefes" in *Annales Academiae Scientiarum Fennicae*, B.102 (Helsinki 1956) 25. He points out that in view of the early collections of the letters of other philosophers, that is, Plato and Epicurus, it is very unlikely that the letters of Aristotle remained unpublished until the second century, and suggests that the Artemon mentioned by Demetrius may well have been a contemporary of Theophrastus.

name of his city, a later practice. When scholars thus argue on the basis of their own conjectures as evidence, it might be salutary to remember that we teach students to respect Socrates because he knew he did not know what he did not know. The truth is that we have no means of knowing who the mysterious "Gadereus" is intended to be, just as we are quite unable to identify either Archedemus or Artemon. These three unknown names provide no evidence at all.

2. *Other "late" references.* As far as references to persons in our treatise are concerned, the unusual familiarity with many who lived in the late fourth and early third century would seem to favour an early date, in fact one almost contemporary or at least within the reach of oral tradition; on the other hand the references to Clitarchus, Praxiphanes, and Sotades would seem to make the first quarter of the century improbable but offer no difficulty if we assume a date about 270 B.C. or later. However, the absence of references to later authors is no argument for an early date, for it was the practice of even later critics to draw their illustrations from the writers of Classical Greece and Alexandria. Nor would it be safe to draw any conclusion from the absence of references to later critics, though we may well feel that in a later work we might expect some reference to Hegesias (250 B.C.) and to the Asiatic style in general, for both were universally condemned by critics from the time of Cicero on, and these references would have been especially apt in connection with the affected style. Indeed it has been suggested that some examples of it, such as "a Centaur riding himself" and the pun on Olympias (187) are typical of Asianism and may well be derived from Asiatic writers of the third century.[50] But if we remember that Hegesias' *floruit* was the middle of that century, a taste for affectation obviously developed before his day, and our author may well be quoting from writers with "Asiatic" tendencies earlier in the century, before the name of Asianism or the reputation of Hegesias had developed. Nor need we regard historical inaccuracies (at 238 Aristides is reproached for not being present at Salamis) or excessive hyperboles as betraying clear traces of the artificiality of the rhetorical exercises of Roman times. Even Isocrates was careless of historical truth and some pretty wild hyperboles are quoted by Aristotle.[51]

[50]By Norden, *Kunstprosa* 1.148 note 1 (quoted by Roberts). We may remember in this connection that Quintilian tells us that "fictitious themes in imitation of lawsuits and of deliberative speeches" began in the time of Demetrius of Phalerum, even if these were not as artificial as the Roman type of declamation which he seems to regard as of more recent origin (cp. Quint. 2.4.41 and 2.10.1).

[51]At *Rhet.* 3.11.15–16. The specific passages said to bear clear traces of the later rhetorical schools (Roberts, p. 251 and Radermacher, pp. 91 and 112) are: the rock of the Cyclops at 115, the Amazon's girdle at 138, the Centaur and the pun on Olympias

Our author mentions certain characteristics of rhetoric in his day. He tells us that his contemporaries are apt to confuse grandeur with eloquence itself (38); that forcefulness is in fashion (245); that the term κακόζηλος was commonly applied to affectation or preciosity (186) and this was apparently a recent coinage (239), which, in word-arrangement, was applied to broken rhythms (189) like those of Sotades; finally, that such affectation when combined with aridity of thought was called ξηροκακοζηλία (189 and 239). We are told also that the orators of the day did not know how to use innuendo without making it ridiculous (287). These are all faults of taste; they are quite insufficient to give any clear indication of date, but they seem quite appropriate to the early Hellenistic period when Cicero tells us the fatty or corpulent Asiatic style came into fashion.[52] Certainly these faults are not particularly characteristic of *Greek* style from 100 B.C. to 100 A.D., and in so far as they were current then, they were certainly not new.

Certain specific phrases are also supposed to betray a late date. For example, Demetrius' use of the expression οἱ ἀρχαῖοι, the old writers or the ancients, to designate the Classical writers. This, we are told, is a late usage. The word is used three times: in 12, the adjective is applied to the loose, unperiodic sentence-structure; we have the same contrast in 244 and we are told again that "ancient" writing is unperiodic because "the ancients were simple men." Obviously, this does *not* mean the Classical writers but those who wrote before periodic structure came into fashion. Aristotle uses the word in exactly the same sense (*Rhet.* 3.9.1) and in the same context, and gives, as an example of the "ancient" manner, a sentence from Herodotus. Indeed Aristotle goes further, for in the previous sentence he compares the period to "the antistrophes of the ancient poets" (τῶν ἀρχαίων ποιητῶν), which must include at least Pindar, and probably the three fifth-century tragedians as well. The truth is that ἀρχαῖος is a very elastic term, like our own word "old," and, if Aristotle could apply it to fifth-century poets, we should not be surprised if a couple of generations later it could include Demosthenes in the one place (67) where Demetrius uses it of the Classical writers as against those of his own day: "the old writers use many figures but they use

---

at 187, the reproach to Aristides at 238, and the obscure phrase οὐ μίγνυται ἀνθρώπῳ at 239. Radermacher also considers the advice on how to address despots at 292–293 to smack of later declamations, though one would have thought it quite as topical in the third century B.C. Alexander was certainly a frequent topic for *suasoriae* and the rock of the Cyclops (but not this phrase) is found in Seneca, *Suas.* 1.12. These were perennial subjects.

[52] *Adipata dictio, Orator* 25.

them so skilfully that they seem less artificial than those who use none."
The contrast between old and contemporary writers is there, but such
expressions may mean no more than half a century. Modern critics of
the twenties and thirties certainly used such expressions to contrast
their contemporaries with the writers of even the late nineteenth century.

In 204, Demetrius says that "the new comedy" uses shorter verses.
We are told that "the triple division of comedy is Alexandrian and this
suggests a later date than Demetrius of Phalerum." How much later?
Does the expression "the new comedy" really imply a tripartite division?
Aristotle already used a very similar expression when he said the difference between crude and polished wit is seen in "comedies old and
new."[53]

In 181, prose of a general rhythmical nature is said to be practised by
Plato, Xenophon, and "the Peripatetics." The objection is that only
"later" writers would thus have referred collectively to the school of
Aristotle and to writers of that school. Perhaps, but we do not know
when the Aristotelians became Peripatetics (*LSJ* traces it back to about
200 B.C.). Is it not the kind of nickname that should be almost contemporary with the first two heads of the school?

The expression οἱ 'Αττικοί to designate the inhabitants of Attica,
where Attic dialect is contrasted with Doric at 175–177, is even less
significant. The adjective is, of course, quite Classical and Aristotle
uses the phrase οἱ 'Αττικοὶ ῥήτορες for the Attic orators (*Rhet.* 3.11.16).
There is no reason to consider this a gloss, but in any case Plato speaks
of "the Attic speech" and "the old Attic speech."[54]

There is one other phrase the meaning of which presents a pretty
problem. In 108, Demetrius says "altogether, ornamental addition
(*epiphônêma*) may be compared to those external displays of riches,
(ornamented) cornices and triglyphs and broad purples (πορφύραις
πλατείαις)." The meaning of this last phrase is very obscure, but the
context requires some ornament used to display wealth, almost certainly
in connection with buildings, probably awnings or drapes of some kind.
The fact that Lucian in the second century A.D.[55] uses a somewhat similar

[53]*Nic. Ethics* 1128a 22: ἐκ τῶν κωμῳδιῶν τῶν παλαιῶν καὶ τῶν καινῶν . . . .

[54]*Cratylus* 398d. We may also remember Aristophanes' phrase "the Attic look" in
Clouds 1176. Demetrius also uses the verb ἀττικίζειν for "to speak Attic" in contrast
to δωρίζειν, to speak or write Doric. The verb is found in the comic writers of the fifth
and fourth centuries.

[55]Lucian, *Demonax* 41: "Seeing one of the grandees taking pride in the width of his
purple—τῷ πλάτει τῆς πορφύρας," but there the previous use of τῶν εὐπαρύφων
which already means wearer of the purple stripe makes the meaning quite clear, and is
not even evidence of ἡ πορφύρα alone for the *laticlavus*.

expression to refer to the *laticlavus,* that is, the broad purple band which Roman senators wore on their toga, is hardly enough to see a reference to it here. In any case the senatorial purple was not a sign of wealth but of caste and prestige, nor did *mere* wealth entitle one to it, certainly not in the first century B.C. or A.D.

Finally, the citing of 172 as a proof of a later date by Roberts, Radermacher, and others seems a good example of faulty logic. Demetrius tells us that certain jibes may be allowed, and he clearly implies that they are allowed because their frequent use ($\chi\rho\acute{\eta}\sigma\sigma\nu\tau\alpha\iota$) has blunted their sting. The two examples he gives are that a tall dark man is called "an Egyptian clematis" and that a fool on the water (whether rowing or swimming is not clear) is called "a sheep at sea," the word "sheep" or $\pi\rho\acute{o}\beta\alpha\tau\sigma\nu$ being common parlance for a stupid fellow also in other contexts. Now we are told by Seneca (*De Constantia* 17) that Chrysippus (280–207 B.C.) mentioned someone who was indignant because he was called a sheep at sea, *vervex marinus*; and from Diogenes Laertius (7.1.2) we learn that in a work on proverbs or saws Chrysippus said that Zeno, who was tall and dark, was called an Egyptian clematis. As both expressions are traced to Chrysippus, this proves, we are told, that Demetrius is extracting them from Chrysippus' collection of proverbs. It surely proves nothing of the kind: it is in no way surprising that two jibes quoted by Demetrius as in frequent use should reappear in a collection of such proverbial sayings by Chrysippus one or two generations later. Proverbs hardly find their way into a collection until they have been in use for a considerable time.[56]

Language and Vocabulary

Both Radermacher and Roberts, and indeed all those who have argued that *On Style* must have been written much later than the traditional date, have put a good deal of emphasis upon the language of the treatise.

[56]We may add one more reference. At 158 Demetrius refers to a legend that "cats grow fatter and thinner as the moon waxes and wanes," and quotes a further elaboration by an unknown writer. Now Plutarch (*Isis and Osiris* 63, 376f) gives a different version, namely that a cat's *pupils* grow larger at the full moon. As it seems established that this and other Egyptian tales were first told in the West by Apion in the first century A.D. and that this is Plutarch's source, Demetrius, Radermacher asserts, must have got it indirectly from the same source and got it wrong. But no one suggests that Apion invented the legend, and if our author was writing in Alexandria, or indeed had been in Egypt at all, he might have heard it from anyone, correctly or incorrectly, and so could anyone else. Such arguments surely have little force. I understand from my colleague Professor R. J. Williams that the story is not found in native Egyptian sources.

It is one of their main arguments, at times their chief argument. The fullest study of the language of Demetrius is that of Dahl, and most of his arguments will be found in Rhys Roberts' edition. In this question of language we are admittedly on very slippery ground, for we have no third-century prose works to give us a standard of comparison. We know that linguistic habits were changing by the second half of the fourth century. The number of word-forms, apart from technical terms, which appear for the first time in Aristotle and Theophrastus is very considerable. The *Rhetorica ad Alexandrum* is of special interest in this respect, for it is a fourth-century text and, being a rhetorical work, it is roughly of the same kind as *On Style*. Even a superficial study of its language and vocabulary makes quite evident that it contains a substantial number of words, expressions, and constructions which would certainly have been condemned as "late" if the date of the treatise had not been so firmly established.[57]

At the end of the fourth century, Greek spread rapidly all over the Near East until it became the common language, the *Koinê* of the Eastern Mediterranean world. All our later authorities agree that this was the time when the florid, over-rhythmic Asiatic style was born; all of them associate this style with the name of Hegesias whom they unanimously condemn, and the *floruit* of Hegesias was as early as 250 B.C. Clearly the degeneration was rapid. Obviously, many changes took place before then.

What kind of Greek, then, would be written in Alexandria in the first half of the third century, and written by the scholars of the Museum who had been attracted there by the patronage of the Ptolemies from all over the Greek world? They studied and edited all the great Classics, they were students of *all* dialects. They wrote Greek, but it is pretty well established that they did *not* write Attic Greek, nor any particular dialect, unless indeed a particular type of Greek was required by convention for a particular genre of poetry. One would expect to find Attic and Ionian, poetic and prose forms appearing cheek by jowl with colloquialisms we know only in Aristophanes; it would be a mixture of the old and the new, and a more heterogeneous mixture than either the later *Koinê* of the New Testament, or the deliberate Atticism of Roman times. We should not be surprised, therefore, to find in a scholarly text of that period both forms and constructions that are specifically Attic, forms in ττ, for example, and even an occasional use of the dual, which we know had almost disappeared. We should also expect a relaxation of that grammatical precision which is so characteristic of the best Classical

[57]See Appendix II.

authors (the beginnings of this process too we can trace in Aristotle), for example, a less exact use of prepositions, a slackness in the use of ἄν with the optative, in short an erratic kind of inconsistency. And this is precisely what we do find.

As for the words themselves, we should always remember that our evidence is incomplete for any period. Unless the method of word-formation is itself late, when we call a word "late" it only means that it does not appear *in our extant texts* before a later period. Even where the manner of derivation is late, we cannot be sure, for the Greeks always formed words very easily, especially compounds. There is surprisingly a large number of words that occur only once in extant literature. Our treatise has sixteen such words.[58]

Where the form is regularly derived from a word in common use in Classical times—when, for example, the verb and the adjective are used in Classical writers but the noun is not, or *vice versa*,—there seems very little point in considering such forms as "late."[59] It is true that later Greek shows a tendency to use compounds, and double compounds (verbs formed with two or even more prepositions) carelessly, where the simple word would do just as well, while the Classical writers are, with occasional lapses, more careful. This tendency too began in the fourth century. Our Demetrius, however, is here, at least on a number of occasions, on the side of precision. He uses double compounds with each preposition having its full meaning so that the double compound is fully justified.[60]

In fact, Demetrius has a tendency to be precise also in his technical terms. We have already seen that he on occasion changes the technical terms of Aristotle, even where he follows him closely, from an apparent desire to simplify. We are very ignorant of the technical rhetorical vocabulary which, by the end of the fourth century, had been developing for well over a century. Plato quotes a few such terms in the *Phaedrus* in order to ridicule them; Aristotle gives us more, but his attitude to rhetorical subtleties is not very different.[61] There are some more rhetorical terms in the *Rhetorica ad Alexandrum*; of Theophrastus we have only a few uncertain fragments on matters of style. Yet, clearly, the vocabulary of rhetoric and criticism had, by this time, reached considerable propor-

[58]As given by Rhys Roberts p. 57.

[59]Examples will be found in Appendix I. See, in particular, ἀποτομία, ἀποφθεγματικός, γνωμολογικός, κρεανομία, λιθοβολέω, ὁλοκληρία, συγκάλυμμα, φιλοφρόνησις.

[60]See, in Appendix I, συγκαταλήγω, ὑποδάκνω, κατασκευάζω, προαναβοάω. Rhys Roberts (p. 229) himself says there are comparatively few such double compounds in our treatise, as compared, for example, with the περὶ ὕψους.

[61]See notes 6 and 13 above.

tions. Most of these terms are, for us, inevitably "late." Moreover, even in the first generation after the foundation of the Museum, the learned men of Alexandria were no doubt adding technical terms of their own. We must therefore expect some "new" and some "late" technical words in Demetrius in any case. There are altogether about twenty. It would be very surprising if there were fewer.[62] These terms do not appear again till the first century, but then we have no extant critical or rhetorical works in which they could appear.

It is perhaps more surprising that some words that are very common in later criticism do not appear in Demetrius at all. The most obvious of these are τρόπος in the sense of "trope," ἀφελής, later applied to the simple style, a word also used by Aristotle for the "simple" period, which Demetrius avoids, as he seems to avoid or not to know the phrase ἐκλογὴ ὀνομάτων, the choice of words, meaning diction. Moreover, Demetrius uses a number of terms in a sense closer to the Classical than to the later meaning.[63]

If we carefully review all the words and expressions suspected of being "late," (as is done in Appendix I), we shall, I believe, conclude that the evidence for a date much later than the traditional one is, as far as language goes at any rate, not convincing. It is true that the effect of such suspicious words is cumulative; if enough words are listed as suspect, the reader is tempted to believe that there must be something in the argument, but we should not forget the truism that poor arguments, however numerous, do not lead to sound conclusions. There are a half-dozen Classical forms used in a "non-Classical" sense. Of the fifty or so words said to be "late" in form, most could pass anywhere and the exceptions are less than a dozen. There are some deviations from the Classical usage in the use of adverbs, prepositions, and syntactical constructions. All this is, I believe, quite consistent with an early third-century date.

Is it, however, consistent with the traditional author? It is true that Cicero regards Demetrius of Phalerum as the best Greek exponent of the middle style, yet sharply marks him off from the Classical writers and regards him as an exponent of a less vigorous, softer style. Quintilian says his style is more suitable for display than for the struggle of the courts. We know from other sources that he was very affected and easy-living as a young man. Cicero actually links him with the later "Asiatics," at

[62]See Appendix I, A, where 20 are listed, but some might be added, from other sections, which contain at least semi-technical words.

[63]See Appendix I under ἀλληγορία, ἀστεϊσμός, δεινότης, ἔμφασις, σημειώδης, ἀπαγγελία.

a time when he was more kindly disposed to the latter than he was in his later years.[64] We may conclude that his affectations did lead him to new ways of style. How would such a man write after some years in Alexandria? How far does an expatriate scholar adopt the ways of speech of his adopted country and of the community in which he lives? The question is hard to answer, especially in the case of a man like Demetrius. We may be quite sure that some non-Attic forms would slip in; yet he was an Athenian, a contemporary of Theophrastus and Menander, and we may well feel it hard to believe that he would write in this somewhat medley mixture of Attic and non-Attic. While other aspects of the treatise, its relationship to Aristotle and Theophrastus for example, would suit Demetrius very well, the language of the treatise may well be felt to be a strong argument against his authorship.

General Critical Views

To infer from the occurrence of the four "styles" here that "the writer lived at a time, considerably later than Aristotle, when the doctrine of the types of style had undergone many developments"[65] is to confuse our author's scheme of four main manners of writing which can all be used together (except that the plain and the grand do not mix) with the far more rigid formula of the separate and distinct three styles which we first meet in the *Ad Herennium*, and then in Cicero, but in no earlier Greek extant texts. The "styles" of Demetrius are much more like qualities of style than χαρακτῆρες in this more rigid sense,[66] and they

[64]On the style of Demetrius of Phalerum see Cicero *De Oratore* 2.95, *Orator* 92, *Brutus* 37, and Quintilian 10.1.33 and 80.

[65]Roberts p. 59; this view seems to be generally accepted.

[66]As is indeed pointed out by Altschul (p. 31, note 21) but he rather surprisingly takes this as evidence of a later date. It should be noted that Solmsen links the four styles with the four virtues which he traces back to Theophrastus (note 44 above). We first meet the formula of the three styles in the *Ad Herennium* 4.8–11. It is there clearly stated (ch. 11, 16) that every orator must use all styles. So in Cicero (e.g. *Orator* 20–21, 75–99) who links the three styles with the three *officia oratoris* (*ibid.* 69: *subtile in probando, modicum in delectando, vehemens in flectendo*).

Dionysius has three kinds (χαρακτῆρες) of diction and three kinds of word-arrangement, but these do not correspond (see *AJP* 73 [1952] 261–267). We do, however, have a passage of Aulus Gellius (6.14) which not only speaks of the three styles and their corresponding vices, but further states that Varro said that Pacuvius was an example of *ubertas*, Lucilius of *gracilitas*, and Terence of *mediocritas*, that is, of the grand, the plain, and the intermediate respectively. As Gellius, however, calls them *virtutes* as well as *genera dicendi*, this need not imply any classification according to "styles" in Varro; he may have given these authors as examples of particular qualities only.

The earliest Greek classification by three styles seems to be a doubtful passage in Tryphon's περὶ τρόπων (Spengel 3, p. 201 = Walz 8, p. 750) where he lists three

seem rather to belong to a time when the three-style formula had *not* become current.

As for the general standpoint of our author, it does not seem to be "that of the Graeco-Roman period, earlier than Hermogenes and (possibly) later than Dionysius."[67] Demetrius does *not* seem to share either the point of view or the concerns of Cicero, Dionysius, Horace, or their successors. They are deeply concerned to restore rhetoric to its Isocratean place as the true philosophy based on a general education, and they insist that the writer, poet, or orator must know life and imitate it. Cicero and Dionysius are vehement in their condemnation of Asianism. There is not a word about all this in our treatise. There is no such comparative criticism as was the fashion in the circle of Dionysius and Caecilius. Demosthenes is not for Demetrius, as he was for Dionysius and Hermogenes, *the* supreme model; even δεινότης is not his above all others, for he shares it with others as well as Demades. Demetrius is aware of the basic formula which differentiates matter from style and subdivides the latter into diction and word-arrangement, but the far more elaborate critical formulae of Dionysius do not appear. There is no trace of the rhetorical *mimêsis* or emulation so important to Cicero, Dionysius, and Quintilian. The whole apparatus of criticism seems very much simpler.

We do not know what the Greek critics of the first century A.D. were concerned with; for the schools of Theodorus of Gadara and Apollonius seem to have concentrated on matters purely rhetorical.[68] We do know, however, that the Romans were extremely concerned with the evil results of declamations and the decay of eloquence. Indeed the treatise *On the Sublime* has been dated in the first century largely on the strength of its concluding chapter on this latter subject. There is nothing of all this in Demetrius, nor of the more specifically Roman controversies between the "moderns" and the "ancients," any more than about Asianism vs. Atticism, Analogism vs. Anomalism, or any other topical question of that period. It is hard to see in what respect our Demetrius can be said to share the standpoint of Graeco-Roman times.

χαρακτῆρες, namely αὐστηρός, μέσος, and ἰσχνός. He gives Thucydides and Antiphon as examples of the first, Demosthenes, Hyperides, Demarchus, and Lycurgus as examples of the intermediate, and Aeschines, Isocrates, Lysias, Andocides, and Isaeus as examples of the simple style. The passage is quite irrelevant where it stands, the classification contrary to that of critics like Dionysius; Spengel brackets it.

[67]Roberts, p. 59. See also note 26 above.

[68]See my "Theodorus of Gadara" in *AJP* 80 (1959) 337–365. To include the author of the περὶ ὕψους as a first-century critic would beg the question of *his* date. In any case the main preoccupations of "Longinus" are quite different from those of Demetrius.

As for the place where our treatise was written, the concern with literature in general rather than with rhetoric would suit Alexandria very well,
and the apparent familiarity with Egypt would tend to confirm an
Alexandrian origin.[69]

External Evidence

There are a few somewhat uncertain references to our treatise in much
later authors. There are also one or two references in Philodemus which
deserve more attention than has been paid to them. Also, the references
to, and fragments of, Demetrius of Phalerum himself, which have recently
been collected by Wehrli,[70] should be examined anew to see what light
they throw on his possible authorship.

These last are somewhat disappointing. The περὶ ἑρμηνείας does not
occur in the list of his works in Diogenes Laertius (early third century
A.D.).[71] The list is not very long, as compared for example with the works
of Theophrastus, though Diogenes tells us that he wrote more than any
contemporary Peripatetic. He also says that Demetrius wrote rhetorical
works, but the only clearly rhetorical title is a *Rhetoric* in two books. There
are, however, some other titles that may be rhetorical: the περὶ πίστεως,
περὶ χάριτος, and περὶ καιροῦ may well have been *On Proof, On Elegance,*
and *On Good Taste*[72] in the rhetorical sense, rather than *On Faith, On
Favour,* and *On Opportunity* in general.[73] The word χάρις is used by our
Demetrius as one of the terms to describe the elegant style, and Radermacher even suggests (p. 95) that our author may have owed a good deal
to this work of the Phalerean. It is, at any rate, a point of contact between
the two, if a slight one.

Both Plutarch and Stobaeus[74] tell us that Demetrius of Phalerum
advised Ptolemy to read books on kingship as he would find written
there the advice his friends did not dare to give him, which may remind
us of *On Style* (292–293) on how despots have to be addressed with care.
More directly reminiscent of that whole section is a passage in

---

[69]See sections 77, 158, 172. We may add 97, for Boll (*Rhein. Mus.* 72 [1917] 27–28)
gives good reason to think that the word σκαφιτής is of Egyptian origin.

[70]See Fritz Wehrli, *Demetrius von Phalerum, Die Schule des Aristoteles* 4 (Basle 1949).

[71]Diogenes Laertius 5.80–81 = Wehrli 74.

[72]The meaning of καιρός and καίριος in criticism comes very close to that of πρέπον,
that is, appropriateness to the occasion. Dionysius complains in *Composition* 12 that
no rhetorician or philosopher has written a treatise on the subject since Gorgias first
dealt with it. For an interesting, if somewhat fanciful, discussion of καιρός in Gorgias
see W. Vollgraff, *L'Oraison funèbre de Gorgias* (Leiden 1952) 21–27.

[73]As R. D. Hicks translates these titles in his Loeb version of Diogenes.

[74]Plutarch, *Reg. et Imp. Apopth.* 189d, Stobaeus 4.7.27 = Wehrli 63.

Philodemus,[75] who says that Demetrius, together with the Sophistic kind of speeches, added to the deliberative and forensic kinds of rhetoric τὸν ἐντευκτικὸν (λόγον) ἄπασι, that is, the speech which knows how to address all audiences and obtain favour with all. Philodemus seems to mean that Demetrius included this under "sophistic" (which in Philodemus means epideictic) rather than that he made it a fourth kind of rhetoric, but, in any case, he obviously attached great importance to methods of addressing, in particular, popular assemblies and ruling princes. This subject may also have been treated in the πρεσβευτικός (how to speak as an ambassador?)[76] which is listed among his works by Diogenes, or in the περὶ καιροῦ.[77] Now this ἐντευκτικὸς λόγος is highly reminiscent of what our Demetrius says about innuendo, which he too specifically links with princes and assemblies (289–293). Here again we have a distinct point of contact between the two Demetrii.

There is another interesting sentence in Philodemus, where he says that "long periods are bad for delivery, as we read also in Demetrius about those of Isocrates. . . ."[78] We should note that the name "Demetrius" is uncertain, though the restoration has been generally accepted, and some commentators have admitted this as a reference to our treatise. The sentence occurs in a discussion of delivery in which just before "the Phalerean" (that name is quite clear) was said to have disliked the delivery of Demosthenes.[79] If the name "Demetrius" is

[75]Rhetorica IV, Col. XI^a (Sudhaus 1, p. 222 = Wehrli 157): καὶ μὴν ὁ Δημήτριος μετὰ τοῦ σοφιστικοῦ γένους τῶν λόγων προστιθεὶς τῷ δημηγορικῷ καὶ δικανικῷ τὸν ἐντευκτικὸν ἄπασι, εἰ μὲν λαμβάνει τὸν τοῖς πλήθεσιν ἐντευκτικὸν καὶ τὸν κατὰ πρεσβείαν τοῖς δυνάσταις . . . διότι δὲ ταὐτοῦ καὶ ταῦτα καὶ τὸ σοφιστικὸν εἶδος ἐποίησεν, λεγέσθω διαμαρτάνειν. We may compare Aristotle's use of ἔντευξις in Rhet. 1.1.12, and Wehrli in his note (p. 79) shows the correspondence of ὁ ἐντευκτικὸς λόγος with the προσομιλητικὴ τέχνη of Plato, Sophist 222 c. This type of rhetoric obviously means "to know how to address various types of hearers," and might also have been discussed in the περὶ καιροῦ (note 72 above). There can be little doubt that Philodemus is referring to Demetrius of Phalerum, as Wehrli and others have taken him to be.

[76]So Hubbell, "The Rhetorica of Philodemus," Trans. Connecticut|Acad. Arts and Sciences 23 (1920) 304, note. "Obtaining favor with all" is Hubbell's translation of ἐντευκτικός.

[77]See note 72 above.

[78]Rhetorica IV. Col. XVI^a (Sudhaus 1, p. 198) = Wehrli 169: πονηρ[ὸ]ν γὰρ ε[ἰ]ς ὑπόκ[ρι]σιν αἱ [μα]κραὶ περίοδοι, καθάπερ καὶ παρὰ [Δη]μη[τρί]ῳ [κ]εῖται περὶ τῶ[ν Ἰ]σο[κρά]τους.

[79]The point seems to have escaped Roberts who says (p. 60): "it is to be noticed that Philodemus speaks vaguely of 'Demetrius' without any addition, and so may, or may not, have Demetrius Phalereus in mind." Hammer (p. 60) admits the reference is to our treatise which was therefore known to Philodemus, but he does not make the connection with Phalereus. A look at Sudhaus' text makes clear that there is no possible doubt that the two passages go together.

correct in the sentence quoted, there is therefore no doubt that it refers to Demetrius of Phalerum, and if the reference is to our treatise, then Philodemus, *in the first century B.C.*, already believed the author of our treatise to be Demetrius of Phalerum.

What Philodemus says of the long periods of Isocrates does accord very well with what we find in our section on forcefulness. From the very beginning of that section we are told that the forceful style requires short phrases rather than clauses (241–242), brevity and lack of smoothness (241–244), vehemence (246), the avoidance of the antitheses and balanced clauses found in Theopompus, the pupil of Isocrates (247). We may have periods but they should be short (252); forcefulness favours harsh sounds and abrupt endings (255–256), but not smoothness or regularly connected clauses (258, 269). Moreover, dramatic delivery is clearly related very closely to forcefulness, indeed at one point all but identified with it (271, and compare 193, where the disjointed word-order is said to be histrionic, ὑποκριτική). Returning to forcible word-arrangement at 299, we are there told that "smooth word-order, *as practised most by the school of Isocrates*" is not suited to forcefulness; it is better to do without connectives (301) and a little later (303) *long, continuous periods* are said to be unpleasant and tiresome in this style. We also remember that our author said (12) that he disliked a style which is entirely periodic like that of Isocrates.

In view of the specific mention of Isocrates at 299, of Theopompus at 247, of the emphasis throughout this section on characteristics of Isocrates' style which are undesirable in the forceful style, and the all but identification of the forceful style with that of delivery and debate, it would seem that Philodemus is indeed referring to our treatise when he says that it is "stated in Demetrius" that the long periods of Isocrates are not suited to delivery, even though where Isocrates is specifically mentioned Demetrius refers to the smoothness of Isocrates' periods rather than to their length. In Isocrates certainly the two went together. It seems, therefore, more than probable that Philodemus believed Demetrius of Phalerum to be the author of our treatise; in any case, we have here a very close similarity of viewpoint between the two Demetrii.

There is one other matter of interest in connection with Demetrius of Phalerum. We are told that, in common with Theophrastus and other cultured Athenians, he was very critical of Demosthenes' delivery; they considered it to lack dignity and simplicity, and they disliked his boldness and violence.[80] Now the attitude to Demosthenes in our treatise is un-

[80]Besides the passage just referred to from Philodemus, see also Plutarch, *Demosthenes* 9 and 11 and other references in Wehrli 162–169.

usual. He is quoted fourteen times in the section on forcefulness, usually with approval though he is once (250) condemned. No other style is illustrated by a quotation from him. At 80 a metaphor of his is quoted to illustrate the difference between a metaphor and a simile. The other three references are illustrations of periods in the first section. In other words Demetrius regards forcefulness as characteristic of the orator, *and that style only*. And even that section he shares not only with Demades but with seventeen illustrations from other writers.

How very different from the picture of Demosthenes which we find in Cicero, Dionysius, and Hermogenes! The δεινότης attributed to him by all the writers of these later centuries is no longer the one quality of forcefulness but an over-all excellence in every kind of style, at times including force but not restricted to it.[81] In our treatise Demosthenes has not reached that supremacy. Not only is he used to illustrate one style only, but other writers are both more frequently quoted and illustrate various styles. As against the eighteen references to Demosthenes, there are thirty-seven references to Homer, twenty to Xenophon, nineteen to Plato, eighteen also to Aristotle, and twelve to Thucydides. Altogether, Demetrius' attitude to Demosthenes is almost as unlike that of later critical texts[82] as his attitude to Aristotle.

There are no other references to our treatise in writers of the Classical period. Ammonius, the commentator on Aristotle (*ca.* 500 A.D.) does refer to the περὶ ἑρμηνείας of "Demetrius" and explains that Aristotle's work of the same name dealt with a different subject.[83] True, he does not add "of Phalerum" but Demetrius of Phalerum is by far the most natural reference in such a Peripatetic context. One feels that if he had not meant the friend and pupil of Theophrastus he would certainly have said so. Specific references to the author as Demetrius of Phalerum do occur in the eleventh century and later, but these are of little value except in so far as they support the tradition of the manuscripts.[84]

Conclusion

None of the arguments in favour of a date much later than the traditional one seem to me at all compelling. On the other hand, our author's

[81]See Appendix I, A under δεινότης.

[82]It is true that "Longinus," *On the Sublime* (33–35), recognises that Demosthenes lacks many virtues which Hyperides possesses, but this is meant to show that those he does possess are by far more important, in a passage which insists that faulty genius is to be preferred to flawless mediocrity.

[83]*In Arist. de Interpretatione*, Berlin edition, 4. 4–5, 966–997a. See Appendix I, A under ἑρμηνεία.

[84]Quoted by Rhys Roberts, pp. 60–61.

familiarity with Aristotle and the way he uses him, his attitude to Demosthenes, his unusual familiarity with people living in the late fourth and early third centuries about whom he gives us a good deal of information not found elsewhere, his general critical outlook, his remarks on contemporary oratory and his silence about later controversies—all these things seem to point to a quite early date. The use of some technical terms in a Classical or near-Classical sense while often ignoring later meanings seems to point in the same direction. There are some references to Alexandrine personalities, on the other hand, which make a date before 270 unlikely. Certainty in such matters is of course impossible to attain, but I incline to the view that our treatise was written about 270 B.C., or not very much later.

As for the author, we have seen that, as far as critical ideas are concerned, there are several points of contact with Demetrius of Phalerum. It must also, I think, be admitted that Ammonius (*ca.* 500 A.D.) regarded him as the author. Far more important, it seems highly probable that Philodemus, in the first century B.C., also attributed our treatise to him. On the other hand, the un-Attic nature of the language does not seem to suit the Phalerean. Moreover, if we accept the evidence of Cicero and Diogenes Laertius quoted above[85]—and in the absence of any evidence to the contrary it seems that we must accept it—Demetrius of Phalerum most probably died shortly after the death of Ptolemy Soter in 283/2 B.C. He cannot then have been the author of our treatise.

This leaves us with a treatise *On Style* probably written in Alexandria not much later than 270 B.C. by an unknown author. This author must, obviously, have had strong Peripatetic connections, and to some extent have shared the critical ideas of Demetrius of Phalerum, whom he had probably known, and with whose writings, as with those of Aristotle and Theophrastus on rhetoric and style, he was no doubt familiar. If his name was also Demetrius—for it was a common enough name—this might help to account for confusion between the two even at an early date.

[85]P. 23.

TRANSLATION OF *ON STYLE*

NOTE ON THE TRANSLATION

THE translator of Demetrius, as of any ancient critical text, is faced with an inherent difficulty: some of his author's illustrations are untranslatable, especially when it is the sound or rhythm of a word or phrase that is in question, or the use of a particular word or particle. To translate the meaning is completely pointless and irrelevant, to pepper one's English version with strings of Greek words is a confession of failure.

I have adopted neither of these expedients, which can only be justified when the Greek text is printed opposite and the translation is intended merely to explain the Greek text. Where the point can be made clear by translation, I have simply translated, sometimes adding the Greek, or some of it, in a note where this seemed helpful. When it was the sound or rhythm of a very short phrase or one word that is in question, the best way seemed to print the Greek word in the text, for even those without Greek could see what is involved. However, where neither was possible or satisfactory, the point that Demetrius is making and his explanation are made clear in the text, but the Greek illustration, omitted in the text, is printed and explained in the footnote. Every such omission is marked by an asterisk in the text.

I believe that this is the only effective way to present this important treatise to all who do not have considerable knowledge of Greek. I hope that, with the explanations given in the notes, even the Greek illustrations will be significant to those who have little or no Greek, and that, after all, is the purpose of a true translation.

The texts of the two standard editions, of Rhys Roberts and Radermacher, are fairly well in agreement. I have followed that of Roberts, except where Radermacher's seemed an improvement, and in those few cases attention is drawn to the discrepancy in the notes. The footnotes are numbered according to the section to which they belong.

ON STYLE

1. Just as poetry is divided into metrical lines, half-lines, hexameters, and the rest, so clauses or *kôla*, as they are called, divide and articulate prose. These clauses may be said to provide pauses both for the speaker and in the subject-matter, and to mark the boundaries of what is said in many places. Without them the discourse would go on indefinitely without pause and simply give a speaker no chance to catch his breath.

2. The intention of these clauses is to mark the end of a thought. It may be a complete thought, as when Hecataeus said at the beginning of his *History*: "Hecataeus of Miletus tells this story." Here the whole thought is contained in one whole clause, and both end together. Sometimes, however, the clause does not complete the whole thought, but a definite part of it. The arm is one whole, yet its parts, such as the fingers or the forearm, have a wholeness of their own. Each part then has a contour of its own, and indeed itself has parts. In the same way a complete thought, if it is extensive, may contain parts, each of which is, in a sense, also a whole.

3. Take the beginning of Xenophon's *Anabasis*: from "Darius and

---

1. By half-lines (ἡμίμετρα, a word which does not seem to recur) Demetrius presumably means short measures in contrast to the hexameter. The idea recurs at 180.

The word κῶλον means limb; it was then applied to the two halves of a race-track. Hence the notion of running oneself out of breath comes naturally in the Greek. The meaning "clause" or "limb" of a sentence is first found in Aristotle, *Rhet*. 3.9.5.

2. Aristotle had said, in *Rhet*. 3.9.4., that the characteristic of a period was that sense and sentence should end together, but the period could consist of one or more clauses. Demetrius adds that, in a period of the latter kind, there should be a similar correspondence between the structure of the sentence and that of the thought expressed, so that each clause should express a specific part of the whole thought. This is a new point, and important.

Hecataeus of Miletus was a geographer and historian who lived early in the fifth century B.C.

3. The sentence of Xenophon reads: Δαρείου καὶ Παρυσάτιδος γίγνονται παῖδες δύο, πρεσβύτερος μὲν ᾿Αρταξέρξης νεώτερος δὲ Κῦρος (Darius and Parysatis had two sons, the elder [was] Artaxerxes and the younger, Cyrus.)

Demetrius is here defining a *kôlon* or clause; as against a *komma* or phrase, it must have a meaning of its own. One might have expected him to divide Xenophon's sentence into three clauses, but, as the elder implies the younger, the sense of the second clause would then have been incomplete.

Parysatis" to "the younger, Cyrus." The whole thought is here completed, and each of the two clauses contains one part of it, but, within
its own limits, a thought is also fully expressed in each clause. In the
first, it is that Darius and Parysatis had two sons, and this thought has a
certain completeness, namely that Darius and Parysatis had sons. The
same is true of the other clause: that the elder was Artaxerxes and the
younger Cyrus. I say then that a clause should in every case fully express
some thought, either a whole thought or a part of it which also forms a
whole.

4. We must not make our clauses very long, for then the sentence lacks
measure and is hard to follow. Even poetry rarely ventures upon a metre
which is longer than the hexameter, for it is absurd for metre to lack
measure so that we forget where the verse began before we get to the end
of it. Lengthy clauses are unsuitable in prose for the same reason. Very
short clauses, however, are also unsuitable, and produce the type of
sentence-structure which is called arid, as in: "Life is short, art lasting,
opportunity fleeting." The structure of this sentence is chopped up, fragmented, and unimpressive because all the clauses are brief.

5. Yet there is a right time for lengthy clauses as, for example, in noble
passages such as Plato's "and this whole universe the god himself at times
helps to guide and direct on its circular way," where the length of the
clause contributes to the elevation of the passage. So the hexameter is
called the heroic metre because its length makes it fit for heroes. The

4. Demetrius quotes only part of the famous first aphorism of Hippocrates and expects his reader to remember the rest of it. The whole sentence runs: "Life [is] short,
art long, opportunity fleeting, experiment precarious, judgement difficult." σύνθεσις
is the word here translated by sentence-structure; it refers to the "putting together"
of words, as against the selection of them. It is often translated by "composition"
but this, though literal, is misleading in English. The best over-all translation is probably
"word-arrangement." The ancients were concerned with three aspects of word-arrangement: the collocation of sounds, the rhythm, and the structure of the clauses and sentence. These are, of course, closely akin, indeed the last two are often confused, and
Demetrius immediately goes on to discuss rhythm. We shall translate σύνθεσις mostly
by word-arrangement, but also by rhythm or structure, according to the aspect of
word-arrangement which is being discussed.

5. The Platonic quotation is from the myth of the *Politicus* (269c) where the god
intermittently leaves the world to its own devices, and then has to control its motion
again. To strengthen his point here, Demetrius quotes two lines from Archilochus
(late eighth or early seventh century, B.C.), namely: ἀχνυμένη σκυτάλη (a sorrowful
message) and τίς σὰς παρήειρε φρένας (who changed your mind?) and one from
Anacreon (sixth century, B.C.) φέρ' ὕδωρ, φέρ' οἶνον, ὦ παῖ (boy, bring the water,
bring the wine). He is here clearly thinking both of length and metre. The metre of the
three lines is, respectively: —UU—UU—, ——U————U—, and UU—U—U——. Greek
scansion is entirely a matter of long and short syllables.

Iliad of Homer could not fittingly be written in the short metres of Archilochus or Anacreon.* The Anacreontic is quite suitable for an old man in his cups, but not for a fighting hero.

6. So there is an appropriate time for the long clause, but other occasions call for short clauses, when our subject is small or trifling. When the Greeks reach the river Teleboas in Xenophon: "This river," he says, "was not large; it was pretty though." The short and abrupt rhythm expresses the smallness and charm of the river. If he had extended the sentence and said: "In size this river was smaller than most others, but in beauty it surpassed them all," the length of his clauses would have been unsuitable, and we would have had what is called the frigid style. But frigidity must be discussed later.

7. Short clauses are also used in forceful passages, for it is both more forceful and more violent to express much in a few words. It was the forcefulness of the Spartans that made them brief in speech. Orders are always short and brief, and every master is monosyllabic to his slaves, whereas supplications and lamentations are lengthy. Homer represents the Prayers as lame and wrinkled and slow, that is, lengthy in speech, as old men are verbose because they are weak.

8. Brevity in sentence structure is well illustrated by the message: "The Spartans to Philip: Dionysius [is] in Corinth." Thus briefly expressed, it is much more forceful than if they had expanded their sentence and said: "Dionysius was once a great ruler like you, but he is now living in Corinth as a private citizen." Expressed in so many words this is no longer a frightening rebuke but a rather didactic statement of fact; it loses both in feeling and in vehemence. As wild beasts gather themselves together before they leap, so there is a drawing together and coiling up of words which makes for forcefulness.

*An asterisk in the text indicates that an illustration is there omitted; it is then quoted in the note (see Introd. to Translation p. 59).

6. Xen. *Anabasis* 4.4.3: οὗτος μὲν ἦν μέγας μὲν οὔ, καλὸς δέ The quotation, as often, is from memory and not quite exact. We are concerned here again with length and rhythm together. The rhythm of the Greek, five trochees following an initial long syllable, would by all Greek critics have been considered a broken rhythm quite unsuitable to any noble utterance.

I read ὁ λεγόμενος ψυχρός (with Roberts), but we should probably understand χαρακτήρ, even though the expression has not been explained. Spengel's conjecture ὁ λόγος ψυχρός, adopted by Radermacher, is unnecessary, though the meaning is much the same. Roberts' translation "the so-called frigid writer" is improbable. The same sentence of Xenophon is quoted for the same reasons at 121.

7. Demetrius has in mind the famous personification of Prayers in the speech of Phoenix to Achilles, *Iliad* 9. 502ff.

8. Sections 7 and 8 qualify the prohibition of short clauses. We shall return to this subject when discussing the forceful manner. See below at 241.

9. Such a brief arrangement of words is called a *komma* or phrase. It is usually defined as being shorter than a clause, like the words just quoted: "Dionysius [is] in Corinth," or like the sayings of the wise men: "Know thyself," or "Follow the god." These short sayings are in the nature of apophthegms or maxims. It takes more skill to compress much meaning into a few words, as whole trees are potentially present in their seeds. A maxim which is expanded into a lengthy statement becomes an instructive piece of information or a piece of rhetoric instead of a maxim.

10. Clauses and phrases together form what we call periods, for a period is a combination of clauses and phrases well fitted together to express the underlying thought. Here is an example from Demosthenes: "Mainly because of my belief that the repeal of this law will benefit the state, but also for the sake of Chabrias' son, I have agreed to speak, to the best of my ability, on their behalf." This period consists of three clauses, it somehow turns and coils back upon itself at the end.

11. Aristotle defines a period as a form of expression which has a beginning and an end, a very right and proper definition. By saying "period" one implies that it had a definite beginning, will come to a definite end, and is hurrying to a close, like runners after the race has started. They too have the end in view from the beginning; hence the word period, by comparison with a circular course that is being run. In general, a period is nothing but a certain arrangement of words. If its circular course is broken up and the structure changed, the content remains the same but there will be no period. If, for example, we unwind the Demosthenic period just quoted, and say something like this— "I shall speak on their behalf, gentlemen. The son of Chabrias is a friend

10. The quotation is from the beginning of Demosthenes' speech *Against Leptines*. The period is more tightly constructed in the Greek where it ends: ὡμολόγησα τούτοις, ὡς ἂν οἷός τε ὦ, συνερεῖν (lit.: I agreed on their behalf, so far as I am able, to speak.) The coiling back (συστροφή) exists because neither the main clause nor the meaning is complete or clear till the last word is spoken.

11. The Greek word περίοδος is a compound of the words ὁδός, way or road, and the preposition περί, round or about, and it implies a coming back upon itself, a circular course. Aristotle's definition, *Rhet.* 3.9.3., is here quoted only in part, for he goes on to say that a period should only be of such length as can be grasped as a unit. The comparison with the footrace comes from the same passage of Aristotle, and the word καμπή, used to indicate the "turn" in the period, also means the "turning point" on the course. A Greek footrace was usually a double course, from the starting point to the turning point and back again. This image explains a good deal of the terminology used by Greek critics in their discussions of the period. It should be noted that when Demetrius "unwinds" the period of Demosthenes, the different clauses, in the Greek, are still joined by connectives, for this was always done in Greek, but the effect is that of unrelated clauses, and the connectives must be left out in translation to obtain a parallel effect.

of mine. Much more dear to me, however, is the state. It is right for me to plead its cause"—the period has disappeared.

12. The origin of the period is as follows. One type of style we call involved; it is that which consists of periods, the style of Isocrates' set speeches, of Gorgias, and of Alcidamas. In their works one period follows another just as surely as one hexameter follows another in the poetry of Homer. Then there is the loose style; this is resolved into clauses which are not integrated with one another, for example, in Hecataeus, most of Herodotus, and the older writers generally. Here is an example: "Hecataeus the Milesian tells this tale. I write these things as I believe them to be true. The stories told by the Greeks are many and, I think, ridiculous." These clauses are thrown together in a heap, as it were; they are not bound or held together; they do not support each other as clauses do in periods.

13. Indeed the clauses of a period are like the stones of a building, which hold together and support a rounded dome, whereas in the loose style the clauses are like stones that have been thrown close but are not fitted together.

14. As a result, the earlier style has a certain polish and neatness, like old statues whose art seems to have a plain spareness, whereas the later style resembles the statues of Pheidias with their combination of splendour and precision.

15. Now, in my opinion, a whole discourse should not consist of a string of periods, like those of Gorgias, nor be altogether in the loose style, as with the writers of old. Rather it should be a mixture of the two. It will then have both elaboration and simplicity and derive charm from

12. Demetrius' term for the involved or periodic sentence structure is συνεστραμμένη which Aristotle uses in the same sense in *Rhet.* 3.9.1., where it is also contrasted with the loose or "strung-along" style of the older writers. This looser style Aristotle calls λέξις εἰρομένη, a term which Demetrius does not use. Instead, he calls it διηρημένη, a word which Aristotle applies to the looser kind of period (3.9.7.), while he calls the more involved period ἀνακειμένη. Demetrius here ignores this distinction between different kinds of periods but later (19) brings forward a tripartite classification of his own. These changes in both terminology and classification seem quite deliberate and, in view of Demetrius' familiarity with the *Rhetoric*, can hardly be accounted for by faulty recollection. This is not the only time he will try to improve on Aristotle. See Introd. pp. 32ff.

13. The comparison with a heap of stones is also used by Dionysius in his *Composition* (ch. 22 *ad fin.*) and was probably a commonplace.

15. Demetrius is here applying to word-arrangement Aristotle's advice that the language should not be too lowly nor too elevated—*Rhet.* 3.2.1 and *Poetics* 22. In the last sentence he is thinking of rhythm rather than of structure. This, if monotonous, can be anticipated by the audience. Cp. Aristotle, *Rhet.* 3.8.1., and "Longinus," *On the Sublime* 41.2.

both, being neither too common nor too sophisticated. Those who pile on the periods become lightheaded like the intoxicated; their audience is nauseated because unconvinced, and sometimes calls out aloud the end of the period, which it foresees, before the speaker has reached it.

16. The shorter periods consist of two clauses; the longest, of four. More than four clauses goes beyond the proper proportions of a period.

17. There are, however, periods of three clauses, and some indeed of one; the latter are called simple periods. Whenever a clause is of a certain length with a turn at the end, we have a single-clause period, as in: "The History of Herodotus of Halicarnassus is here set forth," or again: "Lucid language brings much enlightenment to the reader's mind." Two factors make a simple period: the length of the clause and the turn at the end, and both must be present.

18. In composite periods the last clause must be longer than the others; it must embrace and encompass the rest. Then the period ends with a long and stately clause and will itself be long and stately; otherwise it will be fragmented and limping. Here is a good period: "Nobility consists not in speaking nobly but in performing noble things after saying them."

19. There are three kinds of period, the historical, the conversational, and the rhetorical. The historical is neither too tightly coiled nor too loose, but intermediate between the two. It will not appear rhetorical, or unconvincing through a too carefully rounded structure, while its simplicity gives it a certain dignity suited to history. Such is the first sentence of the *Anabasis*: "Darius and Parysatis had two sons; the elder

17. There is some confusion here, and some contradiction. It is not easy to see how the sentence of Herodotus (1.1) quoted here differs in kind from the sentence of Hecataeus in 12 and 2, or from "most of Herodotus" which was said at 12 to be non-periodic. The confusion may have arisen from confusing Aristotle's use of the term διῃρημένη and Demetrius' own (see note on 12), for here Demetrius fails to distinguish the looser kind of period from the loose style, and Aristotle quoted this sentence of Herodotus as an example of the strung-along or *non*-periodic style. It is true that Aristotle also recognizes one-clause periods (*Rhet.* 3.9.5); to him the essential feature of the period is that sense and sentence end together, and this is implied in 2 and 3 by Demetrius, though not stated. Indeed the existence of the one-clause period leads to some confusion even in Aristotle. Except where he defines it, he too uses the word period in the usual sense of an involved sentence with two or more clauses. It is interesting that the definition of Aristotle, and the two senses of the word period which derive from it, are still found in the current *Oxford English Dictionary*.

18. Demetrius' Greek example, from an unknown source is: οὐ γὰρ τὸ εἰκεῖν καλῶς καλόν, ἀλλὰ τὸ εἰπόντα δρᾶσαι τὰ εἰρημένα in which the thought is not completed until the last word is spoken.

[was] Artaxerxes, the younger, Cyrus." Its closing words make a firmly based and safe ending.

20. The rhetorical period is of the involved and circular kind; it requires a well-defined utterance and a gesture of the hand brought round with the rhythm, as in the sentence: "Mainly because I believe that the repeal of this law will benefit the state, but also for the sake of Chabrias' son, I have agreed to speak, to the best of my ability, on their behalf." From its very beginning such a period has something involved about it which shows that it will not end simply.

21. The conversational period is still looser and simpler than the historical. It scarcely shows that it is a period, like this: "I went to the Piraeus yesterday with Glaucon, the son of Ariston, to pray to the goddess, at the same time wanting to see how they would celebrate the festival, since they were doing so for the first time." The clauses are thrown together one upon the other as in the loose, unperiodic style, and when the end comes we hardly realize that this is the end of a period. So the conversational period should be written in a manner intermediate between the involved and the loose style; it is like both, and a mixture of them. These then are the different kinds of periods.

22. Periods can also consist of antithetic clauses. The antithesis may be either in the subject-matter, as in "sailing over a continent and marching over the sea," or in both words and matter, as is indeed the case in this very sentence.

19. This sentence was quoted in 3 in a different context. By a safe and stable ending Demetrius means mainly a solid rhythm. In the Greek this is —∪——, thus ending with a spondee, and only one short syllable in the last four. One may compare what Dionysius of Halicarnassus says of the ending of periods in the elegant style in his *Composition* ch. 23.

20. For this sentence of Demosthenes see also 10 and 11.

21. The quotation is the first sentence of Plato's *Republic*, and Demetrius was probably aware of the well-known story that at Plato's death tablets were found among his belongings, which showed he had tried many different arrangements of the simple words in this very sentence. See note 3 to Introd. I have given the whole sentence in the text but Demetrius only quotes a few words from the beginning and the end.

There is a certain verbal confusion at the end of this section. The involved and the periodic styles are the same (12), and this has now been divided into three kinds of period: the rhetorical, the historical, and the conversational. The conversational is still a period, though less tightly integrated than the other two, so much so that it is here said to be halfway between the involved or periodic (to which it belongs) and the non-periodic. This is an exaggerated way of pointing a difference, and Demetrius seems to be almost trying to escape his own categories.

22. The quotation, not quite accurate, is from Isocrates' *Panegyric* 58e, and refers to Xerxes' bridging the Hellespont and digging a canal through Mount Athos. Presumably the reader is intended to identify and remember the whole sentence. Demetrius here

23. There are clauses where the antithesis resides in the words only, as where Helen is compared to Heracles: "to the one Zeus gave a dangerous and laborious life, to the other he granted a beauty ever coveted and ever admired." Here both the articles and the connectives are in antithesis, each to its own kind, and so with other words throughout the sentence: "gave" is in antithesis to "granted," "laborious" to "admired," "dangerous" to "coveted," and the correspondence goes on throughout, like being in antithesis to like.

24. Clauses in which there is no true antithesis may yet appear antithetical because they are cast in that form, like the jocular words of the poet Epicharmus: "At one time I was among them, at another time I was with them." He has said the same thing twice and there is no contrast, but his manner imitates antithesis and is likely to deceive. His use of antithesis was probably a jest, and at the expense of the rhetoricians.

25. There is also *paromoiôsis*, where the clauses have similar sounds at the beginning, as in "swayed by gifts, waylaid by words," or at the end, like the beginning of Isocrates' *Panegyric*.* Another kind of paromoiôsis is the *isokôlon*, where the clauses have an equal number of syllables, as in Thucydides.* That is isokôlon.

---

takes up what in Aristotle was the main difference between the simpler and the more involved period, which he called antithetic in *Rhet.* 3.9.1–7, and continues to follow Aristotle in the next sections.

23. Correspondences of length, rhythm, and sound are of course much clearer and more exact in the Greek (*Encomium of Helen* 17), a typical Isocratean sentence with carefully balanced clauses, which Demetrius quotes in part as follows: τῷ μὲν ἐπίπονον καὶ πολυκίνδυνον τὸν βίον ἐποίησεν, τῆς δὲ περίβλητον καὶ περιμάχητον τὴν φύσιν κατέστησεν.

24. The fragment of Epicharmus quoted is: τόκα μὲν ἐν τήνοις ἐγὼν ἦν, τόκα δὲ παρὰ τήνοις ἐγών. Aristotle uses the same example, in slightly different words, *Rhet.* 3.9.10.

25. The first quotation (cp. *Rhet.* 3.9.9), translated in the text, is *Iliad* 9.526, where Phoenix reminds Achilles that even the gods can be influenced by gifts and prayers: δωρητοί τε πέλοντο, παράρρητοί τ' ἐπέεσσιν. The next example of paromoiôsis (the homoioteleuton of the next section), the beginning of Isocrates' *Panegyric*, is also used by Aristotle (*Rhet.* 3.9.7): πολλάκις δ' ἐθαύμασα τῶν τὰς πανηγύρεις συναγαγόντων, καὶ τοὺς γυμνικοὺς ἀγῶνας καταστησάντων (I have often wondered at those who established these gatherings and instituted the athletic contests), the point being that both clauses end in -ντων, but the effect is probably helped by the rhythm: both last words are four-syllable genitive participles, ending in a spondee (——).

In the last example (Thucydides 1.5), the two clauses have exactly the same number of syllables ὡς οὔτε ὧν πυνθάνονται ἀπαξιούντων τὸ ἔργον, οἷς τε ἐπιμελὲς εἴη εἰδέναι οὐκ ὀνειδιζόντων, that is, when asked, men admitted being pirates, (and neither did those questioned disclaim it, nor those who had questioned them censor it).

Aristotle had restricted the word paromoiôsis to the first kind here mentioned: similarities of sound at the beginning or the end (*Rhet.* 3.9.9). As the Greek adjective means

26. *Homoioteleuton* applies to clauses which end with the same sounds. Indeed they may end with the same word: "When he was alive you spoke ill of him, now he is dead you write ill of him"; or they may end with the same syllable only, as in the sentence just quoted from Isocrates' *Panegyric*.

27. The use of such clauses is risky; they are not suited to forceful speech because their pedantic artificiality destroys the forcefulness. We see this in Theopompus' attack on the friends of Philip,* where the assonances between the clauses and the antitheses are bad art and destroy the force of the passage. Anger needs no display of skill to express itself; in such attacks the words should be spontaneous and simple.

28. Such devices are, as I have shown, useless in forceful passages or in those that express passion or the speaker's character. The expression of emotion should be simple and unpolished, and the same is true in expressing the character of a speaker. In Aristotle's work *On Justice* a man laments the position of Athens. If he said: "What city have they taken from the enemy equal to their own, which they have lost?" he would be speaking with passion and in sorrow. But if he uses paromoiôsis and says: "What city have they ever taken, to equal their own which they have forsaken?" he will certainly not arouse either passion or pity, but only the tears of laughter, as we call them. Such badly applied rhetorical art in emotional passages is like jesting at a funeral, as the saying goes.

29. Yet these devices are sometimes useful, as when Aristotle says:

"similar" generally, Demetrius seems quite justified in using it as the generic term. Aristotle called balanced clauses with an equal number of syllables parisôsis. Demetrius, who makes it a species of paromoiôsis, calls this ἰσόκωλον, an expressive term. Homoioteleuton (next section) is used in the same way by both writers.

26. The quotation is also used by Aristotle in *Rhet.* 3.9.9, but it has not been identified. Each clause ends with κακῶς. Any pair of rhymes will illustrate the effect of homoioteleuton, but as the Greeks did not know rhyme, which involves a recurrent metrical pattern, the effect was different, and only one of various forms of assonance.

27. The quotation from Theopompus, a fourth-century historian of high reputation, is a good example of the absurd jingles and crudities into which Isocrates' fondness for these figures led even some of his famous pupils: ἀνδρόφονοι δὲ τὴν φύσιν ὄντες, ἀνδρόπορνοι τὸν τρόπον ἦσαν, καὶ ἐκαλοῦντο μὲν ἑταῖροι, ἦσαν δὲ ἑταῖραι which might be mildly and inadequately rendered: "Slayers by nature, waylayers by habit, they were the king's friends in name, his companions in shame."

28. The passage from Aristotle is not known. In the rewritten version the first clause ends with ἔλαβον, the second with ἀπέβαλον, and it is this jingle which Demetrius condemns as undignified, and losing its force.

29. Another unknown passage of Aristotle. In the Greek both clauses end with τὸν μέγαν, which is a clear homoioteleuton, a species of paromoiôsis. Note that most of the examples in 25–29 are cases of assonance, that is, of the more restricted Aristotelian sense of paromoiôsis. See on 25.

"I was driven from Athens to Stagira by the great king, and from Stagira to Athens by the great storm." Take away the second "great," and you destroy the charm of the sentence. Such clauses contribute to extravagance of language, as do many antitheses in Gorgias or Isocrates. So much for paromoiôsis.

30. An *enthymeme* differs from a period in that the period is a rounded kind of sentence-structure and derives its name from this, whereas the force and substance of the enthymeme lies in the thought. It is true that the period is the rounded form of the enthymeme also, as it is of all other content, but the enthymeme is a thought expressed either in contradiction or as a consequence.

31. The proof of this is that if you resolve the structure of the enthymeme, you destroy the period, but the enthymeme remains the same. For example, one might resolve such an enthymeme of Demosthenes: "If any one of them had been convicted, you would not have proposed this bill; and if you are now convicted, no one else will propose it." Break this up into: "Show no mercy to those who propose unconstitutional bills; if they had been stopped, this man would not be putting forward this proposal; nor will anyone else do so if he is now convicted." The course of the period is here broken up, but the enthymeme is still there.

32. In general terms, the enthymeme is a kind of rhetorical syllogism; whereas the period does not reason at all; it is only an arrangement of words. We use periods in every part of a speech, in the exordium for example, but enthymemes do not occur in every part. The enthymeme is something over and above the words as it were; the period is in the words themselves. The former is an imperfect syllogism, the latter is no syllogism, perfect or imperfect.

33. It is an accidental quality of an enthymeme to be a period, when it is expressed in periodic structure, but it is not the same as a period, just as a building may be white but is not essentially so. We have now dealt with the difference between a period and an enthymeme.

34. Aristotle defines the clause as "one of the two parts of a period"; then he adds: "there is also the simple period." Now this definition obviously implies that a period has two parts. Archedemus takes

30. The enthymeme is said by Aristotle to be to rhetoric what the syllogism is to logic, and he explains it as an argument or proof based on the probable only, an imperfect syllogism, *Rhet.* 1.2.8–9. See App. I, A under ἐνθύμημα.

31. From Demosth. *Against Aristocrates* 99.

32. The enthymeme proves something: it will therefore naturally occur in the third part of a speech, that is, the proof and refutation. The period is a matter of style, not of content.

34. For Archedemus and his correction of Aristotle here see Introduction p. 35, with note 41, and p. 42.

Aristotle's definition and the addition, and gives a definition which is both clearer and more complete: "A clause is either a simple period or a part of a composite period."

35. We have explained what a simple period is. When Archedemus says "a part of a composite period," he does not appear to limit the period to two clauses, but to admit three or more. We have set out the proper limits of a period.

Let us now proceed to discuss the types of style.

THE FOUR STYLES

36. There are four simple types of style: the plain, the grand, the elegant, and the forceful. The rest are combinations of these, but not all combinations are possible: the elegant can be combined with both the plain and the grand, and so can the forceful; the grand alone does not mix with the plain; these two face one another as opposite extremes. That is why some critics recognize only these last two as styles, and the other two as intermediate. They class the elegant rather with the plain, because the elegant is somewhat slight and subtle; while the forceful, which has weight and dignity, is classed with the grand.

37. Such a theory is absurd. With the exception of the two opposite extremes mentioned (the plain and the grand), we find combinations of all these types in the Homeric epic, in the works of Plato, Xenophon, Herodotus, and many other writers who display a frequent mixture of grandeur, forcefulness, and charm, so that the number of types is such as we have indicated, and the manner of expression appropriate to each will be seen in what follows.

35. For four clauses as the best limit of a period see 16 above.

36. Demetrius names his four "styles" ἰσχνός, μεγαλοπρεπής, γλαφυρός, and δεινός. ἰσχνός means thin, dry, plain, or lean; our own word "spare" is especially close when applied to a person's physique. μεγαλοπρεπής is the opposite and offers little difficulty: it is the grand, impressive, or magnificent. γλαφυρός seems to mean hollow in Homer, who uses it of caves and ships; in classical times it means polished or smooth and, when applied to persons or style, neat, delicate, subtle, or elegant. As for δεινός, which means forceful or intense, see Appendix I, A under δεινότης.

37. Is Demetrius here rejecting the well-known formula of the three styles—the plain, the grand, and the intermediate as it is known in critical history? His saying that the elegant and the forceful were by some people not recognized as separate "styles" but classed *between the other two*, the grand and the plain, which are then the only two "styles," would make one think so, but this is really quite different from three recognized styles. It is rather a way of classifying everything under two headings and two only— the plain and the grand, and even these are not so much "styles" in the later sense, as manners or qualities. We have seen elsewhere that Demetrius uses the word χαρακτήρ

THE IMPRESSIVE STYLE

Impressive Word-Arrangement

38. I shall begin with the grand or impressive manner which is today called eloquence. Grandeur resides in three things: the content, the diction, and the appropriate arrangement of words. This last is impressive, as Aristotle says, if it is paeonic in rhythm. There are two kinds of paeon: the initial paeon which consists of one long followed by three shorts, for example, ἤρξατο δέ, and the final paeon, its opposite, in which three shorts are followed by one long, for example, Ἀραβία

39. In impressive speech, the clauses should begin with the initial paeon and the final paeon comes later. We may take an example from Thucydides.* Why did Aristotle advise this? Because the start and opening of a clause should impress at once, and so should the end. We will achieve this by using a long syllable in both places. A long syllable has a natural dignity; it impresses at the start and leaves a strong impression at the end. All of us particularly remember the initial and final words and are affected by them but what comes in between has less effect on us, as if it were hidden and obscured.

40. This is obvious in Thucydides. In almost every instance, his impressiveness is wholly due to long-syllable rhythms. The grandeur of

---

in a much looser sense than the more rigid three-style formula implies (Introd. pp. 24–25 and notes).

We seem here to be much closer to the Aristotelian formula that the language should be neither too humble nor too grand, but somewhere in between (e.g. *Rhet.* 3.2.1). This Peripatetic mean of style is a quite different conception for with them *the mean only is right*, and it is not static but will vary according to the particular circumstances (see Introduction p. 14 and note 14).

Those to whom Demetrius here refers, he clearly says, recognized only *two* main manners or styles (not three) and insisted that everything should come under one heading or the other. At any rate he is right to point out that elegance and simplicity are not the same, and if forcefulness is indeed more akin to grandeur, they are quite distinguishable. It is interesting to note that even Dionysius is still confused between the two meanings of μέσον, an Aristotelian mean or a mixture of extremes (*Composition* 21). It should be added, however, that at a later date the flowery or elegant was sometimes identified with the middle style (e.g. Cicero, *Orator* 69 and see Radermacher 94–95).

38. What Aristotle really says is discussed in the Introduction, pp. 36–37.

39. The example from Thucydides is 2. 48: ἤρξατο δὲ τὸ κακὸν ἐξ Αἰθιοπίας (the evil began in Ethiopia), its total rhythm is —∪∪∪ ∪∪∪——∪∪∪—, but all that concerns us here are the paeons at the beginning and at the end.

40. Demetrius exaggerates the importance of rhythm; he practically ignores many other factors even in word-arrangement, namely the importance of collocations of harsh sounds stressed by Dionysius of Halicarnassus in his *Composition* ch. 22, when describing the austere word-arrangement in Thucydides, and cp. 48 below. However, there is no doubt that heavy rhythms are a distinct feature of Thucydidean prose. No examples are given in this section. See Introd. p. 17.

the man is many-sided, but it is this kind of word-arrangement which is the sole, or at any rate the main, factor in his greatest effects.

41. We should realize, however, that if we cannot have a paeon exactly at the beginning and at the end of each clause, we can still make our arrangement generally paeonic by at least beginning and ending with long syllables. This would seem to be what Aristotle advises us to do but he goes into details about the two kinds of paeon for no purpose except greater accuracy. Hence Theophrastus gives as an example of the grand manner a clause* of which the rhythm does not consist of exact paeons, yet it is paeonic in its general effect. We should therefore incorporate paeons into our prose; it is a measure mixing long and short, and less risky than others. The long syllables give dignity, while the shorts preserve the character of prose.

42. As for the other metres, the heroic is stately but unsuited to prose; it resounds too much. It is not a good rhythm, indeed it is not a rhythm at all when it becomes a mere succession of long syllables,* for the number of longs is far too great for prose rhythm.

43. The iambus (∪ —) is commonplace and like the rhythm of ordinary speech. Many people converse in iambics without knowing it. The paeon is a mean between the heroic and the iambic and is a mixture of the two. One should use the paeonic rhythm in impressive passages in some such way as we have indicated.

44. Lengthy clauses also make for grandeur, as in "Thucydides of Athens wrote this account of the war between the Peloponnesians and

41. Here Demetrius makes an important advance when he speaks of the *general* rhythmic character of a clause without trying to analyze it into exact feet. It is interesting that he attributes this point of view to Theophrastus, for this sensible attitude to rhythm in prose was lost to other critics. It is not found in Dionysius, Cicero, or Quintilian who concern themselves far too much with rhythmical feet.

The sentence quoted from Theophrastus is τῶν μὲν περὶ τὰ μηδενὸς ἄξια φιλοσο-φούντων (they were philosophizing about matters of no importance), the rhythm of which is ——∪∪∪—∪∪—∪∪∪∪——. We should especially note that it neither begins nor ends with a paeon, and is yet termed generally paeonic.

42. Demetrius' example here is an unidentified clause: ἥκω ἡμῶν εἰς τὴν χώραν in which all the syllables are long. Now the term "heroic metre" usually refers to the hexameter of six feet, in which the last foot must be a spondee (— —) but the first four may be either dactyls (— ∪ ∪) or spondees, while the fifth foot should be a dactyl, though sometimes replaced also by a spondee. Why Demetrius ignores the dactyl here is a puzzle. His example has only four feet in any case, and can only be said to be heroic in the same general sense as the clause from Theophrastus was called paeonic. Compare this and the following sections with Aristotle, *Rhet.* 3.8.4.; he too condemns the "heroic" metre as unsuited to prose, and the iambic as too conversational.

44. This first sentence of Herodotus has already been quoted in 17. The sentence from Thucydides begins his History.

the Athenians," and "The history of Herodotus the Halicarnassian is here set forth." To end quickly with a short clause lowers the dignity of the sentence even if there is grandeur in the thought or in the words.

45. A rounded sentence-structure also contributes to grandeur, as in Thucydides': "After flowing from Mount Pindus through Dolopia and the land of the Agrianians and Amphilochians, and passing inland by Stratus, the river Achelous, as it makes its way to the sea near Oeniadae, surrounds that city with a marsh, thus making a winter attack on it impossible because of the water." All the grandeur of this sentence is due to its periodic structure, and to the fact that Thucydides never allows himself or his reader to pause.

46. Now break up the sentence and say: "The river Achelous flows from Mount Pindus; it runs into the sea near Oeniadae; it turns the nearby plain of Oeniadae into a marsh; the water forms a natural protection against winter attacks." Written like this, there are many pauses, but the grandeur has vanished.

47. Long journeys seem shorter if one stops frequently at an inn; on the other hand, a deserted road makes even a short journey seem long. The same is true of clauses.

48. A harsh joining of sounds often makes for impressiveness, as in: "Aias the massive aimed always at Hector's bronze casque." The clash of sounds is not in other ways euphonious but its very exaggeration suggests the greatness of the hero. Smoothness and euphony have no place in the grand style, except occasionally. Thucydides almost always avoids what is smooth and even; his word-order stumbles like men walking along a rough path. For example: "from other outbreaks of disease the year, it was agreed, was free." This could have been put more easily and pleasingly, as "all agreed that the year was free from other diseases," but it is no longer impressive.

49. Harsh-sounding words make for grandeur, as does the juxtaposition of harsh sounds in the arrangement of words. "Shrieking" (κεκραγώς)

---

45. Thuc. 2.102. The general periodic effect can be rendered in translation but the periodic structure is much tighter and more effective in the inflected Greek.

48. The line from Homer, *Iliad* 16.358, is: Αἴας δ' ὁ μέγας αἰὲν ἐφ' Ἕκτορι χαλκοκορυστῇ; both the repeated "a" and "ai" sounds, and the gutturals, contribute to the harshness. In the sentence of Thucydides Demetrius would seem to have both the harsh sounds, the hiatus, and the jerky construction in mind (2.49): ὅτι τὸ μὲν δὴ ἔτος, ὡς ὡμολόγητο, ἄνοσον εἰς τὰς ἄλλας ἀσθενείας ἐτύγχανεν ὄν. Note the repeated dentals at the beginning and the sibilants and dentals later. However, he only rewrites the end ἄνοσον εἰς τὰς ἄλλας ἀσθενείας ὄν ἐτύγχανεν, where he eliminates the monosyllabic ending, but this is not a change in *sound* but in smoothness. The translation in the text can only illustrate his point in a general way.

has a harsher sound than "calling" (βοῶν), and "bursting" (ῥηγνύμενον) than "going" (φερόμενον). Thucydides uses all these harsh words; he chooses his words to fit his arrangement of them, and *vice versa*.

50. We should also arrange our words in the following manner: those that are not very vivid should come first, and the more vivid second and last. The sense of vividness then increases from one word to the next. The opposite order gives a feeling of weakness, of lapsing, as it were, from the stronger word to the weaker.

51. Plato has the following example: "When a man allows music to play upon him, and to flood through his ears into his soul," where the second verb is much more vivid than the first. He then goes on: "when the flood does not cease but puts a spell upon him, it weakens and melts his spirit." Here "melts" is a stronger word than "weakens" and closer to poetry. If the second word had been first, the addition of "weakens" would have seemed rather feeble.

52. Homer too, in his description of the Cyclops, continually increases the hyperbole and seems to rise higher and higher with it: "He was not like a mortal man but like a wooded hilltop," and he goes on to speak of a high mountain towering over its fellows. The things mentioned first are big, but they seem small as bigger things follow.

53. Connectives should not correspond exactly, a δέ after a μέν, for instance, for there is something petty in precise writing. Impressiveness requires a certain disorder, as in a passage of Antiphon* where we have μέν used three times before one answering δέ occurs.

54. However, it often happens that a succession of connectives magnifies even trifling things. Homer joins together the names of the Boeotian

51. The quotation is from *Rep.* 3.411a-b.

52. Homer: *Odyssey* 9.190.

53. The logical connections between clauses and sentences were always expressed in Greek by conjunctions and other connectives. Aristotle rightly pointed out the importance of connectives in writing good Greek (*Rhet.* 3.5.1); that these should correspond according to their nature, and that a μέν should be followed by a δέ. Demetrius denies such exact correspondence to be suited to the impressive style. μέν and δέ is the simplest way to express an antithesis in Greek, but the antithesis is often so weak as to be untranslatable without undue emphasis.

We do not possess the context of the sentence here quoted from Antiphon (480–411 B.C.): ἡ μὲν γὰρ νῆσος ἣν ἔχομεν δηλὴ μὲν καὶ πόρρωθέν ἐστιν, ὑψηλὴ καὶ τραχεῖα, καὶ τὰ μὲν χρήσιμα καὶ ἐργάσιμα μικρὰ αὐτῆς ἐστι, τὰ δὲ ἄργα πολλά, σμικρᾶς αὐτῆς οὔσης. (The island we occupy is visible from afar, high and rough, and the parts of it that are workable and cultivated are small, but the uncultivated parts are large, considering its size.) Actually the δέ answers the last μέν only. μέν was used alone when the second member of an antithesis remained unexpressed.

54. Lists of names had a great appeal for epic writers. In *Iliad* 2.497–508 Homer gives a list of about 22 Boeotian cities, each joined to the other by τε or καί. Demetrius,

cities, in themselves ordinary and unimportant, by a string of connectives and this gives them a certain weight and impressiveness: "And Schoinos and Scolos and many-topped Eteonos . . . ."

55. Expletive connectives should not be used as mere empty fillers, like superfluities or excrescences, as some writers use δή (then, indeed) without reason, and νυ (now), and ποτε (ever), but only when they contribute to the impressiveness of what is said.

56. So in Plato's "And in the heavens then (δή) the great Zeus," and Homer's "when they came then (δή) to the ford of the wide-flowing river." Thus placed near the beginning of the clause the connective separates it from what precedes and adds a certain impressiveness. To amplify the beginnings of sentences lends dignity. If Homer had merely said: "When they came to the ford of the river" this would have seemed but a trivial description of one particular event.

57. The particle δή is also frequently used to express strong emotion, as in Calypso's words to Odysseus, "God-born son of Laertes, wily Odysseus, do you then (δή) long so much for your beloved land?" If you remove the expletive, you will destroy the emotional tone. Altogether, as Praxiphanes says, such particles were employed instead of groans and lamentations, like αἲ αἲ (Ah! Ah!) or φεῦ (Alas) or ποιόν τί ἐστι (what is it?). And he points out too that the connective καὶ νύ κε in Homer's line* is appropriate to lamentation and has the same effect as a word expressing sorrow.

58. Praxiphanes says that those who use expletives as mere fillers are like actors who add a word here and there without reason, as if one said:

> This country, Calydon, of Pelops' land
> Alas!
> The opposite shore, fertile and happy plains
> Ah me! Ah me!

who refers to the passage by quoting one line only, considers this more impressive than a mere enumeration without connectives.

55. Radermacher is surely right to question the reading πρότερον (rather or before) which is hardly a connective particle. I have adopted the reading ποτε in the text; περ has also been suggested.

56. Plato, *Phaedrus* 246e and Homer, *Iliad* 14, 433 or 21.1. Demetrius means that the use of δή in these examples gives emphasis by breaking the flow, creating a pause, and thus contributes weight and dignity.

57. Demetrius quotes the first four words only of the Homeric line καὶ νύ κ' ὀδυρομένοισιν ἔδυ φάος ἠελίοιο (the light of the sun set upon their lamentations) from the scene of Patroclus' burial, *Iliad* 23.154. The same line also occurs in *Odyssey* 16.220, and 21.226. For Calypso's words see *Odyssey* 5. 203.

Praxiphanes, pupil of Theophrastus (*ca.* 370–285 B.C.), was a grammarian and literary critic. His works are lost.

Just as here "Alas" and "Ah me" only distract the audience's attention, so connectives scattered everywhere without reason have the same effect.

Figures of Speech

59. Connectives then can make the word-arrangement impressive, as we said. Figures of speech are themselves a kind of word-arrangement. For to say the same thing twice by repetition, by *epanaphora* or by *anthypallagê*, is to order and arrange the words in a different way. We must assign to each style the figures that are appropriate to it. The following are appropriate to the grand style which is our present concern.

60. First there is anthypallagê (the substitution of one case for another). When Homer says: "The two rocks, one reaching to the sky ..." he uses a much more impressive construction than if he had used the usual genitive: "Of the two rocks, one reaching to the sky ...," for what is customary is trivial and fails to arouse wonder.

61. Nireus is not himself important in the *Iliad*, and his contribution is even less so, three ships and a few men, but Homer makes him appear important and his contribution great instead of small by using and combining two figures, epanaphora and *dialysis*. "Nireus brought three ships," he says, "Nireus, son of Aglaïa," "Nireus, who was the most beautiful man." The epanaphora as a figure of speech in connection with the same name, and the dialysis give an impression of abundant possessions, even though it is only two or three ships.

---

60. Anthypallagê means the substitution of one case for another, here the nominative for the genitive. In the Homeric lines referred to (*Odyssey* 12.73) Circe is warning Odysseus about Scylla and Charybdis, and she says: οἱ δὲ δύω σκόπελοι, ὁ μὲν . . . and then (27 lines later) ὁ δέ that is, (the two rocks, one ... the other ...). This leaves us with a suspended nominative, and the normal grammatical form of expression would have been τῶν σκοπέλων ὁ μὲν . . . ὁ δέ . . . , that is, "Of the two rocks, the one ... the other." Demetrius is quite right, the ungrammatical construction is more vivid.

61. Epanaphora is the repetition of the same word at the beginning of succeeding clauses, here also succeeding lines. Dialysis (disconnection) is the name here given to lack of connectives, elsewhere also called asyndeton (see on 53). The passage from Homer is *Iliad* 2.671–674, in the Catalogue of ships. Aristotle uses it also in *Rhet.* 3.12.4 as an example of asyndeton and it was a favourite with critics and rhetoricians:

> Nireus from Syme brought three curved ships;
> Nireus, son of Aglaïa and of Charopus;
> Nireus, most beautiful of all the Greeks
> Who came to Troy, saving Achilles only.

And Nireus is never mentioned again.

62. Although Nireus is mentioned only once in the action, we remember him as well as Achilles and Odysseus who are talked about in almost every line. This is due to the effectiveness of the figure of speech. If Homer had said: "Nireus, the son of Aglaïa brought three ships from Syme," he might as well not have mentioned him. At banquets a few well-arranged dishes give an impression of plenty; the same is true in discourse.

63. Frequently, however, impressiveness can be achieved by the opposite of lack of connectives, namely by *synapheia,* as in: "On this campaign went the Greeks and the Carians and the Lycians and the Pamphilians and the Phrygians." Here it is the repetition of the same connective which gives the impression of large numbers.

64. In such a phrase as "high-arched, white-crested" on the other hand, it is the absence of the connective "and" which makes for greater impressiveness than if he had said "high-arched and white-crested."

65. Impressiveness by means of figures is also attained by varying the case, as in Thucydides: "First to step on the gangway to land he fainted, and as he fell among the oars . . . ." This is much more impressive than if he had retained the same case and said: "he fell among the oars and lost his shield."

63. The source of the quotation is unknown. The term synapheia is here used of the repetition of the *same* connective (καί). This figure is called *polysyndeton* by Quintilian (9.3.51). There is no contradiction between this and the two previous sections or with what follows, only the realization that similar results may be obtained by different means, and that the same means may lead to different results in different contexts. See Introd. p. 27.

64. Demetrius expects his readers to remember Homer's description of the waves breaking on the shore in *Iliad* 13.798-800. ἐν δέ τε πολλά | κύματα παφλάζοντα πολυφλοισβοῖο θαλάσσης | κυρτὰ φαληριόωντα, πρὸ μέν τ' ἄλλα, αὐτὰρ ἐπ' ἄλλα... (Many a clashing wave of the loud-roaring sea, high-arched, white-crested; first one comes, then another . . .).

65. The sentence of Thucydides (4.12) which we are expected to remember from a brief and inexact quotation runs as follows: καὶ πειρώμενος ἀποβαίνειν ἀνεκόπη ὑπὸ τῶν Ἀθηναίων, καὶ τραυματισθεὶς πολλὰ ἐλιποψύχησέ τε καὶ πεσόντος αὐτοῦ ἐς τὴν παρεξειρεσίαν ἡ ἀσπὶς ἀπερρύη ἐς τὴν θάλασσαν καὶ ἐξενειχθείσης αὐτῆς ἐς τὴν γῆν οἱ Ἀθηναῖοι ἀνελόμενοι . . . (He tried to land and was cut down, many times wounded and near death, and as he fell among the oars, his shield slipped into the sea and, as it was drifting to shore, the Athenians picked it up . . .). The sentence contains two examples of Thucydides' very free and vivid use of the genitive absolute, contrary to strict grammatical rules. It begins with two participles in the nominative agreeing with Brasidas, the subject of the following main verbs, but then switches to a genitive absolute though the subject is still Brasidas. The subject now becomes the shield which falls into the sea, but its drifting to shore is described by another genitive absolute, and the subject now changes to the Athenians. It is indeed a vivid sentence, but hardly smooth syntax! Dionysius (*Second Letter to Ammaeus* 4) objects, in this

66. *Anadiplôsis* also heightens the effect, as when Herodotus says: "The serpents in the Caucasus are large, large and numerous." The repetition of "large" gives weight to the style.

67. One should avoid crowding the figures, for this argues a lack of taste and indicates an uneven style. It is true that the old writers use many figures, but because they use them skilfully, their style is more natural than that of those who do not use figures at all.

68. Opinions vary about the clashing of vowels (in hiatus). Isocrates and his school took care to avoid it; others have paid no heed to it at all. We should neither arrange our words so that they ring in our ears through haphazard collisions, for these interrupt our flow with stops and jerks, nor altogether avoid such collisions. Total avoidance of hiatus would, it is true, make our words flow more smoothly, but the result would be flat and unmusical, without the euphony which often results from a clash of vowels.

69. We should in the first place note that customary speech, which certainly favours euphony, itself does bring vowels together within such words as Αἴακος and χιών (snow); indeed there are words which consist entirely of vowel sounds, for example, Αἰαίη and Εὔιος.These words are no harsher than others; indeed they are perhaps more musical.

70. Poetic forms such as ἠέλιος (sun) and ὀρέων (of mountains) with their deliberate lengthening of the words and the resulting clash of

---

same sentence, to the use of the word παρεξειρεσία to describe the projecting oars, as one word used where a phrase is needed. Demetrius does not use the word anthypallagê here, as he did in 60 above.

66. Anadiplôsis is the immediate repetition of a word. This sentence is not found in Herodotus' description of the Caucasus, but a near-anadiplôsis does occur at 1.203, where he says of the Caucasus: ἐὸν ὀρέων καὶ πλήθει μέγιστον καὶ μεγέθει ὑψηλότατον (of mountains in number the greatest, and in greatness the highest). The reading is uncertain at the beginning of this section. I have translated Radermacher's δέ που instead of Roberts' δ' ἔπους, that is, "of a word." The meaning is little affected.

67. For this use of "the writers of old," οἱ ἀρχαῖοι see Introd. p. 44.

68. Isocrates was notorious for his avoidance of hiatus, that is, the clash of vowels which comes from a word which ends in a vowel being followed by one which begins with a vowel.

69. All Demetrius' examples are proper names, except χιών.

70. The example (omitted in translation) of sounds that lose by being elided is an unidentified sentence: πάντα τὰ νέα καὶ καλά ἐστιν (all that is young is also beautiful) where the last two words would normally be elided into καλ' ἐστιν or, and this is the form he gives, καλά 'στιν to avoid the hiatus.

When a Greek critic speaks of the music of language, or that of any particular word or phrase, we should always remember that this involved five factors: the actual sound of the letters, their length or shortness (on this the scansion was based), the pitch indicated by accentuation, the stress accent (which is not known), and the breathings.

vowels, are more euphonious than the shorter forms ἥλιος and ὁρῶν. The resolving of one syllable into two clashing vowels introduces an added effect not unlike singing. There are many other words which, when run together by elision or contraction, are less harmonious and, when resolved with resulting hiatus, they are more euphonious.* Running the sounds together is both harsher in sound and more commonplace.

71. The priests of Egypt, when singing hymns to their gods, utter the seven vowels in succession and men listen to the singing sound of these vowels instead of to the flute or the lyre, because it is so euphonious. It follows that to remove the hiatus is to deprive language of its song and its music. But this is perhaps not the time to pursue the subject further.

72. The grand style favours the clash of long vowels. This is obvious in Homer's λᾶαν ἄνω ὤθεσκε (he pushed the stone uphill). The line acquires length through the juxtaposition of long vowels; it imitates the violent straining of the stone uphill. The same is true in the phrase of Thucydides τὸ μὴ ἤπειρος εἶναι (not being the mainland), and you will find clashing diphthongs in that sentence of his which describes the founding of Epidamnus by the Corcyraeans.*

73. As the clash of the same long vowels or diphthongs makes for impressiveness, the clash of different sounds may have the same result, and it provides variety as well—as in ἠώς (dawn) or οἵην (such). Not

---

It was the combination of all these factors which made that "music" to which the Greeks were so extraordinarily sensitive.

The lengthening of ἥλιος to ἠέλιος, for instance, involves not only the insertion of a short ε sound, but a change of breathing from rough to smooth (i.e. the omission of an initial "h" sound), the shift of the rise in pitch (the acute accent) from the first vowel to the second, thus making the initial η unaccented. In ὁρέων for ὁρῶν we have a change of pitch, rising on the έ instead of going up and down (the circumflex) on the ῶ. In the last example there is the dropping of an accented α and the acute is transferred to the ε of ἐστιν. It is the total effect that Demetrius has in mind, even though only hiatus is specifically mentioned.

71. The seven vowels in Greek are α, ε, η, ι, ο, υ, ω, which one may roughly transcribe into a, e, ê, i, o, u, ô. While the two circumflexed sounds were always long, a, ι and υ could be long or short.

72. The Sisyphus passage, Odyssey 11. 595–598, was a favourite with the critics, and we have a detailed and penetrating discussion of it in Dionysius of Halicarnassus, Composition ch. 20. Here, however, Demetrius only quotes three words and is concerned with the hiatus between the last two.

The first quotation from Thucydides is at 6.1, and here too he only quotes three words with a hiatus between the first two. The last quotation is from Thucydides 1.24. It too has many long syllables: ταύτην κατῴκησαν μὲν Κερκυραῖοι οἰκιστὴς δὲ ἐγένετο . . . (the Corcyraeans colonized it. The founder was . . .), but our immediate concern is the hiatus in οι and in ε in the last four words.

73. It is interesting to find him actually mentioning the breathings as a factor in the music of language (see on 70 above).

only are the sounds different, but the breathings also, one being rough and the other smooth, so that there is much variety.

74. In songs too there can be musical variations on the same long vowel, like song upon song, so that the clash of similar vowels can be regarded as part of a song or a musical variation. This is enough about the clash of vowels and about the impressive kind of word-arrangement.

Impressive Subject-Matter

75. The grandeur may lie also in the subject matter—a great and notable battle on land or sea, or when there is talk of the heavens, or of the earth. When one hears a person discoursing on an impressive subject one is at once apt to think his style impressive even when it is not. One should consider the manner of his discourse, rather than the matter, for an important subject may be dealt with in a trifling and quite unsuitable manner. Some authors, like Theopompus, are considered forceful when in fact it is their subject, not their style, that is forceful.

76. Nicias, the painter, used to say that to choose a great subject is in itself no small part of the painter's art and that he should not fritter away his talent on trifling themes like birds or flowers. Rather he should choose cavalry charges or naval battles as his subjects, where he could introduce many horses galloping, rearing or crouching, many bowmen shooting, many riders falling from their chargers. Nicias considered the choice of theme to be itself a part of the art of painting just as it is of the poet's art. We should therefore not be surprised if, even in prose, great subjects have their own impressiveness.

Impressive Diction

77. The grand style requires the diction to be distinguished, out of the ordinary, unusual. It will then have weight, whereas current and customary language makes for clarity, but it is also commonplace.

Metaphors

78. In the first place, we should use metaphors. They contribute more than anything else to delight and impressiveness of style. They should not be too numerous, however, or our prose will turn into dithyramb, nor too far-fetched, but arise spontaneously from a true likeness in things. For example, a general, a pilot, and a charioteer all rule over something;

75. Theopompus was a fourth-century historian, a pupil of Isocrates. How close the forceful and the grand manner are akin is shown by the fact that Demetrius slips into mention of forcefulness in the last sentence, even though it is the grand or impressive style he is here discussing. What is said here is repeated in 240.

76. Nicias was a famous fourth-century painter.

77. This last sentence repeats what Aristotle said both in *Poetics* 22.1 and in *Rhetoric* 3.2.2. Reading in the last clause ($\sigma a\varphi\grave{\eta}s$) $\mu\grave{e}\nu$ $\dot{a}\epsilon\acute{\iota}$, $\tau\hat{\eta}$ $\delta\acute{\epsilon}$, in preference to Roberts' $\mu\grave{e}\nu$ $\lambda\epsilon\iota\tau\acute{\eta}$ $\delta\acute{\epsilon}$ because, as Roberts himself points out (p. 290) Demetrius does not use the word $\lambda\iota\tau\acute{\eta}$ elsewhere and the form is improbable.

one can therefore safely call the general the pilot of his city, or again the pilot the ruler of his ship.

79. Not all metaphors, however, are interchangeable like those just mentioned. The poet (Homer) could call the lower slopes of Ida its foot, but he could not call a man's foot his slope.

80. Whenever a metaphor seems too bold, we can change it into a simile, which is safer. A simile is an extended metaphor, as when instead of: "then the orator Python, rushing upon us, a torrent of words" you add to it and say: "then *like* a torrent of words, the orator Python. . . ." Now you have a simile which is a safer method of expression, while the first is a metaphor which is more chancy. Plato is thought to take more chances because he uses metaphors more freely than similes, while Xenophon makes greater use of similes.

81. Aristotle thought that the best type of metaphor is the so-called active metaphor, by which inanimate things are represented as acting like living things, as in Homer's reference to the arrow as "sharp-pointed, eager to fly into the throng," and to the waves as "high-arched, foam-crested," for these epithets imply the actions of living creatures.

82. Some things are expressed more clearly and properly by a metaphor than by the proper terms themselves, as, for example: "the battle shivered." The meaning could not be more truly or lucidly expressed by changing the phrase and using the proper terms. The confused motion of spears and their continuous subdued sound are rendered by "the shivering battle." At the same time the poet is using the active type of metaphor just described, for he says that the battle shivers like a living creature.

78. For Demetrius' indebtedness to Aristotle in the whole discussion of metaphors, see Introd. p. 37. Strictly speaking the pilot should be the "general" of his ship. To say the pilot "rules" his ship is a transference from genus to species, whereas to call the general the "pilot" of the city is from species to species.

79. This is a sound point that Aristotle does not make in his discussion of metaphors, and Demetrius may well be deliberately improving on him. The reference is to *Iliad* 20.218.

80. The quotation is from Demosthenes, *On the Crown* 136. The simile as an extended metaphor, μεταφορὰ πλεονάζουσα, is an adaptation of Aristotle's saying that a simile is a metaphor with some words added, in *Rhet.* 3.10.3, διαφέρουσα προσθέσει. For Demetrius' improved view of the simile in prose see Introd. p. 37.

81. The reference is to *Rhet.* 3.11.3–4, where Aristotle says that such metaphors put the action vividly before our eyes—ἐνέργεια means vividness as well as action in Aristotle—and he praises Homer for thus personifying lifeless things, τὰ ἄψυχα ἔμψυχα λέγειν. He gives the same examples, namely *Iliad* 4.126 and 13.799. The latter Demetrius has also used above as an example of asyndeton or dialysis in section 64. The point is that "eager" implies feeling in the arrow and thus personifies it to that extent, while "high-crested" implies a helmet and compares the wave to a helmeted warrior.

82. *Iliad* 13.339.

83. We should not forget, however, that the effect of certain metaphors is paltry rather than impressive, even though the metaphor is intended to achieve grandeur, as when Homer says that "the wide sky trumpeted about them." A noise ringing through the high heavens should not be compared to the sound of a trumpet, unless indeed one were to defend Homer by saying that the high heavens resounded as if the whole sky were trumpeting.

84. Let us then consider this other kind of metaphor which makes for triviality instead of grandeur. Metaphors should be transferred from the greater to the smaller and not *vice versa*. Xenophon says, for example: "On the march a part of the line surged out" and compares the disorder in the line to the surge of the sea. But if one were to reverse this and say that the sea swerved, the metaphor would be inappropriate and certainly trivial.

85. When they consider metaphors too bold, some writers try to make them more acceptable by adding an epithet, as Theognis speaks of the bow of an archer in the act of shooting as "a tuneless lyre." To call a bow a lyre is a bold metaphor, and it is softened by the adjective "tuneless."

86. Common usage is a good teacher in all things, but especially in the use of metaphor. We do not notice that it expresses almost everything

83. *Iliad* 21.388. This too implies the personification of the active metaphor. Demetrius sees the point at the end.

84. *Anabasis* 1.8.18. The Greek words are more specific than the translation as in ἐξεκύμηνέ τι τῆς φάλαγγος the word ἐξεκύμηνε (surged) is a compound of κῦμα, wave, and similarly in ἐκφαλαγγίσασαν τὴν θάλασσαν, the word translated "swerved" is actually a compound of the word phalanx.

Sections 83 and 84 really continue the thought of 79, namely that in the Aristotelian proportional metaphor, $a/b = c/d$, you cannot always transfer d to a or b to c, for to compare the greater with the smaller is ineffective and unimpressive. Swerving is to the military line as surging is to the sea, but you should not say the sea "swerved." The objection to "the sky trumpeted" is of the same kind, except that it is redeemed by being an active metaphor. Incidentally, the "foot of the mountain" in 79 is an exception to the rule that the smaller should be compared to the greater and not *vice versa*, but this seems to have escaped Demetrius' notice. It too is an "active" metaphor.

85. Aristotle also cites this metaphor, but without naming the author: *Rhet.* 3.11.10 and *Poetics* 21.8; he also speaks of adding *negative* epithets which, he drily remarks, is a process that can go on ad infinitum (*Rhet.* 3.6.7), since each thing is *not* an infinite number of things. Demetrius does not restrict this section to negative epithets though his example, taken from Aristotle, is of this kind. The quotation may be from the didactic poet, Theognis of Megara (sixth century B.C.) or from the tragic poet of the late fifth century B.C.

86. The actual Greek is λευκὴ φωνή, literally "a white voice." The others, ὀξὺς ἄνθρωπος, τραχὺ ἦθος, μακρὸς ῥήτωρ, can be translated with surprising literalness, though our "rough character" has associations which are absent from the Greek.

by metaphors because they are inoffensive, like "a clear voice," "a sharp man," "a rough character," "a lengthy speaker," and so on. These metaphors are so appropriate that they seem like proper terms.

87. I make the art—or is it the naturalness?—of common usage the criterion of a good metaphor in prose. For usage has produced some metaphors so successfully that we no longer need the proper term and the metaphor has usurped its place, as in "the eye of the vine" and other such expressions.

88. Certain parts of the body* derive their names not from a metaphorical usage but from their physical resemblance to other objects.

89. When we turn a metaphor into a simile, as mentioned above, we should aim at brevity, and add only the word "like" (ὥσπερ) before it. Otherwise it will not be a simile but a poetic comparison. When Xenophon says: "As a noble hound leaps at a boar without caution," or again: "Like a horse let loose, kicking and prancing in a meadow" he is no longer using similes but poetic comparisons.

90. Such poetic comparisons should not be freely used in prose, but with the greatest caution. And this is a sufficient outline on the subject of metaphors.

Compound Words

91. We should also use compound words but we should avoid dithyrambic formations such as "the heaven-portented wanderings" and "the fiery-lanced host of stars." Our compounds should be like those which are formed by usage, for in usage I see the universal criterion of good diction. It forms without challenge such words as lawgiver,* and the like.

92. A compound word, because of its composite nature, will also provide a certain ornamental variety and dignity, as well as brevity. One word

87. The "eyes of the vine" means the buds, and ὀφθαλμός was used in many other common metaphors. A modern equivalent would be "the eye of a needle."

88. The instances given in this section are σφόνδυλος which means both vertebra and the whorl of a spindle; κλείς key and also collar-bone; and κτένες ribs, incisor teeth, and also the comb of a loom.

89. *Cyropaideia* 1.4.21. The distinction here is between the prose simile and the Homeric kind here called παραβολὴ ποιητική (poetic comparison). It is a distinction that needed making and is not made by Aristotle. See Introd. p. 37.

91. The Greek examples in the last sentence are νομοθέτης, lawgiver, and ἀρχιτέκτων, but architect is not an English compound, nor is master-builder a single word.

92. Demetrius' example, σιτοπομπία for ἡ πομπὴ τοῦ σίτου is not particularly impressive either in Greek or in English. One can easily think of compound words which can be avoided only at the cost of considerable circumlocution, for example, eyelid, flagstaff, and in certain contexts "the staff on which the flag was hanging" might be more impressive. This last point is reminiscent of Aristotle who says that to attain weight (ὄγκος) circumlocutions should be used, *Rhet.* 3.5.

will take the place of a whole phrase, "corn-supply," for example, instead of "the supplying of corn," and this is much more impressive. Sometimes, however, this greater effect is better obtained by resolving one word into a phrase, for example, by saying "the supply of corn" instead of "the corn-supply."

93. A word replaces a whole phrase, for example, when Xenophon says: "it was impossible to catch a wild ass unless the hunters took up positions at intervals and hunted in relays." By the word "relays" he means that some riders pursued the animal from behind, while others met it head on so that the wild ass was caught between them.

We should be careful not to combine words already compound. Such double combinations are not suitable in prose.

New Words

94. Newly-coined words are usually defined as words used to imitate some emotion or action like "sizzled" and "lapping."

95. These words are impressive because they imitate noises, and mostly because they are strange. The poet is not using existing words, for this is their first occurrence. Making a new word is thought to be a clever thing, as if one were creating a usage of one's own. For by creating new words one seems to act in the same way as the originators of language.

93. Xen. *Anabasis* 1.5.2. The word translated "relays" is διαδεχόμενοι, which is a compound word so that this is not a digression. Nor is the picture given in the translation strictly accurate for, though the word does mean "in turn," the first group of hunters drives the animal to the second and the animal is caught ἐν μέσῳ, in between the two groups, that is, both hunting it at the same time.

In the last sentence I read with Roberts διπλᾶ τιθέναι τὰ διπλᾶ ὀνόματα, which makes better sense and seems nearer the Mss than Radermacher's πολλὰ τιθέναι.

94. These two examples are Homeric. σίζω, to sizzle, is used of the Cyclops' eye, *Odyssey* 9.394, when the burning stake is driven into it. Later uses of the word are mostly found in the comic poets. λάπτω is used of wolves and dogs in *Iliad* 16.161, and this word came into more general use.

95. The phrase πεποιημένα ὀνόματα means simply newly-made words, and so does the noun ὀνοματοποιΐα, while the transliterated "onomatopoeia" refers, in English, to words coined to imitate sound. Aristotle refers only to πεποιημένα in the more general sense, *Poetics* 21.9 and *Rhet.* 3.2.5, where he adds that they should be used but rarely. But, obviously, new words were frequently coined for onomatopoeic effect, so that a certain confusion arose which is reflected in this paragraph: the examples are onomatopoeic, though other examples, which are not so, follow. The confusion was evidently common and is found in Quintilian who defines ὀνοματοποιΐα quite generally in 8.6.31 and 9.1.5, yet also uses the word in our sense of onomatopoeia, and indeed seems to differentiate it from πεποιημένα ὀνόματα, mere new coinages or unusual derivatives, in 1.5.72. From 8.6.31 we learn that new coinages were not favoured by the Romans, compared with the Greeks.

96. When coining a new word we should aim at clarity and remain within the bounds of usage. The new coinage should be analogous to existing words, for one should not appear to use Scythian or Phrygian expressions when writing Greek.

97. We should make new words where no existing names are available, as when someone called the kettledrums and other instruments used in effeminate ritual "lewderies" or when Aristotle spoke of an elephant-driver as an "elephanteer." Or we may make new derivatives from existing forms, as someone called a man who rows a boat a "rowman," and Aristotle spoke of a man who dwelt alone as "selfsome."

98. We read in Xenophon: "The army battle-shouted." He makes a kindred verb from the battle-shout the army was raising continually. As I said, this is a risky business, even for a poet. Any compound word, however, is a sort of coined word, for what is composite must have been built from its parts.

99. *Allêgoria* (hidden meaning) is also impressive, especially in threats such as that of Dionysius: "Their grasshoppers will sing to them from the ground."

100. If he had simply said that he would ravage the country of Locris, he would have sounded angrier but more commonplace. As it is, he uses allêgoria to camouflage his meaning. What is implied is always more frightening, for different interpretations are possible. What is clear and obvious is likely to be considered commonplace, like men without their clothes.

101. That is why mystic formulae are expressed by means of allêgoria, to frighten people and make them shudder as they do in the dark and at night. Allêgoria is not unlike darkness and night.

97. The Greek examples translated here are, in the order given: κιναιδίαι, this, however, was only a new application of an existing word, not a new coinage—ἐλεφαντιστής, σκαφίτης, and αὐτίτης. σκαφίτης also occurs in Strabo (17.817). αὐτίτης is used elsewhere, but to refer to new wine. Radermacher (p. 89) believes it to be, here and in 144, an error for μονώτης which does occur in our texts of Aristotle (*Eth. Nic.* 1.8 and 5.8). ἐλεφαντιστής occurs in the *Hist. Anim.* 2. 497 and 610. κιναιδίαι has not been traced anywhere in this sense.

98. Curiously enough, the word ἐλελίζω, which Xenophon used in *Anab.* 5.2.14, was not new, except in its context perhaps, for it had been used in the sense of raising a shout by both Euripides and Aristophanes.

100. Allêgoria seems to be used here in the same general sense as the figure which Aristotle (*Rhet.* 3.11.6) defines as τὸ μὴ ὃ φησι λέγειν, that is, "to mean something else than one says," rather than in our more restricted sense of allegory (see Appendix I, A). Aristotle uses the same example, with the variation of αὐτοῖς for αὐτοῖς, that is, "their grasshoppers will sing to themselves on the ground." The meaning is, of course, that the whole city and country will be devastated.

102. A succession of such veiled expressions should, however, be avoided, for then we would be writing riddles like that of the doctor's cupping-glass, "I saw a man who had welded bronze upon another man." The Spartans too used many veiled threats, as when they said to Philip: "Dionysius [is] in Corinth," and on many other occasions.

103. Sometimes it is impressive to express a thought briefly, and most impressive not to express it at all, for there are things which increase in importance by not being spoken but implied.

At other times, however, to be brief is to be trivial, and grandeur is found in repetition, as when Xenophon says: "The chariots drove on; some drove through the lines of their friends, others through the lines of their foes," which is much more impressive than if he had said: "The chariots drove on through the lines of friend and foe."

104. An oblique construction is frequently more impressive than a straightforward one: "The decision was of charging the Greek lines and breaking through them," instead of "They decided to charge and break through."

105. Words similar in sound and an apparent lack of euphony may also contribute to impressiveness. For what is not euphonious often gives an impression of weight. In the line which describes the attack of Ajax upon Hector* the combination of these two factors makes us realize

102. The line about the cupping-glass is used by Aristotle both in *Rhet.* 3.2.12 and in *Poetics* 22.5. For Dionysius in Corinth see 8–9 above.

103. The Greek for "to pass over in silence," that is, not to express what is implied, is *aposiôpêsis*. Repetition here is *dilogia*, that is, repeating words from one clause to another. It should not be confused with epanophora, which refers to the repetition of the same word at the beginning of each clause in sections 61–62, nor with anadiplôsis which was used in section 66 to indicate the immediate repetition of a word. Here we are concerned with the same word or words being used anywhere in the two clauses. The two figures, of course, merge into one another.

The quotation is from *Anabasis* 1.8.20, and the repetition is that of the word αὐτῶν which it is impossible to translate; it is a curious use of the word even in the Greek: τὰ δ' ἅρματα ἐφέροντο, τὰ μὲν δι' αὐτῶν τῶν φιλίων, τὰ δὲ δι' αὐτῶν τῶν πολεμίων. Incidentally, this is also a homoioteleuton (see section 26).

104. The reference is to *Anabasis* 1.8.10: ἡ δὲ γνώμη ἦν ὡς εἰς τὰς τάξεις τῶν Ἑλλήνων ἐλώντων καὶ διακοψόντων. The "obliqueness" consists partly in the use of the abstract noun "decision" instead of the verb. This is easy to translate, but the effect is not the same because we use abstract terms much more freely. The more important point is the use of ὡς with genitive future participles—an involved way of putting it, in Greek, and obviously not translatable. The Greek for oblique construction is τὸ πλάγιον, which also means an oblique case, whereas εὐθύς also means the nominative. Now an oblique or involved construction inevitably means the use of more oblique cases, and fewer nominatives.

105. Demetrius here quotes only in part *Iliad* 16.358, which he quoted in full, as an example of dysphony in section 48 (see note). There the main point was the recurrence

the greatness of Ajax better than his shield of seven layers of ox-hide.

106. The so-called *epiphônêma* might be described as an added ornamentation. It is most impressive in prose. One part of a passage serves
to express the thought, the other part is added to embellish it. In the
following lines of Sappho the thought is expressed in these words:

> The mountain-hyacinths are trodden down
> By shepherds' boots

and then comes the epiphônêma:

>   and on the ground
> The purple blooms lie bleeding.

This has obviously been added to what precedes, as a beautiful ornament.

107. Homer's poetry is full of these ornamental additions. For example:

> I've put the arms away, out of the smoke.
> They are already quite unlike the armour
> Odysseus left when he set out for Troy.
> And I bethought me of a graver matter:
> I feared that, flushed with wine and prone to quarrel,
> You wound each other.

Then comes the added phrase:

>   Steel makes men reckless.

108. Altogether, the epiphônêma may be compared to those external
displays of riches: cornices, triglyphs, and broad purples. The epiphônêma
too is a sign of riches, verbal riches.

109. The enthymeme might be thought to be a kind of epiphônêma,
but it is not. It is added in order to prove something, not to embellish.
However it may be added at the end, like the epiphônêma.

110. The maxim too is an addition like the epiphônêma, but it is not an
epiphônêma. It often stands at the beginning, although at times it fills
the place of an epiphônêma.

---

of harsh sounds at the end of the line. Here our attention is drawn more to the repetition
of the long a and αι sounds in Αἴας ὁ μέγας αἰέν . . . but we are meant to remember
the line as a whole which contains both repetition of sound and lack of euphony, and is
quoted here as a combination of both.

106. The epiphônêma as the word implies is added at the end, an extra statement
as it were, after the main thought has been expressed.

107. *Odyssey* 19.7–13.

108. For the meaning of "broad purples" see Introd. pp. 45–46.

109. For the enthymeme see sections 30–33.

110. For the maxim, γνώμη, see section 9. It is a statement of general significance,
but, when it comes at the end, it might well have been regarded as a special kind of
epiphônêma, though it is usually longer. It would be hard to distinguish the ornamental
addition or epiphônêma of section 107: "Steel makes men reckless" from a maxim.

111. A line like: "Fool! He was not to escape his evil doom" is not an epiphônêma either. It does not come at the end and it does not beautify. Indeed, it is quite unlike an epiphônêma and more like a form of address or a rebuke.

112. Even a blind man can see, as the saying is, that poetic language gives a certain grandeur to prose, except that some writers imitate the poets quite openly, or rather they do not so much imitate them as transpose their words into their own work, as Herodotus does.

113. When Thucydides, on the other hand, takes over some expression from a poet, he uses it in his own way and makes it his own. The poet said of Crete, for example,

> Crete lies in the midst of the wine-dark sea,
> A land comely and fertile, ocean-bound.

Homer uses the word "ocean-bound" with impressive effect. Thucydides considers it a fine thing for the Sicilians to have a common policy, since they are the denizens of one land, and that ocean-bound. He uses all the same words as the poet; he says land instead of island but calls it ocean-bound in the same way. Yet one feels that he is not saying what Homer said. The reason is that he uses the word not in order to impress but to underline the need for a common policy.

So much for the grand manner.

Frigidity

114. Every attractive quality has as its neighbour a specific weakness: rashness is close to bravery, and shame is close to respect; similarly, successful styles have certain faulty styles lurking nearby.

We shall deal first with the fault which borders on the grand style. We call it frigidity, and Theophrastus defined the frigid as that which overshoots its appropriate expression. For example, to say "Unbaséd goblets cannot tabled be" instead of "goblets without a base cannot be put on a table" is frigid because the trivial subject cannot carry such weighty words.

115. Frigidity, like grandeur, arises in three ways: it may be in the thought, as when a certain writer said in describing the Cyclops hurling a rock at the ship of Odysseus: "As the rock hurtled through the air, goats were grazing upon it." This is frigid because the thought is exaggerated and impossible.

111. See *Iliad* 12.113.
113. Thuc. 4.64, and *Odyssey* 19.172 (cp. 259 below).

116. There are, according to Aristotle, four sources of frigidity of diction. ⟨It is due to the use of unnecessary epithets⟩ as in Alcidamas' "damp sweat," or to a compound where the nature of the double word is dithyrambic, like "lone-journeyed" or some such overelaborate word; or it may be due to a metaphor such as "pallid and tremulous troubles." These then are the four kinds of frigidity of diction.

117. The arrangement of words is frigid when the rhythm is poor, as when, in a phrase, all the syllables are long.* This deserves censure, for it is not like prose.

118. On the other hand, a succession of metrical phrases is equally frigid. Some writers write like that, but the metres are obvious because they follow one another. Verse is out of place in prose, and therefore frigid, as is everything which is too metrical.

119. Generally speaking, pretence and frigidity are alike. The writer who deals with a trivial subject in weighty language is like a man who pretends to qualities he does not possess, undeterred by his lack of them, or like a man who boasts about trifles. To discuss trivialities in an exalted style is, as the saying is, like beautifying a pestle.

---

116. The lacuna indicated in the text must have contained not only some such expression as is added there, but also a reference to the fourth kind. This we can supply from the passage of Aristotle which Demetrius is obviously following, namely *Rhet.* 3.3.1–4, where the four causes of frigidity are: (i) too elaborate compounds, (ii) too unusual words (γλῶτται), (iii) too long, too frequent, or unsuitable epithets, and (iv) poor use of metaphors, in that order. It is the second of these, the poor use of unusual words, which has dropped out of our texts. Aristotle, however, does not mention any other kind of frigidity except that of diction (κατὰ τὴν λέξιν). The frigid metaphor quoted by Demetrius: τρέμοντα καὶ ὠχρὰ τὰ πράγματα seems to be a variation of that which Aristotle quotes from Gorgias: χλῶρα καὶ ἄναιμα τὰ πράγματα. Demetrius is probably quoting from memory. The examples are much more numerous in Aristotle under each section.

Alcidamas was a fourth-century rhetorician. Aristotle says that for him epithets were not a seasoning, they were the whole dish.

117. Demetrius gives one example, the unidentified phrase: ἥκων ἡμῶν εἰς τὴν χώραν, πάσης ἡμῶν ὀρθῆς οὔσης, of which he gave the first five words as an example of "heroic" metre in 42. All the syllables are long.

118. Demetrius adopts the general view of Aristotle, *Rhet.* 3.8, who says prose must have rhythm but not metre, but Aristotle does not discuss metre in connection with frigidity. It is very doubtful whether Demetrius gains anything by thus extending the meaning of frigidity. He is led to do so by making it the one vice to which the grand style is peculiarly liable, and wanting it to apply to the three divisions of that style namely content, diction, and word-arrangement.

119. Another proverb of similar meaning was (165) "beautifying a monkey," both referring to inappropriate or wasted effort.

120. Yet some people say we should discourse in the grand manner on trivialities and they think that this is a proof of outstanding oratorical talent. Now I admit that Polycrates, the rhetorician, eulogized ⟨Thersites⟩ as if he were Agamemnon and in so doing used antitheses, metaphors, and every device used in encomia. But he was doing this in jest, not writing a serious eulogy, and the dignified tone of the whole work was itself a game. Let us be playful by all means, but we must also observe what is fitting in each case: that is, we must write in the appropriate manner, lightly when our subject is slight, impressively when it is impressive.

121. Xenophon says of the small, pretty river Teleboas: "This river was not large, it was pretty though." The short sentence, and its ending with "though" makes us almost see the little river. But when another writer says of a similar stream "from its source in the mountains of Laurium it flows into the sea," one would think he was describing the cataracts of the Nile or the Danube pouring into the sea. All such writing is called frigid.

122. Small matters can be magnified in another way without inappropriateness, and sometimes this has to be done. We may, for example, want to exalt a general after a slight military success, or the punishment inflicted by the Spartan ephor who had a man whipped for playing ball earnestly and in an un-Spartan way. One is at once struck by the trifling nature of the offence, but we can dramatize its importance by saying that to ignore the formation of bad habits in small things is to open the door to more serious crimes, and that, therefore, it is the lesser, not the graver, infractions of the law that must be punished more severely. We shall then bring in the proverb about "work begun is work half-done" as applying to these trivial offences, or indeed as showing that no offence is trivial.

123. A trivial success may thus be greatly magnified without doing anything inappropriate. Just as it is often useful to minimize what is important, so the unimportant may be magnified.

120. Some name has obviously dropped out. It may have been any lowly or weak character. The suggestion of Thersites, the ugly and obstreperous rank-and-filer of *Iliad* 2 will do as well as any other. He is mentioned as an object of ridicule in 163.

121. This sentence of Xenophon, *Anab.* 4.4.3, was quoted in section 6, where it is praised for its rhythm and brevity. The Greek οὗτος δὲ πόταμος ἦν μέγας μὲν οὔ, καλὸς δέ with the unusual ending in δέ, balancing οὔ, is more abrupt than the English rendering. The source of the other quotation is unknown.

122. The proverb comes from Hesiod, *Works and Days* 40, ἀρχὴ τὸ ἥμισυ παντός (the beginning is one half of the whole).

124. The most frigid of all devices is the hyperbole. It is of three kinds; one thing is said to be like another, as in "they run like the wind"; or one thing may be made superior to another, for example, "whiter than snow"; or, thirdly, what is said is impossible: "her head reached unto heaven."

125. Every hyperbole is really impossible. Nothing is whiter than snow, no horse can run like the wind, but the type mentioned just now is especially called so. It is precisely because every hyperbole states an impossibility that every hyperbole is thought to be frigid.

126. Hence comic poets use hyperbole very freely, and they make the impossibility a source of laughter, as when someone said hyperbolically, in connection with the insatiability of the Persians: "their excrements covered the plains," and again "they carry oxen between their jaws."

127. Of the same type are the well-known "balder than a cloudless sky" and "healthier than a pumpkin." As for Sappho's phrase "more golden than gold," although it is expressed as a hyperbole and is indeed an impossibility, it is the more charming because impossible. Indeed it is a most admirable feature of the divine Sappho's art, that she extracts great charm from devices which are in themselves questionable and difficult.

So much for frigidity and hyperbole, and we now turn to the elegant style.

THE ELEGANT OR POLISHED STYLE

128. The elegant manner has a certain bright playfulness of expression. Its charm may be either serious and dignified as in poetry, or it may be more commonplace and comic, like jibes. Such are the witticisms we find in Aristotle, Sophron, and Lysias. It was said of an old woman, for example, that "her teeth were easier to count than her fingers," and of a

124. The first two examples are used by Dolon of the horses of Rhesus: "they are whiter than snow, and run like the wind" in *Iliad* 10.437. This certainly does not seem frigid. The third is from *Il.* 4.443 and describes Eris or Strife. Here Demetrius' criticism is more justified.

125. We should remember that we are still dealing with the impressive style; Demetrius considers that the hyperbole is not suited to it.

126. The source of these quotations is unknown.

128. As stated in the introduction pp. 30–32, there is a confusion of thought here. Demetrius is speaking of two quite different things, elegant charm, and wit which may be charming but is not always so, for example, Lysias' joke (see 262) in the text. He is straining the meaning of χάριτες which he uses as equivalent to γλαφυρός, and under which he includes all forms of wit. It would be little use trying to find an English word

man that "he made as many drachmas as he deserved strokes of the lash." Such clever sayings are like jibes in every respect and close to the laughter of comedy.

129. Homer's description of Nausicaa which begins "The Nymphs played with her; Leto's heart was gladdened" and ends with: "And she outshone them all, but all were lovely" is an example of the more dignified and serious charm.

130. Homer sometimes also uses witticisms to make a passage more forceful and more expressive, and his playfulness increases the fearful effect. Indeed he is the inventor of grim jests, as when he makes his repulsive character, the Cyclops, say to Odysseus: "I shall eat Nobody last, and the others first." That is the Cyclops' gift of hospitality. Nothing Homer says about him makes the Cyclops as terrifying as these striking words, not his eating two of Odysseus' friends at one meal, nor the big rock that serves him as a door, nor his huge club.

131. Xenophon too uses this kind of device and achieves forcefulness by means of wit, as in the case of the armed dancing-girl. "A Paphlagonian asks a Greek whether their women accompany them to war. 'Yes,' is the reply, 'and it was they who put the king to flight.'" The witticism is doubly forceful; it implies that they were accompanied by Amazons rather than women, and it reflects on the king if he was so weak as to be put to flight by women.

Elegant Subject-Matter

132. Such then are the different kinds of charm and wit. Some are inherent in the subject-matter: gardens dedicated to the Nymphs,

---

to cover all this. Rhys Roberts' "pleasantry" is possible but he himself does not apply it consistently.

It seems best to recognize that Demetrius' classifications here are faulty. His "elegance" can certainly cover both elegant charm (the Nausicaa scene) and elegant wit. Grim or vulgar wit he should, however, have excluded.

For purposes of translation we may render χάριτες in the over-all sense as "charm and wit," without trying to unify the two ideas.

129. *Odyssey* 6.105–109.

130. *Odyssey* 9.369. When asked his name, Odysseus answered it was "Nobody" (Οὖτις). Hence the jest when later the Cyclops called to the others outside that "Nobody" was killing him. Demetrius tells us that Homer here aims at δείνωσις (intensity) and ἔμφασις. For these words see App. I, A. The word δείνωσις should be noted here and in the next section for this type of witticism is out of place here and belongs really to the forceful style (cp. 292–296).

131. Xenophon, *Anabasis* 6.1.13, not an exact quotation.

132. Hipponax was an iambic poet of the sixth century, alleged to be the inventor of parody.

bridal songs, loves, all the poetry of Sappho. Such subjects have a charm and brightness of their own, even when treated by Hipponax. No one could sing a bridal song in anger; no style can turn Eros into a Fury or a Giant, or laughter into tears.

133. One kind of charm then lies in the subject matter though the language can also increase the charm of things:

> When the pale nightingale, Pandareus' daughter,
> Utters her lovely song, and spring is near.

The nightingale is a charming little bird, and spring is naturally delightful, but the lines are much embellished by calling the nightingale "pale," and the "daughter of Pandareus." These expressions are the poet's own.

134. On the other hand, a subject which is naturally unpleasing and distasteful can often be brightened by the writer. Xenophon seems to have been the first to discover this. He takes that unhumorous and distasteful character, the Persian Aglaitadas, and makes him the occasion of an elegant jest when he says: "it is easier to strike fire from you than laughter."

135. This is the most effective kind of wit, and it especially depends on the writer. For the subject was naturally unpleasant and opposed to wit, as Aglaitadas certainly was, but Xenophon shows that it is possible to be playful even on such subjects, as if one could be warmed by cold and cooled by heat.

136. As we have now explained the different kinds of charm and wit, their nature and also wherein they inhere, we will proceed to show the sources from which they originate. Charm and wit, we said, are either inherent in the subject-matter or due to the expression of it. We will now indicate their sources in both cases, and begin by charm of expression.

137. First comes the charm which is due to brevity, when the same thought expressed at length would be in poor taste, and it is the rapidity of expression which makes it attractive. We read in Xenophon: "And he said: 'In truth there is nothing Greek about him, for I myself have seen that he has both his ears pierced, like a Lydian.' And so he had." The brevity of the final clause "And so he had" makes for elegance, and if the thing had been put into more words: "What he said was true, he

---

133. In Greek legend the nightingale was a maiden changed into a bird. The reference is to *Odyssey* 19.518. There is a point which is missed in translation: Demetrius approves of "pale" also, presumably, because Homer uses the lengthened form χλωρηΐs instead of χλωρά. He has told us in section 70 that such lengthened poetic forms contribute to impressiveness, they evidently also contribute to elegance and polish.

134. Xen. *Cyropaedia* 2.2.15.

137. Xen. *Anabasis* 3.1.31.

evidently had had his ears pierced" the result would have been a simple statement without charm.

138. It is often a sign of wit to express two things at once, as someone described the sleeping Amazon: "Her bow lay ready-strung beside her, her quiver was full, her shield lay by her head; but they do not loosen their girdles." The same expression refers both to the custom of loosening the girdle and that she did not loosen her girdle (to sleep), two meanings in one phrase. This brevity has a certain elegance.

Elegant Arrangement

139. The second source of elegance is the arrangement. What is said last may have charm yet have none if put first or second, as when Xenophon says of Cyrus that "he also gave him presents: a horse, a robe, a necklace, and a promise not to further ravage his country." Here it is the last gift, "a promise not to further ravage his country," which has wit because the gift is of an unusual and peculiar nature. But it is its place in the sentence that makes it witty; it would be less attractive if it headed the list and Xenophon had said: "he gave him as a present a promise not to further ravage his country, a horse, a robe, and a necklace." As it is, he has put the usual gifts first, then he adds the strange and unusual, and all this adds up to a witticism.

140. The charm derived from the use of figures of speech is obvious, especially in Sappho. It is achieved, for example, by anadiplôsis, where the bride exclaims: "Maidenhood, maidenhood, thou hast left me, whither hast thou gone?" and the reply makes use of the same figure: "No longer shall I come to thee, no longer shall I come." This is clearly more charming than if the words were not repeated and there was no figure. Yet anadiplôsis seems to have been devised rather as a means of forcefulness. Sappho, however, can use even the most forceful figures charmingly.

141. She sometimes obtains a charming effect by *anaphora*: "O Evening

138. Quotation unknown. The two meanings are that the Amazon was a virgin and that she slept ready-armed.

139. *Anabasis* 1.2.27.

140. Anadiplôsis was a figure to be used in the impressive style at 66; here we are told that it is mainly a means to forcefulness, but that it can be used to achieve elegance, at least by Sappho.

141. Sappho's words are: Ἕσπερε, πάντα φέρεις, φέρεις ὄϊν, φέρεις αἶγα, φέρεις ματέρι παῖδα.

For anaphora, there called epanaphora, the repetition of the same word at the beginning of succeeding clauses, see 61–62 (the Nireus passage). There it was said to achieve impressiveness.

Star, all things you bring; you bring the sheep, you bring the goat, you bring the child to its mother." Here the charm lies in the repetition of the words "you bring" in the same place in succeeding clauses.

Elegant Diction

142. One might mention many other kinds of charm and wit, of which some are due to the choice of words, or the use of a metaphor, as in the lyric verses on the cricket: "he pours a shrill song from under his wing, when he flutes his song that flies o'er the fiery depth."

143. Or the charm may be due to the use of a dithyrambic compound: "Pluto, black-winged lord . . . ."* This is more comic and playful, and suited to the satyr-drama.

144. Or again it may be due to a commonplace derivation, as when Aristotle said: "The more of an isolate I am, the fonder I have become of stories," or it may be a word coined for the purpose, as he also said in the same passage: "The more of a selfsome isolate I am, the fonder I am of stories." The word "isolate" is more commonplace, and "selfsome" is coined from self.

145. Many words have charm when applied to a particular thing, as in: "This bird is a flatterer and a rascal." Here the bird is mocked like a person, and the words are not usually applied to birds. These then are the kinds of charm due to the actual words.

146. Comparison too can be charming, as when Sappho says of a man of great beauty: "He shines among his peers like the Lesbian singer among strangers." The comparison is charming rather than impressive, which it would have been had she said "like the moon among the stars," or "like the brightness of the sun," or made some other more poetic comparison.

147. Sophron, too, uses the same device where he says: "Look, my dear, the boys are pelting the men with leaves and twigs as innumerable as the mud which, they say, the Trojans showered upon Ajax." There is charm and wit in the comparison which makes fun of the Trojans as if they were boys.

142. The quotation here: πτερύγων δ' ὑποκακχέει λιγυρὰν ἀοιδὰν ὅτι ποτ' ἂν φλόγιον καθέταν ἐπιπτάμενον καταυλεῖ, is uncertain as to text, meaning, and author. It is attributed to Alcaeus by some (Bergk fr. 39), to Sappho by others (J. M. Edmonds, *Lyra Graeca* I, fr. 94). However, the metaphor is obviously καταυλεῖν, to play the flute.

143. The meaning here too is obscure, and the author of the quotation unknown, but the point lies in "black-winged": δέσποτα Πλούτων μεγαλοπτερύγων, δεινὸν πρὸ πτερύγων αὐτὸ ποίησον . . . .

144. The passage from Aristotle is unknown: ὅσῳ γὰρ αὐτίτης καὶ μονώτης φιλομυθέστερος γέγονα. Both derivatives mean "alone." Cp. 97.

148. Sappho achieves a witty charm all her own by means of *metabolê*. She says something, then changes it as though she were changing her mind: "Raise high the hall, you builders. A bridegroom is coming as tall as Ares, much taller than a big man." She seems to be correcting herself, because she used an impossible hyperbole, and because no man is as tall as Ares.

149. The same device is found in Telemachus: "Two dogs were tied before the court, and I can give their names—but what are their names to me?" He too achieves an attractive effect by changing his mind in the middle of the sentence and suppressing the names.

150. There is a certain charm, too, in borrowing from the verse of another writer. Aristophanes is mocking Zeus because he does not blast the wicked with his thunderbolt "but strikes his own temple, and Sunium, the foreland of Athens." One feels that he is no longer mocking Zeus, but Homer, and the Homeric line where the words "and Sunium, the foreland of Athens," also occur, and this increases the attractive effect.

151. Veiled meanings (allêgoria) too, at times, have a certain gossipy wit about them, like the well-known: "Delphians, your bitch is with child"; or Sophron's scene about the old men: "Here I am with you, all greybeards together, ready to sail, indeed expecting a journey beyond the seas, for at our age the anchor is always weighed." And then his allêgoria about the widows and the fish,* but such things are vulgar and too much like the mime.

148. The word metabolê, which usually has the quite general meaning of "change" is here used as a technical name for this particular figure of self-correction. Quintilian (9.3.38) uses it as the name of a quite different figure, namely to express the same idea several times in different words.

149. We know of no Telemachus as a writer or critic to whom this might refer. It has been suggested that the quotation is from a story *about* Telemachus, but that is not the natural meaning of the Greek.

150. Demetrius is no doubt right that this kind of semi-quotation can have a certain charm or wit. But one doubts his reason; it is the Athenians' pride in one of the very few references to Athens in Homer which Aristophanes is laughing at, plus the fact that Sunium was a deserted cape which cannot have offended Zeus. Homer's line was as familiar to the Athenians as "To be or not to be" is to us, and, though Demetrius does not say so, this sort of familiar quotation is especially suited to comedy. The reference is to *Odyssey* 3.278, and *Clouds* 401.

151. The mime was a homely sort of prose-drama, which realistically depicted scenes from daily life. The mimes of Sophron were famous, but only the merest fragments remain.

The point of the first quotation about the Delphian bitch is quite obscure. The second is clear: old men must be ready for the journey of death. Of the third, σωλῆνες, γλυκύκρεον κογχύλιον χηρᾶν γυναικῶν λίχνευμα, no translation will be attempted.

Allêgoria was discussed at 99–102 as contributing to impressiveness. See App. I, A.

152. There is also the witty charm of the unexpected as where the Cyclops says: "I shall eat Nobody last," for neither Odysseus nor the reader expected such a tribute to hospitality. Or, as Aristophanes says of Socrates: "He melted some wax, took up a pair of compasses, and filched a coat from the wrestling-school."

153. The witticisms in these cases derive from two sources: not only are they unexpected, but they have no connection with what has gone before. This kind of *non-sequitur* is called a *griphos*. A good example of it is the speech which Sophron puts in the mouth of Boulias, whose statements have no logical connection with one another. Another example is Menander's prologue to *The Woman from Messenia*.

154. Clauses with paromoiôsis frequently have a charming or witty effect, as when Aristotle said: "From Athens I was driven to Stagira by the great king, from Stagira to Athens by the great storm." By ending both clauses with the same word he attains a certain graceful wit. If you leave out the word "great" in the second clause, this charm disappears also.

155. Implied censure sometimes is very like a witticism. So, in Xenophon, Heraclides, the companion of Seuthes, approaches each of the guests at dinner and urges him to give Seuthes whatever he can. The point is witty, and there is a camouflaged rebuke.

156. These then are the kinds of charm and wit which depend on style and the sources which produce them. Elegance of thought or subject-matter includes the use of saws and proverbs, for proverbs have a natural charm. Sophron speaks of "Epioles who throttled his father" and elsewhere he says: "from one claw he drew the whole lion"; "he

152. The Cyclops' words were quoted in 130, also as an example of χάρις (see on 128) but to illustrate the grim type of jest. Demetrius is no doubt justified in quoting it also as an example of the unexpected, παρὰ προσδοκίαν, though it is very different from the slighter witticisms we have here been dealing with, and from Aristophanes' rather feeble *non-sequitur*, *Clouds* 179.

153. Demetrius does not quote here, and we know nothing of the passages referred to. For Sophron see on 128.

154. For paromoiôsis and homoioteleuton see 25–26. This saying of Aristotle is quoted in 29, and we were there told that such clauses made for μεγαληγορία or extravagance of language although the word χάρις or charm is there also used of this particular example. The Greek clauses do end with the same word μέγαν.

155. *Anabasis* 7.3.15–20. The remainder of Xenophon's ten thousand had just taken service with Seuthes, an outlaw Thracian prince (400 B.C.). Heraclides approaches envoys on their way to another monarch with gifts, and Xenophon who had nothing to give, and embarrasses them both.

156. The meaning of the first proverb, about the man who throttled his father, is quite obscure to us. The others are fairly clear: "to draw the lion from the claw" is to reconstruct a whole picture or situation from one small detail or circumstance, to build

polished a wooden soup ladle"; "he split his cinnamon grain" thus multiplying the display of wit by using two or three proverbs at once. Indeed one might collect almost all the proverbs in existence from the works of Sophron.

157. A fable told at the right time also has charm. It may be one that is well known, as Aristotle says of the eagle that he dies of hunger as his beak grows more and more crooked and that he suffers this fate because he was once a man and wronged a guest. In this case the fable is familiar and common property.

158. We also fashion fables to make them appropriate and suitable to our subject-matter. Someone, when talking about cats, stated that they wane and grow fat with the moon; he then added: "Hence the story that the moon is the mother of cats." The fiction itself has charm; moreover, the fable which makes the cat the child of the moon makes an attractive point.

159. Relief from fear provides an occasion for wit, as when a man has been afraid without reason, mistaking a strap for a snake, or a pot for a hole in the ground, but these occasions are more suited to comedy.

160. Similes too have great charm, as when you say that a cock is like a Persian because he wears a stiff crest, or like a king because of his purple plumage, or because we leap up at the crow of a cock as at a shout from a king, and are afraid.

161. The charm of comedy is derived mostly from the use of hyperbole. Every hyperbole states an impossibility, as when Aristophanes, aiming at the insatiable greed of the Persians, says: "they baked oxen in their baking pans instead of bread," or another writer said of the Thracians "Their king Medoces used to carry a whole ox between his teeth."

---

a whole case on very little evidence. For "polishing a ladle" Rhys Roberts quotes a pleasant version from A. S. Way: "He had such an artistic soul, that he polished the scullery-bowl"; though the Greek proverb seems to have referred to wasted effort. "Splitting cinnamon seed" probably refers to miserliness; we might translate "skinning a flint," as Roberts does; it might also refer to oversubtlety, like our "splitting hairs." The prominence given by Demetrius to proverbs is quite unusual; cp. 119, 122. It is also worth noting that Sophron (470–400 B.C.) is rarely mentioned by other critics.

157. Aristotle, *Hist. Anim.* 9. 32.

158. Plutarch tells a different Egyptian story (*Isis and Osiris* 63) that the pupils of the cat's eyes grow wide at the full moon. See Introd., note 56.

161. For hyperbole see 124–126. In the grand style it was said to lead to frigidity. Here it is discussed as a form of witticism, of the kind which (see on 128) is included under elegance and charm. The Aristophanic reference is to *Acharnians* 86–87, where an envoy returned from Persia tells a marvellous tale about the Persians, full of incredible exaggerations. Serving an ox baked in a pan (where one would expect loaves) is one of them. The other passage is unknown.

162. The following expressions are of the same kind: "healthier than a pumpkin," "balder than a cloudless sky," and Sappho's "far more musical than a harp," "more golden than gold." The charm and wit of all these sayings derive from the hyperbole.

163. Charm and comic laughter are different. They differ first in subject-matter. To charm belong such subjects as the gardens of the nymphs, and the loves; these do not provoke laughter, whereas Irus and Thersites do. Indeed the two kinds of subject are as far apart as Thersites and Eros.

164. A second difference is in the language used. Charm is expressed by means of embellishment through beautiful words. These contribute most to charm as, for instance, "the earth with its variegated embroidery of flowery garlands" or "the pale nightingale"; but ridicule or comic laughter requires current everyday language as in Aristotle's "the more isolate and selfsome I become, the fonder I am of stories."

165. Moreover, stylistic ornament distracts the attention from a joke; people admire but do not laugh. One should be moderate in the use of literary graces: to deck a joke with stylistic embellishments is like beautifying a monkey.

166. That is why Sappho's language is delightful in its beauty when she sings of beauty, love, springtime, or the kingfisher; every beautiful word is woven into her poetry, including those she has coined herself.

167. But she adopts a quite different manner to ridicule the boorish bridegroom or the porter at the wedding; she uses commonplace and prosaic rather than poetic language; these poems of hers are more easily spoken than sung; they are not attuned to the dance or the lyre, unless indeed one can speak of a choral rhythm in conversation.

168. The difference is great, and it is deliberate. The writer with charm

162. Three of the four examples have been cited in 127 which goes on to note Sappho's capacity to use risky figures with charm. The whole of 127 would be more in place here, for it adds nothing to the discussion of frigidity.

163. For Thersites see note on 120; Irus is the beggar Odysseus finds in his palace (*Odyssey* 18).

164. Demetrius seems in these sections (163–169) to be establishing a new distinction between γελοῖον, ridicule, and χάρις, charm, though so far he has included all jests, charming or crude, under χάρις = γλαφυρόν. He seems to be feeling his way to a threefold division: (a) poetic charm, (b) graceful wit, (c) ridicule, which is forceful rather than elegant. But this difference is not properly worked out, and, except briefly in these sections, he confuses the two. See Introduction pp. 30–32.

The quotation from Aristotle has already been used at 97 and 144. Actually, αὐτίτης is not ordinary language, except in the sense (intended here) that it is not graceful or poetic, and derived from a common word.

165. On beautifying a monkey see 120.

and the comic writer have different ends in view, the one aims to delight us, the other, to make us laugh; and our reaction is quite different too: in the one case we laugh, in the other we admire.

169. They derive from different sources. Satyr-drama and comedy, it is true, combine laughter and charm. Tragedy has many graces of style, but laughter is its enemy. No one can conceive of a playful tragedy, for he would, in fact, be writing satyric drama instead of tragedy.

170. Even thoughtful men indulge in ridicule on appropriate occasions, at feasts and parties for example, and also to rebuke extravagance. And so we have Telauges "the pouch," the poetry of Crates, and the eulogy of pea soup which one might well read to a company of spendthrifts. The Cynic manner is, generally speaking, of this kind, for such jests take the place of saws and maxims.

171. A man's jokes give some indication of his character; they may indicate a lack of seriousness or of self-control, as with the man who stopped a libation of wine with the words "Peleus instead of Oineus." The words, the antithesis, the careful thought betray a cold and unpleasant character.

172. Personal jibes imply a sort of simile, and the antithesis between the terms of the comparison is witty. Men may use such comparisons as calling a tall dark man "an Egyptian clematis," or speaking of "sheep at sea" when they see a fool at the oars. For such expressions as these are in general use, but otherwise we should avoid personal jibes as we would personal abuse.

170. The reference to Telauges is obscure. There is little doubt that a proper name is intended, for it recurs at 291 and Aeschines on Telauges is also mentioned by Athenaeus 5.220a. Here a pun may be intended ($\tau\eta\lambda\alpha\upsilon\gamma\dot{\eta}s$ = far-shining) and (as Roberts suggests p. 240) "far-gleaming pouch" may have been a jocular expression for a fat man. The point is lost to us.

Crates of Thebes (ca. 365–285 b.c.) became a disciple of Diogenes the Cynic in Athens. He wandered all over the Greek world preaching the simple life. He injected into Cynicism a kindliness that was lacking in Diogenes, and wrote a great deal of poetry and prose in a satirical but friendly vein. The Cynic serio-comic manner described in later texts was developed by him, by Bion of Borysthenes and by Menippus. All three were writing during the first half of the third century.

171. The point of the pun is uncertain. Presumably the offence lay in the poor pun on the heroic names Peleus ($\pi\tilde{\eta}\lambda os$ = mud) and Oeneus ($o\tilde{\iota}vos$ = wine) to say in effect Mud instead of Wine as the libation was poured on the ground—whether this showed a lack of respect for the occasion or the heroes is not clear. Roberts (pp. 240–241) quotes references to this same pun in Athenaeus 9.383c and Eustathius ad Iliad. p. 772.

172. The meaning seems to be that certain expressions, like those quoted, are allowed in common parlance, and their sting is blunted by usage, but that we should avoid others. See Introd. p. 46.

173. The use of words that we call beautiful also contributes to charm of style. Theophrastus defined beautiful words as follows: the beauty of words depends on their appeal to the ear, to the eye, or on the esteem in which our mind holds them.

174. Words such as "rosy-hued," or "a complexion fresh as a flower," are pleasing to the eye because what is pleasant to see is pleasing when mentioned. On the other hand, words like "Callistratus" and "Annoôn" are pleasant to the ear, because the double "l" and double "n" have a certain resonance.

175. Attic writers generally add an "n" to certain words and use the (accusative) forms $\Delta\eta\mu\sigma\sigma\theta\epsilon\nu\eta\nu$ and $\Sigma\omega\kappa\rho\alpha\tau\eta\nu$ for reasons of euphony. Words whose associations are more highly esteemed are, for example, "ancient" instead of "old," for the ancients are more esteemed.

176. Musicians classify words as smooth, rough, well-knit, or weighty. A smooth word is one which consists entirely, or for the most part, of vowels, like "Aias." A word like "crunching" is rough, and this particular example of roughness was formed to imitate its own action. A well-knit word is one which has characteristics of both and mixes both kinds of sound equally.

177. Weight is due to three factors: broad sounds, long sounds, and the use of certain forms, as when we use $\beta\rho\sigma\nu\tau\dot{\alpha}$ for $\beta\rho\sigma\nu\tau\dot{\eta}$ (thunder).

173–175. There is a certain ambiguity in the terms used in 173, but fortunately Demetrius goes on to explain their meaning. The appeal to the ear is clear: the sound of certain words is more pleasing, more euphonious, than that of others. By words pleasing to the eye, however, is obviously *not* meant the look of the word on the page (a thought which would hardly occur to an ancient writer, as they always read aloud) but, as explained in 174, certain words recall a pleasing visual picture to mind (to the eye of the mind?). The third source of beauty is $\tau\dot{o}$ $\delta\iota\alpha\nu\sigma\dot{\iota}\alpha$ $\dot{\epsilon}\nu\tau\iota\mu\sigma\nu$ and Demetrius quotes as an example that $\sigma\dot{\iota}$ $\dot{\alpha}\rho\chi\alpha\dot{\iota}\sigma\iota$ is $\dot{\epsilon}\nu\tau\iota\mu\dot{o}\tau\epsilon\rho\sigma\nu$ than $\sigma\dot{\iota}$ $\pi\alpha\lambda\alpha\iota\sigma\dot{\iota}$. Both words mean exactly the same, namely the "ancients" or "men of old." The difference here must be that $\dot{\alpha}\rho\chi\alpha\dot{\iota}\sigma$ has nobler or more esteemed associations because it derives from $\dot{\alpha}\rho\chi\dot{\eta}$ and is connected with the whole family of words derived from that root. This is partly lost in translation but a parallel might be found, for example "emperor" and "king," since men have called themselves "emperors" for precisely this reason. This third source of beauty in words, then, does not lie in any difference of meaning, but in the fact that of two words of similar meaning one is "more highly esteemed" than the other. This is due to its associations in the past, or to its own family connections.

How far Demetrius' explanations, beyond the bare quotation in 173, are derived from Theophrastus is not clear. There is, however, a close connection between Theophrastus' definition and Aristotle, *Rhet.* 3.2.13.

176. I have translated $\beta\dot{\epsilon}\beta\rho\omega\kappa\epsilon$ (eating) somewhat freely by "crunching," as more or less equivalent in harshness of sound and also onomatopoeic.

177. The broad $\bar{a}$ of $\beta\rho\sigma\nu\tau\dot{\alpha}$ as against the Attic $\beta\rho\sigma\nu\tau\dot{\eta}$ is the only difference between them but it ensures the first factor, broadness, and thus makes $\beta\rho\sigma\nu\tau\dot{\alpha}$ the heavier word.

The former derives roughness from its first syllable, from the second it receives length because of the long sound, and it has broadness because of the Doric form, for the Dorians broaden all their sounds when speaking. This is why comedies were not written in the Doric dialect, but in the sharper Attic, for Attic speech has a certain compactness and popular flavour, and is more suited to such displays of wit.

178. But these things should be discussed in detail on another occasion. Of the words we have mentioned, the smooth only are to be used as having a certain elegance.

Elegant Arrangement: Rhythm

179. Elegance also depends on the arrangement of the words. This is not an easy subject to discuss, for no previous writer has had anything to say about elegant word-arrangement. However, I must do the best I can.

180. We shall achieve a pleasing charm if we base the order of our words on some rhythmic measures or half-measures. These must not be obvious in the connected text, but a careful examination of each individual phrase enables us to detect that they are metrical.

181. Even a mere resemblance to metrical measures will achieve the same graceful effect, which is not directly perceived but delights the reader. This device is most frequently found in Peripatetic writers as well as in Plato, Xenophon, and Herodotus, and often in Demosthenes, but Thucydides avoids this type of elegance.

182. One can find examples of this, for instance in Dicaearchus,* where the two clauses have a certain metrical effect at the end, but this remains unperceived because the words are closely linked together without any pause. The effect is very pleasing.

183. Plato's elegance, however, is often due to the rhythm; it is somewhat prolonged, without well marked clause-endings or much in the way of long syllables. Well-marked endings are plain or forcible, long syllables are impressive; but Plato's clauses seem to slide into each

179. It is discussed by Dionysius in his *Composition*, ch. 23. It is unlikely that any later writer would be unaware of Dionysius' work.

182. Two consecutive phrases of Dicaearchus are quoted here: ἐν Ἐλέᾳ τῆς Ἰταλίας (in Italian Elea) where we have two "final paeons" (see 38–39) separated by a long syllable, and πρεσβύτην ἤδη τὴν ἡλικίαν ὄντα (already an old man in years) where there are a lot of long syllables and a "final" paeon ends just before the last syllable.

183. Demetrius does not quote here, except for the last phrase, and seems to expect his hearers to remember *Republic* 3.411a-b, but he does quote from it in the next section. The well-marked ending is ἔδρα and μῆκος refers not to the length of the passage but the presence of many long syllables.

other, they are neither altogether metrical nor unmetrical. There is the passage on music for example, after the words: "We said just now."

184. Take one sentence,* and then another.* This is clearly elegant and like a song. And if you change the order of words at the end you destroy the charm of the passage, which lies in the rhythm itself, not either in the thought or the language.

185. Again, Plato has a delightful rhythm where he speaks of musical instruments,* and if we invert the order of his words we get a quite different effect. The next sentence about the shepherd's pipe,* by its greater length and longer syllables, somehow imitates the sound of the pipe. This would be clear to anyone who changed the order of the words.

Affectation

186. So much for that difficult subject, elegance which is due to the arrangement of the words. We have also discussed the ways and means of achieving the elegant style. And just as the frigid style lay close to the grand, so the elegant has its own neighbouring vice. This I call the affected style, and it is the name commonly given to it. Like all the others, it is due to three factors.

187. Affectation may be due to the thought expressed, as when someone spoke of "a Centaur riding himself," or the remark made to Alexander

---

184. The first sentence quoted is μινυρίζων τε καὶ γεγανωμένος ὑπὸ τῆς ᾠδῆς διατελεῖ τὸν βίον ὅλον. (Singing and taking delight in song he spends his whole life.) Here we have 15 short to 10 long syllables, and four shorts at the end, which certainly does not make a firm ending or ἕδρα. Change the order of the last three words, says Demetrius, to ὅλον τὸν βίον and you lose the elegant rhythm. In fact you do get a more "solid" ending with only two shorts preceded by two longs (the last short probably lengthened by position).

The second quotation is τὸ μὲν πρῶτον, εἰ τι θυμοειδὲς εἶχεν, ὥσπερ σίδηρον, ἐμάλαξεν (in the first place, if there was anything spirited about him, the music would temper it, like steel). This is really three clauses or phrases, each of which ends with a short syllable preceded by a long one and the sounds are certainly of the kind that run into one another without pause, that is, "n" followed by a vowel in each case.

185. Demetrius here quotes two parts of a sentence of Plato at *Rep.* 3.399 d, but his quotations are not exact according to our texts. His first quotation is λύρα δή σοι λείπεται κατὰ πόλιν (the lyre is left for you in the town) ending with four short syllables, which, he says, would be quite different if written as κατὰ πόλιν λείπεται. The words he quotes on the shepherd's pipe are: καὶ αὖ κατ' ἀγροὺς τοῖς ποιμέσι σύριγξ ἄν τις εἴη. (And for the shepherds in the fields there would be the pipe.) (Plato has νομεῦσι but this makes little difference.) Here we have 12 long syllables to 3 short, and the ending U — —.

186-187. κακόζηλον is affectation, preciosity, or just bad taste. It is an attempt at polish or wit that does not come off. Alexander's mother was, of course, called Olympias. The sources of these quotations are unknown.

when he was planning to take part in the races at Olympia: "Alexander, run your mother's name."

188. Or the particular words may be affected; for example: "laughed the sweet-complexioned rose." Laughter is here an unsuitable metaphor, and no man of accurate judgment would use the compound "sweet-complexioned" even in poetry. Then again someone said: "the pine whistled an accompaniment to the gentle breeze." These are matters of diction.

189. Then there is the anapaestic arrangement of words which is very like broken and trivial metres, especially the feeble Sotadeans.* The line seems to have lost its form, like the men who in the legend are changed into women. So much for affectation.

The Plain or Simple Style

190. In the plain style we should deal also with simple subjects which are appropriate to it, as when Lysias says: "I have a small house with two floors, with the same amount of space above and below stairs."

The diction must consist of current and usual words throughout, for the more usual is always more trivial, while the unusual and metaphorical is impressive.

Lucidity

191. Compounds should not be used, for they too belong to the opposite style, nor should new coinages or any other words which contribute to impressiveness. The diction should above all be lucid; and lucidity can be attained in a variety of ways.

188. The first example is: ἐγέλα που ῥόδον ἡδύχροον and the second: ὅτι λεπταῖς ὑποσύρισε πίτυς αὔραις. Neither passage is known, but we would not object to them or consider them affected (λεπταῖς is a conjecture of Radermacher's adopted by Roberts). Demetrius objects to the word ἡδύχροος itself, not only to its use here (literally it means sweet-coloured), because the two components do not belong to the same categories taste and colour; no colour is sweet.

189. Sotades wrote early in the third century B.C. and his name became identified in all later critical writings with tripping, broken metres. Demetrius gives two examples: the first is σκηλᾱς καυμᾰτῐ κᾰλῡψ́ον (having dried in the heat, cover up). The second is a "metamorphosis" of *Iliad* 22.133: σειῶν Πηλιᾰδᾰ μελῐην κᾰτᾰ δεξῐον ωμον (brandishing over his right shoulder the Pelian ashen spear) into σειῶν μελῐην Πηλιᾰδᾰ δεξῐον κᾰτ' ωμον, which breaks up the metre, the line ending with three trochees, and might well be called an unmanned hexameter.

190. The same is said of these two dictions at 77.

191. For compound words Demetrius here uses διπλᾶ ὀνόματα, the Aristotelian term. See on 91–93 above. Newly-coined words were discussed, as contributing to grandeur, at 94–98.

192. First, by using current terms, and secondly by using connectives. A disconnected and disjointed word-arrangement always and everywhere leads to obscurity, because the looseness obscures the beginning of clauses. This is the case with Heraclitus; his notorious obscurity is for the most part due to lack of connectives.

193. A style which omits the connectives is more suited to debate; this manner of expression is also called histrionic and indeed it requires an actor's delivery. A written style, on the other hand, should be easy to read; it is closely integrated and, as it were, made safe by connectives. That is why Menander, whose style lacks connectives, is mostly acted, while Philemon is read.

194. The following example will show how disconnected clauses are histrionic: "I conceived thee, I bore thee. I nurse thee, my dear." These disconnected clauses compel a histrionic delivery, even against one's will. But if you bind the clauses together and say "I conceived thee and I bore thee, and I nurse thee," you lower the emotional tone considerably by adding the connectives. And what is unemotional is not histrionic.

195. There are other aspects of the actor's art which deserve study. In the play of Euripides, Ion snatches his bow and threatens the swan which is defiling the temple statues. The running to his bow, the looking up into the sky while talking to the swan, provide the actor with many gestures, and the whole composition of the rest of the scene has the actor in view. But we are not now discussing acting.

196. Lucid writing should avoid ambiguities. It should use the figure called *epanalêpsis*. This means the use of the same connective after a considerable interval: "As for Philip's achievements—the conquest of Thrace, the capture of the Chersonese, the siege of Byzantium, the refusal to surrender Amphipolis—as for all these, I shall not mention them . . . ." The connecting words "as for," when repeated, remind us of the main point, and put us back at the beginning.

---

192. Demetrius uses two words for lack of connectives, namely ἀσύνδετον, the usual term, and διαλελυμένον or λύσις. The latter, however, has a more general meaning, and is also used to indicate the loose, that is, non-periodic structure in 13, 15, 21, 46. For the use of connectives in the impressive style see 53–58. Aristotle too refers the obscurity of Heraclitus to poor use of connectives, *Rhet.* 3.5.6.

193. On the difference between written and spoken style see Aristotle, *Rhet.* 3.12.1–2. Philemon (361–262 B.C.) was one of the great writers of new comedies. On this judgment and its possible relation to the date of our treatise see Introd. p. 40.

194. The example is a fragment of Menander.

195. See *Ion* 158–184.

196. The quotation sounds Demosthenic, but it has not been identified. The particle repeated in the Greek and translated by "as for" is μέν.

197. Lucidity often requires that words should be repeated. Brevity is more pleasing than lucid. Just as we sometimes fail to see distinctly a man who runs past us, so what we say may be misunderstood if said too quickly.

198. Oblique constructions should be avoided; they are, as Philistus' style shows, obscure, but shorter. An example of oblique and therefore obscure construction is found in Xenophon: (Syennesis had retreated) "because he heard Tamos to be commanding triremes sailing from Ionia to Cilicia, both those of the Lacedaemonians, and those of Cyrus himself." The straightforward construction would be: "because many Lacedaemonian and Persian ships which Cyrus had built for this purpose were expected on their way to Cilicia. They were sailing from Ionia. Tamos the Egyptian was in command of them." This may well be longer, but it is clearer.

199. In general, we should follow the natural order of words, as in "Epidamnus is a city on the right as one sails into the gulf of Ionia." The subject comes first, then the description of it, as a city, and the rest follows.

200. The order may be reversed, as in: "There is a city, Ephyra." It

198. At the beginning of this section I have followed Radermacher, taking συντομώτ-ερον δέ with what precedes, rather than qualifying the example from Xenophon that follows, with Roberts.

The word πλαγιότης, translated "oblique construction," also refers to oblique cases, as εὐθεῖα, straightforward, is used for the nominative. Here, however, we are concerned with more than "the avoidance of oblique cases" which is incidental to the avoidance of oblique constructions in which the main idea is grammatically subordinated (cp. 104). This is indeed the case in the half-sentence quoted from *Anabasis* 1.2.21: καὶ ὅτι τριήρεις ἤκουεν περιπλέουσας ἀπ' Ἰωνίας εἰς Κιλικίαν Τάμον ἔχοντα τὰς Λακεδαιμονίας καὶ αὐτοῦ Κύρου. Syennesis withdrew because the fleet of Cyrus was expected behind him in Cilicia, but this is grammatically subordinated to his hearing that Tamos was in command of it, a construction which only becomes clear when we come to the words Τάμον ἔχοντα. There is no doubt that, as Demetrius says, such involved constructions must be avoided in the plain style, and it is indeed an "oblique" way of stating a main idea. The translation can render only this general point. In the Greek, Demetrius' re-writing, which states the main idea first and then adds the provenance of the fleet and the command of Tamos as separate sentences, naturally uses less oblique cases too. But it is the expression of the main idea "obliquely" that Demetrius is criticizing, or at least telling us to avoid when writing in the plain manner.

Philistus wrote a history of Sicily early in the fourth century B.C. He was a Syracusan general.

199. Thuc. 1.24. It is interesting to remember that Dionysius of Halicarnassus, *Comp.* 5, denied that there was any natural order of words in Greek. He exaggerated, but the order of subject, object, verb is frequently disturbed for a variety of reasons. See J. D. Denniston, *Greek Prose Style* (Oxford 1952) 41–59.

200. *Iliad* 6. 152.

is not that we approve of one word-order or condemn the other; we were merely pointing out the natural kind of arrangement.

201. In narrative one should begin with a nominative, for example, "Epidamnus is a city . . ." or with the accusative, as in "It is said that the city of Epidamnus . . . ." The other cases (at the beginning) will bring a degree of obscurity and are a positive torture to both speaker and audience.

202. One should try not to round out the sentence at length. "For the Achelous, flowing down from Mount Pindus inland by the city of Straton runs into the sea." The sentence should end at once and thus give the reader a rest, that is, "the Achelous flows from Pindus and runs into the sea." In this way it is much clearer, just as roads are which have many signposts and resting places. The signs act as guides, whereas a road without signs and everywhere the same is hard to make out even if it is short.

203. So much for lucidity, a few remarks chosen from many things that might be said. And lucidity belongs to the plain style above all others.

Plain Word-Arrangement

204. The word-arrangement in this style should first avoid long clauses, for length always makes for impressiveness, just as among metres the hexameter is called heroic because its length is suitable for heroes, whereas the new comedy has confined itself to the shorter iambic trimeter.

205. We shall therefore, for the most part, have trimeter clauses and sometimes phrases. Such is Plato's "Yesterday, I went down to the

201. To begin with a nominative is to put the main subject first, the natural order recommended in 199. If the narrator is reporting at second hand, he will use some phrase like "it is said," and this will put the indirect speech in the accusative and infinitive in Greek; this is what Demetrius means by beginning with an accusative: that is, one still begins one's narrative with the main subject, now in the accusative. Both are straightforward constructions and suited to the simple style. But if we begin with any other case, for example, a genitive or a dative, the relationship it expresses is at first obscure and not cleared up till later in the sentence and the main subject (the thing we are talking about) is at first uncertain.

202. This sentence from Thucydides is quoted in full at 45 where its periodic structure is said to be suitable for the impressive style. For the image of the road cp. 47. For the use of Hermae as signposts as early as the sixth century see P. Friedländer and H. B. Hoffleit, *Epigrammata* (Berkeley 1948) 139–140.

205. By trimeter clauses (or phrases), τρίμετρα κῶλα, Demetrius means that they fall into short units with natural pauses between, as the trimeter consists of three units of two feet. A trimeter was so divided in theory, though in good verse there would in

Piraeus, with Glaucon . . . ," for there are plenty of rests and pauses. So too Aeschines says: "We sat down on the benches in the Lyceum, where the judges direct the games."

206. Moreover, the clauses should come to a firm and definite end, as those quoted do. For prolonged endings belong to the grand style, like Thucydides' "The river Achelous, flowing from Mount Pindus . . ." and so on.

207. The plain style should also avoid the clash of long vowels and diphthongs, because these long sounds make for weight. If vowels must clash, let them be short,* or a short with a long, as in ἠέλιος, at any rate shorts in one way or another. In general, this manner of writing appears trivial and commonplace, and that is its very purpose.

208. Figures that are packed with meaning should be avoided, for whatever is peculiar is unusual and out of the ordinary. On the other hand, vividness and persuasiveness are most acceptable to the simple manner. Let us therefore discuss these.

Vividness

209. First as to vividness. It is produced mainly by precise language and by omitting and excising nothing as, for example, "the man channeling water . . ." (in Homer) and the whole simile. It is vivid because all the circumstances are mentioned and nothing is left out.

---

fact be no such regular pauses. He also has in mind (204) the contrast between the conversational trimeter of comedy and the longer heroic hexameters. In both these ways the clauses will be to plain prose as the trimeter is to verse. He quotes a few words from the first sentence of the *Republic* (cp. 21) which might be divided κατέβην χθὲς/εἰς Πειραῖα/μετὰ Γλαύκωνος and an otherwise unknown fragment of Aeschines the Socratic, where the pauses seem to be: καθήμεθα μὲν/ἐν Λυκείῳ/οὗ οἱ ἀθλοθέται/ τὸν ἀγῶνα διατιθέασι.

206. We saw in 183 that the elegant manner has no well-marked clause ending, but that, as here, such an ending was said to belong to the plain or the forcible manner, while long endings (i.e., long sounds) belong to the grand. The sentence of Thucydides has already been discussed in 45 and 202.

207. As an example of the clash of short syllables, Demetrius gives πάντα μὲν τὰ νέα καλά ἐστιν with a hiatus of short vowels between the last two words. Both this example and ἠέλιος are also mentioned in 70, where (68–74) the use of clashing *long* vowels is said to be appropriate in the impressive style.

208. For the expression σημειώδη σχήματα see Appendix I, A.

209. *Iliad* 21.257: "As when a man running a channel from a dark spring guides the flow of water along his plants and his gardens, and holding a mattock in his hands, clears the obstacles from the trench, and all the pebbles are loosened by the babbling water, and the dripping water suddenly rushes along into a steep place and runs faster than the man who guides it . . . ."

210. So with the horse race in honour of Patroclus, where he says: "their hot breath on Eumelus' back" and "they ever seemed to climb upon his chariot." All this is vivid because no detail of what is happening, or has happened, is left out.

211. It follows that repetition often contributes to vividness more than saying something once, as in "When he lived you spoke ill of him, now he is dead you write ill of him." The repetition of "ill of him" makes the accusation more vivid.

212. In this connection Ctesias is often accused of verbosity because of his repetitions. This criticism may often be true, but the resulting vividness of this writer has often been missed. The same words are repeated because they are thus more expressive.

213. For example: "A certain Stryangaeus, a Mede, dragged a Sacian woman from her horse. For among the Sacians the women fight as the Amazons did. When he saw how young and comely she was, he let her escape. Later, after peace was made, he found himself passionately in love with her but she refused him. He decided to starve to death, but he first sent the woman a letter in which he reproached her: 'I saved you. I was the means of your being saved, but you are the means of my having died.' "

214. Here one who prides himself on his brevity might perhaps object that the repetition in "I have saved you" and "I was the means of your being saved" is pointless, since the meaning is the same. Yet if you delete either clause you destroy at the same time both the vividness and

210. Homer does add detail, but it is his selection of precise and vivid details, rather than the omission of none which attains extraordinary vividness in this passage, *Iliad* 23.379–381, and elsewhere. "Longinus" sees this much more clearly in *On the Sublime*, ch. 10.

211. In 26 the same sentence is quoted as an example of homoioteleuton, which it more truly is. On the other hand, dilogia (repetition) was found effective in the impressive style in 103 and the example there given also implied homoioteleuton, in fact the repetition of several words, with one word changed, from the first clause to the second. In 197 dilogia was also said to contribute, as here, to the plain style (without explanation or example), because it produces clarity. That seems nearer the truth. A different kind of repetition, anadiplôsis is explained in 66, 140, 276.

212. For ἔμφασις and ἐμφατικός see App. I, A. Ctesias wrote a history of Persia in the late fifth or early fourth century B.C.

213. This is presumably an example B. of dilogia from Ctesias, but we should note that, though there is a good deal of repetition there is no homoioteleuton. We may therefore conclude that these were incidental in the previous examples, and that dilogia simply means the repetition of words from one clause to the other. It is hard to share Demetrius' enthusiasm for this passage.

the passionate tone which results from it. Then the added clause, with the past tense "my having died" instead of "dying," is more vivid because it implies that all is over. It has happened, and this is more forceful than to say it will happen or is happening.

215. And this poetic writer—for one might rightly call Ctesias a poet—is an artist in vividness throughout his work.

216. So in the following example. A writer should not immediately say what has happened; he should do so gradually, keep the reader in suspense and make him share the anxiety of the characters. Ctesias does this where news comes of the death of Cyrus. When the messenger arrives, he does not say at once that Cyrus is dead. In the presence of his mother Parysatis this would be brutal or, as we say, to talk like a Scythian. He first reports the victory. The queen is delighted but anxious. Then she asks: "What about the king?" "He escaped." She interrupts: "He can thank Tissaphernes for this," and again she asks: "Where is Cyrus now?" The messenger answers: "Where all good men must camp." Ctesias proceeds thus step by step, as if reluctantly, and so, as we say, breaks the news. His picture of the messenger, unwillingly reporting the disaster, is very vivid and in character, and the reader is made to share the queen's increasing anxiety.

217. Vividness also results from describing the circumstances. It has been said, for example, of a peasant walking that "his steps were heard from afar as he approached" as if he were pounding the ground rather than walking.

218. Or as Plato says of Hippocrates: "He blushed, for the day was now breaking, and I could see him." Anyone can see that this passage is very vivid, and the vividness is due to the careful use of words, reminding us that Hippocrates had come to visit Socrates before dawn.

219. Harsh collocations of sound also contribute to vividness, as, for instance, "he dashed (their heads against the rock) and their brains splattered," or the line describing the flight of horses across the plain in the *Iliad*;* the cacophony imitates the irregularity of motion. For every imitation (of sound) is vivid to some extent.

---

217. This is much the same as was said in 209–210.

218. *Protagoras* 312a. This is the scene where young Hippocrates, having heard that Protagoras is in town, comes to Socrates before dawn eagerly seeking an introduction. It is indeed a very vividly drawn scene.

219. The first quotation is from *Odyssey* 9.289, the Cyclops being the subject; the other, from *Iliad* 23.116, is the famous πολλὰ δ' ἄναντα κάταντα πάραντά τε δόχμιά τ' ἦλθον (up and down, this way and that the horses went), one of Homer's famous examples of onomatopoeia.

220. New coinages are also vivid because they are made to imitate sound, like "lapping up." If Homer had said "drinking" he would not have imitated (the sound of) dogs drinking and there would have been no vividness; and the addition of the word γλώσσησι (with their tongues) increases the vivid effect. This sketchy discussion of vividness must suffice.

Persuasiveness

221. Persuasiveness requires two things: clarity and the avoidance of the unusual, for people are not persuaded by what is obscure or unfamiliar to them. We should therefore avoid uncommon or swollen language when we are trying to be convincing. And, in the same way, we should arrange our words firmly and steadily, without seeking rhythmical effects.

222. These then are the means of persuasion, and further, as Theophrastus says, one should not spell out everything in precise detail, but leave some things for the hearer to work out and understand for himself. When he grasps what you have not expressed, he will be more than your reader, he will be a witness on your behalf and more kindly disposed towards you, for you have given him the opportunity to exercise his intelligence and he feels he has done so. To express everything as to a fool is to accuse your reader of being one.

Epistolary Style

223. We shall now deal with the style of letter-writing, as this too requires the simple manner. Artemon, who edited the letters of Aristotle, says that letters and dialogues should be written in the same way, for a letter is like one side of a dialogue.

220. Here Demetrius is considering only one type of new words, the onomatopoeic in our sense (see note on 94). The subject of new coinages was more fully discussed in 94–98. There onomatopoeic words were recommended for their impressive effect, and λάπτοντες was also quoted. Actually Homer uses the past participle λάψαντες which, with its sibilant sound, and that of γλώσσησι, increases the onomatopoeic effect. It results from the combination of gutturals, labials, and sibilants (*Iliad* 16.161).

222. This is one of the most interesting statements attributed to Theophrastus. However, it seems to contradict what was said in 209–210, that vividness requires no detail to be left out. There Demetrius expresses his point badly (see notes), and the contradiction is largely verbal. We should not resolve it by saying that vividness and persuasiveness are different qualities that may be pursued by different and even contradictory means, for both are the aims of the simple manner, which seeks to attain both at once. We do not know the context in Theophrastus, but the basic idea is Aristotelian, for he connected the success of happy phrases with man's eagerness to learn, in *Rhet.* 3.10.1, and with brevity.

223. Nothing is known of this Artemon, or of his date. See Introd. p. 42.

224. There may be something in what he says, but it is not the whole story. A letter should be written rather more carefully than dialogue, though not obviously so. Dialogue imitates impromptu conversation, whereas a letter is a piece of writing and is sent to someone as a kind of gift.

225. Who would talk to a friend as Aristotle writes to Antipater on behalf of the aged exile? He says: "If this man is to journey over all lands as an exile without hope of return, then, clearly, there can be no reproach cast upon such men, if they wish to seek a home in the underworld." Anyone who talked like that would not be conversing but giving a lecture.

226. Disjointed sentences frequently occur (in conversation) but they are out of place in letters. In written work disjointed clauses are obscure; nor is the imitation of conversation appropriate, as it is in an actual debate. The *Euthydemus* provides an example: "Who was it, Socrates, to whom you were speaking yesterday in the Lyceum? You had a big crowd around you." And a little further: "He seemed a stranger of some sort, the man you talked to; who was he?" This imitative manner as a whole is more suited to oral delivery; it is not appropriate in written letters.

227. The letter, like the dialogue, should be very much in character. You might say that everyone draws, in his letters, an image of his personality. A writer's character may be seen in all his works, but nowhere so clearly as in his letters.

228. The length of a letter should be kept within bounds, and so should its language. Letters which are too long, or too dignified in language, are in fact not letters at all, but treatises with a superscription added. Many of Plato's letters are like that, and so is that of Thucydides.

229. The structure of a letter should be loose. It is ridiculous to construct periods, for then one is not writing a letter but a forensic speech. And it is not only ridiculous, it is not even friendly, for, as the saying goes, one should call a spade a spade to one's friends.

226. *Euthydemus* 271a. Dialogue too is written down, but Demetrius refers to it as actual conversation which it imitates, since actual conversation is the effect it aims to produce.

The text of the first sentence of this section in uncertain, though the general meaning is clear.

228. We have letters of Plato, some of which are generally considered to be genuine. We have no genuine letters of Thucydides. The writing of "letters" which purported to be by some great writer became a recognized literary genre, probably as early as the fourth century. See Introd. p. 29 and note 34.

229. The Greek saying is τὸ σῦκα σῦκα, literally to call figs figs.

230. We should realize that there is not only an epistolary style, but also epistolary content. Aristotle, who seems to have been a most successful letter-writer, says in one of them: "I am not writing to you about this; it is not a suitable subject for a letter."

231. Anyone who discusses logic or natural science in a letter is no doubt writing, but he is not writing a letter. A letter should be a brief expression of one's friendly feelings, expressing a simple topic in simple language.

232. The beauty of a letter lies in the expression of affection and courtesy, and also in a frequent use of old saws and proverbs. This is the only kind of wisdom a letter should contain, for old sayings are a kind of popular and common wisdom, whereas the writer who expounds general reflections and urges a way of life upon you is not chatting with a friend in a letter, but preaching.

233. It is true that Aristotle does, here and there, pursue an argument in a suitable fashion in his letters. Wishing to teach that cities, whether large or small, have an equal claim on benefactors, he says: "The gods are equal in both, so that, since the Graces are gods, you should find them in both equally." What he is trying to prove is appropriate to a letter, and so is the proof itself.

234. Letters are at times written to cities and kings; these should be somewhat more distinguished in style. One must adjust them to the personage to whom they are addressed. However, though more distinguished, they should not become a treatise instead of a letter, like the letters of Aristotle to Alexander or the letters of Plato to the friends of Dion.

235. In general, the style of a letter should be a mixture of two styles, the elegant and the plain. So much about letter-writing, and also about the plain style.

Aridity

236. The faulty style which is akin to the plain is called aridity. It again shows itself in three things. First in the thought, as when someone said of Xerxes that he came down to the sea "with all his men." This belittles the matter by saying "with all his men" instead of "with all of Asia."

232. The last words are: οὐ δι' ἐπιστολῆς ἔτι λαλοῦντι ἔοικεν ἀλλὰ μηχανῆς, that is, he is playing the part of a *deus ex machina*, talking like a god to a mere mortal. The meaning seems clear. The texts offer some difficulty, but the διά which most editors insert before μηχανῆς is probably superfluous; we can understand διά from δι' ἐπιστολῆς.

233. There is a play on the word χάριτες, Graces or favours.

237. Aridity of diction occurs when an important subject is described in trivial words, like Gadêreus' description of the battle of Salamis. Or as someone said of Phalaris the tyrant that he "brought some troubles to the inhabitants of Acragas." A great naval battle, or the cruelty of a tyrant should not be expressed by words like "some" or "trouble" but by impressive words suited to the subject.

238. The word-arrangement is arid when there is an excess of short phrases, as in the *Aphorisms* of Hippocrates: "Life (is) short, art lasting; opportunity fleeting, experiment precarious." Or again when, on an important subject, a clause is abruptly cut off and not completed, as when someone said, reproaching Aristides for his absence from the battle of Salamis, "Demeter came unbidden to take part in the battle, but Aristides not." This abruptness is inappropriate and out of place; it should be used in other contexts.

239. Often the idea itself is frigid, or affected as we now call it, while the abrupt structure masks the audacity of it. An example is what was said of the man who had relations with a dead woman: "It is not the woman he embraces again." The meaning even the blind can see, as the saying is, but the compact structure masks to some extent the audacity of the matter. The result is what is called arid affectation which consists of two faults, affectation of idea and aridity of word-arrangement.

THE FORCEFUL OR INTENSE STYLE

240. As for forcefulness, it follows from what has been said that it, too, shows itself in the same three ways as the previous styles. Certain things are forceful in themselves so that those who speak about them are thought to be forceful even when they do not speak forcefully. When Theopompus, for example, describes the Piraeus with its flute-girls and brothels, and the male flute-players as singing and dancing, he uses words

237. Who Γαδηρεύς was or whether the correction to ὁ Γαδαρεύς the man from Gadara, is right, and if so who this man was, we have no means of knowing. The usual identification with Theodorus of Gadara, the tutor of Tiberius, is mere guesswork. (See Introd., p. 42.) Phalaris was the cruel tyrant of Acragas who, in the sixth century B.C., roasted his victims alive in a brazen bull.

238. For this aphorism of Hippocrates see on 4 where it is condemned generally, not under any particular style. For the falsification of history (Aristides was present at Salamis) see Introduction p. 43.

239. For arid affectation, ξηροκακοζηλία see App. I, A. The point of the saying quoted is not as clear to us as it obviously was thought to be by Demetrius, but then the text is very uncertain.

240. The same was said of Theopompus in 75, and there it seemed out of place; here it fits the context perfectly.

which have an intensity of their own; although his style is feeble, it is considered forceful.

241. As regards word-arrangement, forcefulness follows if, firstly, short phrases take the place of clauses. Length dissolves vehemence, and a more forceful effect is attained where much is said in a few words. An example of this is the warning of the Spartans to Philip: "Dionysius [is] in Corinth." If they had amplified this and said: "Dionysius has lost his throne and is now a beggarly schoolteacher in Corinth," this would have been a statement of fact rather than a taunt.

242. The Spartans were always naturally inclined to brevity of speech. Brevity is more forceful and commanding, while it is more appropriate to speak at length in requests and supplications.

243. *Symbola* (tokens) also have force, because they resemble brevity of speech. From a little that is said one must understand a great deal, just as in the case of tokens. In this way "The grasshoppers will sing to you from the ground" is more forceful for being spoken by allêgoria than if he had simply said: "Your trees shall be cut down."

244. The periods should be securely knotted at the end, for the periodic structure which brings us round to an end is forceful, while a looser structure is simpler and a sign of simpler character. All early writers used this simpler style, for the ancients were simple men.

241. We first met "Dionysius in Corinth" in 7–8, where we were told that short clauses are used to secure forcefulness and this example was given with much the same comment as here. It is there also an example of brevity of structure, and the two passages agree.

In 99–102 allêgoria in the sense of veiled meaning is discussed as contributing to the grand and impressive style and "Dionysius in Corinth" is there given as an example of such allêgoria. The means used to secure intensity are not infrequently the same as contribute to impressiveness or grandeur.

242. Cp. what was said in 7.

243. *Symbolon* is probably not here used as a technical term to mean "symbolic expressions" or the like, but has its ordinary sense of "token." It referred particularly to two pieces of coin, bone, or the like which together made a whole, each piece being kept by one of two persons in widely separated places as a means of identifying each other's representatives who, of course, carried the other piece. Hence a symbolon has a far greater significance than appears on the surface, and this section compares the symbolon in this respect to those pithy and pregnant sayings which also imply a good deal more than their surface meaning.

Like "Dionysius in Corinth," the grasshoppers were also quoted as examples of allê-goria contributing to impressiveness in 99.

244. The ancients, οἱ ἀρχαῖοι, here obviously does not mean the writers of the classical period, as it clearly does in 67, but the early writers who were also mentioned at 12 as having a loose sentence-structure. See Introd. p. 44.

The rounded period was mentioned as essential to the grand style in 45, but there the emphasis was on the tight structure of the whole period; here it is rather on its coming to a clear, definite end, that is, on its being definitely separated from what follows.

245. And so, in the forceful style, we should avoid the old-fashioned in character and rhythm, but rather resort to the forcefulness now in fashion. The rhythm should make the sentence come to a definite stop, as in the first sentence of Demosthenes' speech against Leptines* which clings to the rhythm I mentioned.

246. Violence contributes to forcefulness in word-arrangement, for harsh sounds are often forceful, like rough roads. We have an example in the same passage of Demosthenes.*

247. We should avoid antitheses and balanced clauses in the periods. They make for weight but not for forcefulness, and frequently result in frigidity instead of force, as in Theopompus' attack on the friends of Philip* where the antithesis destroys the intensity. The excessive elaboration, or rather the poor technique, attracts the attention of the reader who is quite untouched by anger.

248. The subject itself will often compel us to adopt a compact and forceful word-arrangement, as in this passage of Demosthenes: "If any one of them had been convicted, you would not have proposed this bill; and, if you are now convicted, no one else will make such a proposal." The subject itself and the steps in the argument clearly demanded a word-arrangement that grows out of them; no one could easily have constructed the sentence differently, not even if he did violence to the subject-matter. For in adopting a certain sentence-structure we are often carried along by the subject like people running downhill.

249. It also contributes to forcefulness to put the most forceful expression at the end as Antisthenes did.* Its force will be blunted in the

245. Demetrius has already quoted this sentence of Demosthenes in 10 as a good example of a period of which the structure corresponds to the thought, and in 20 as an example of the involved rhetorical period. Here he quotes the last few words ὡμολόγησα ἅ τούτοις, ὡς ἄν οἰός τέ ὡ, συνερεῖν (I have agreed, as far as I am able, to speak for them).

No particular rhythm has been mentioned; what Demetrius means, presumably, is a definite rhythmical conclusion, that is, long syllables.

246. Demetrius quotes the end of another sentence from *Against Leptines* 2: (ἀφείλετο) ὑμᾶς τὸ δοῦναι ὑμῖν ἐξεῖναι (he has deprived you of the power to grant exemptions).

247. The words of Theopompus were quoted to much the same effect in 27, where see note.

248. The same sentence of Demosthenes is quoted in 31, where Demetrius is establishing the difference between a period and an enthymeme, and the argument involved is there explained.

249. Demetrius here quotes an example from Antisthenes of which the meaning is quite obscure: σχέδον γὰρ ὀδυνήσει ἄνθρωπος ἐκ φρυγάνων ἀναστάς which seems to mean: "A man will pretty certainly suffer if he stands up from brushwood." Moreover, the particular words are not startling or forceful; the force must lie in the expression as

middle of other words. For if anyone changes the order of the words,* though he says the same thing, he will not be thought to do so.

250. The kind of antithesis which I condemned in Theopompus is inappropriate even in Demosthenes, where he says: "You were the temple-servant, I was the initiate; you were the teacher, I the pupil; you were a minor actor, I was a spectator; you were hissed, I hissed." The exact correspondence of parallel clauses is poor art; it is more like a jest than an expression of anger.

251. When being forceful, it is appropriate to use periods continuously, although this is not suitable in other styles. For if one period follows another the effect will be as of metre following metre, and a forceful metre at that, like choliambs.

252. These continuous periods should at the same time be short, that is, periods of two clauses, for the effect of periods consisting of many clauses is beautiful rather than forceful.

253. Brevity is so useful in this style that it is often even more forceful *not* to say something, as when Demosthenes says: "Now I might remark—but I myself certainly do not wish to say anything offensive, and my accuser has the advantage in slandering me."

254. And, by the gods, even obscurity is frequently forceful. For what is implied is more forceful, whereas what is explained is thought commonplace.

255. Sometimes discordant sounds (*kakophônia*) are forceful, especially if the subject matter demands it, as in Homer's line: "The Trojans

---

a whole. Rhys Roberts suggests the reference may be to a fugitive. We are told that the force is lost if the order is changed to σχέδον γὰρ ἐκ φρυγάνων ἀναστὰς ἄνθρωπος ὀδυνήσει.

The usage recommended, however, is clear enough, and we may compare 50–53 above, where we were told that, in the impressive style, the most vivid word should come last; several clear examples are given there.

250. The reference to Theopompus looks back to 247. The passage from Demosthenes occurs in *On the Crown* 265, where the orator attacks Aeschines for his poor circumstances in youth. Our objection is not so much to a poor use of antithesis as to extreme bad taste.

251. In 15 we had the general advice that periods should be mingled with short sentences. Here an exception is made, though Demetrius adds in the next section that these periods should be of limited length. The choliamb is an iambic trimeter, with the last iambic foot replaced by a spondee.

253. Brevity and aposiôpêsis were also mentioned at 103 as means to the impressive style, but it is there added that sometimes brevity is feeble. We also had brief kommata in 41.

255. The Greek word kakophônia is not as strong as our "cacophony"; it is the equivalent of dysphônia in 48 and 105. The reference is to *Iliad* 12.208: Τρῶες δ' ἐρρίγησαν

shivered when they saw the writhing snake." This could have been said more euphoniously while preserving the metre,* but then neither the poet nor the snake would have seemed as forceful.

256. From this example we can deduce similar examples: instead of πάντα ἂν ἔγραψεν we might write ἔγραψεν ἄν and παρεγένετο οὐχί for οὐ παρεγένετο.

257. Sometimes forcefulness may be attained by ending with a connective like δέ or τε. We are taught to avoid such endings but they are often useful, as in "he gave him no praise although he deserved it, he insulted him though"; or like "Schoinos and Skolon too . . . ," but in the Homeric lines the connectives at the end give an impression of grandeur.

258. A sentence like the following (with repetition of the connective τε)* will sometimes be forceful too. For pleasant smoothness is characteristic of the elegant, not of the forceful manner, and these (two) styles seem most opposed to one another.

ὅπως ἴδον αἴολον ὄφιν. The discord is in the last three words since it is only the order of these that is reversed in the more euphonious versions: ὄφιν αἴολον εἶδον. In the original version the o and i sounds of ὄφιν are lengthened (— — instead of U U) and the recurrent "o" sounds emphasized. Certainly εἶδον is more neutral both in sound and meaning.

256. Demetrius means that we may re-write these two phrases to make them more forceful. παρεγένετο οὐχί (he was not present) is certainly harsher in sound because of the more jerky rhythm at the end (i.e. the short final word and the hiatus), and the same is true, though less obviously, with ἔγραψεν ἄν (he would have written).

257. What Demetrius has in mind is the abrupt, jerky effect in structure and rhythm of thus ending on a short, monosyllabic, normally unemphatic, particle. By opposite means this may attain something of the same effect as the more weighty definite ending he recommends at 244. Translation is here inadequate, for such phrases as "he insulted him though" or "he insulted him too" render something of the abruptness, but not the rhythm. The effect is rather like ending a sentence with a preposition which we "are taught not to do," for example, "this should not be put up with."

Even in the Greek, however, the effect seems too slight to be forceful in the first example he gives: εὐφήμησεν μέν, ἄξιον ὄντα, ἠτίμασε δέ. We do not have the context, but this does not seem very different, on the face of it, from the sentence from Xenophon on the river Teleboas, also ending in δέ which was quoted in 6 as an example of the appropriateness of short clauses and in 121 to illustrate vividness. In a long period, a sudden short ending might certainly be forceful. Demetrius' readers are obviously expected to remember the whole passage from which he quotes. For the Homeric passage on the Boeotian cities see on 54, and as Demetrius himself says, it is irrelevant here and belongs to the grand style.

258. The example omitted in the translation is ἀνέτρεψεν δὲ ὑπὸ τῆς ἀφροσύνης τε ὑπὸ τῆς ἀσεβείας τε καὶ τὰ ἱερά τε τὰ ὅσιά τε (he overthrew, both by his folly and his impiety, things both sacred and holy; our "both" . . . "and" being in each case expressed by the repetition of τε after each noun). The repetition of τε follows the

259. Forcefulness of a kind often results from an admixture of play-fulness, as in comedy and all works written in the Cynic manner. So Crates says:

"There is a land of Pêra (= wallet) in the midst of the wine-dark ocean."

260. Another example is Diogenes' announcement at Olympia. After the race in armour he ran forward and proclaimed himself Olympian victor over all men in personal worth and beauty. The words excite both laughter and wonder, and have a gentle hidden sting in them.

261. Still another example is what Diogenes said to the beautiful youth. In wrestling with him Diogenes had an erection, and when the boy got scared and leapt away "Don't worry," said the philosopher, "I'm not your equal there." The surface meaning is funny, but the hidden significance has a certain forcefulness. And this is true of all Cynic dis-course as a whole. To put it briefly: it is like a dog that fawns and bites at the same time.

---

thought of the previous section, and this excessive repetition might well be effective in delivery, with proper pauses.

We should note here the surprising statement that the elegant and the forceful seem at opposite extremes, ἐναντιώταται, since we were told earlier (36) that all the styles, except the plain and the grand, could be mixed and it was these last two alone which faced each other as opposite (ἐναντιωτάτω). However the contradiction may not be as violent as it is usually taken to be, for, strictly speaking, we are told here that the elegant and the forceful *seem* (or are thought) to be extremes. This may be the case in certain instances or in the working out of certain effects, even though they can be mixed in other contexts.

259. This is an obvious parody of the well-known Homeric line, *Odyssey* 19.172, on *Crete*, quoted in 113: Κρήτη τις γαῖ' ἐστι μέσῳ ἐνὶ οἴνοπι πόντῳ. This parody is the first line of a satirical poem of Crates, quoted by Diogenes Laertius (6.85). He, however, seems to read τύφῳ for πόντῳ, and this is read in this passage by Roberts and others. It is not surprising that there were different versions of this rather obscure line. There is an obvious pun on πήρη, which might be a proper name but certainly means the wallet characteristic of the Cynic wandering philosophers, and the Cynic philosophy is represented as a refuge for mankind. For the Cynic manner with its combination of jest and didactic intent, its use of parody and ambiguity (cp. 170) see C. Wachsmuth, *Sillographorum Graecorum Reliquiae*[2] (Leipzig 1885) 69–75 and his discussion of Crates' poem on p. 196. The reading τύφῳ at the end of the line would mean the land of Wallet amidst a wine-dark *fog* (the fog of other philosophies?).

260. The word καλοκαγαθία (lit. beauty and goodness, here translated "personal worth and beauty") was the word appropriated by the "best" people, like our "gentle-man," but it did express the Greek ideal of physical beauty allied to moral worth. The claim was both unexpected and, on the face of it, absurd, but it focused attention, and the philosopher would then explain what *he* meant by καλοκαγαθία.

261. We should probably understand κέρκῳ (= *membrum virile*) after ταύτῃ. Diogenes (400–325 B.C.) is the famous Cynic who lived in a tub.

262. Orators too will sometimes use this sort of pointed jest as they have done in the past. As Lysias said to the old woman's lover that "her teeth were easier to count than her fingers." These words put the old woman in a most forceful and ridiculous light. And so with Homer's "I shall eat Nobody last."

Forceful Figures

263. We shall now discuss how forcefulness can arise from use of figures. First, from figures of thought; for example that which is called *paraleipsis*: "I make no mention of Olynthus, Methone, Apollonia, and the thirty-two cities in Thrace." With these words the orator has said all he wanted to say, and he says he will not mention them in order to give the impression that he has even more dreadful things to say.

264. Aposiôpêsis, which was mentioned before, has the same character; it also makes for forcefulness.

265. The figure of thought called *prosôpopoiia* can also be used with forceful effect: "Consider that it is your forefathers who are reproaching you and saying such things to you, or Greece, or your own city in the form of a woman . . . ."

266. Or as in Plato's Funeral Speech: "Children, that your fathers were brave men . . . ." He does not speak in his own person but in that of their fathers. To bring them in as *dramatis personae* makes the passage much more real and forceful; indeed it becomes a dramatic presentation.

267. The different figures and forms of thought may be used as stated.

262. Lysias' witticism is given as an example of "elegant" writing in 128, and Homer's in 130, as an example of grim humour which is also included under the same style. They are more in place here than with the poetic graces with which they were first discussed. (See on 128 and 163–164.)

263. Paraleipsis should be distinguished from aposiôpêsis: the latter is really to suppress certain things, while the former is to pretend to pass them over while actually mentioning them. Demosthenes, *Philippic* 3.26.

264. The reference is probably to 253 where aposiôpêsis is also said to be forceful, but in 103 it was a means to impressiveness. In 44 the verb ἀποσιωπᾶν does not seem to be used in a technical sense, but means simply to cease quickly to speak, that is, to speak in short clauses. The present section adds nothing, but the mention of aposiôpêsis follows naturally upon paraleipsis (see previous note). No example is given here.

265. Prosôpopoiia is to personify and make the personification speak. The source of the quotation is unknown.

266. Plato, *Menexenus* 246d.

267. For anadiplôsis (the immediate repetition of a word) see 66 where it contributes to impressiveness, and 140 where it makes for elegance when used by Sappho, though we are there told that it more naturally leads to forcefulness. See Introduction p. 27. The quotation is from Aeschines, *Ctesiph.* 133.

We have said this much by way of examples. As for figures of speech, a varied choice of them will make the style more forceful.

There is anadiplôsis: "Thebes, Thebes, our neighbouring city, has been snatched from the middle of Greece." The repeated word gives forcefulness.

268. Then there is that called anaphora, as in: "You call him against yourself as a witness, you call him against the laws as a witness, you call him against the people as a witness." This is a triple figure. It is, as already stated, an epanaphora, because the same words are repeated at the beginning of each clause; it is an asyndeton because there are no connectives; it is an homoioteleuton because every clause ends with the same words. The forcefulness is due to the combination of all three figures. If one said: "You call him as a witness against yourself, the laws, and the people," the figures would disappear, and so would the force of the passage.

269. We should realize, however, that lack of connectives, more than anything else, produces forcefulness: "He walks through the market, puffing out his cheeks, raising his eyebrows, keeping in step with Pythocles." If you join these clauses by connectives, the effect is much gentler.

270. The figure called *klimax* should also be used, as Demosthenes uses it in: "I did not say these things and then refuse to move a proposal; I did not move a proposal and fail to go as an envoy; I did not go as an envoy and fail to persuade the Thebans." This passage is like a man climbing higher and higher. If you were to put it like this: "After my speech, and after moving a proposal I went as an envoy, and persuaded the Thebans," he would be narrating facts, but saying nothing forceful.

271. In general, figures of speech give the speaker an opportunity for histrionic delivery in debate, that is for forcefulness, and this is especially true when connectives are omitted. So much for figures of both kinds.

268. Demetrius uses anaphora and epanaphora as synonyms, cp. 61 of the Nireus passage, and 141. Both mean repetition of the same word to begin succeeding clauses. Homoioteleuton (26) is, of course, repetition of the same word or sounds at the end of succeeding clauses. We should note that in 61 anaphora contributes to the grand style, in 141 it contributes to elegance or polish, and here to forcefulness. See Introd. pp. 27–28. The reference is Demosthenes, *Embassy* 442.

269. *Embassy* 442 (314).

270. Demosthenes, *On the Crown* 179, a passage frequently quoted by other critics, and the most famous example of klimax (ladder). This figure, which Quintilian (9.3.56) calls *gradatio* consists of a series of steps, each of which is repeated before going on to the next, that is, a b, b c, c d, and so on.

Forceful Diction

272. The diction should in every respect be the same as in the grand style, except that it is not used with the same end in view, and metaphors too contribute to forcefulness; for example: "Python, that bold torrent of oratory rushing upon you . . . ."

273. Similes too can be used, as by Demosthenes where he says: "This decree made the danger which then threatened the city pass away like a cloud."

274. Long comparisons, however, are unsuited to forcible passages because of their length: "As a noble inexperienced hound leaps at a boar recklessly . . . ." There is beauty and precision in this image, but forcefulness requires a vehement brevity, like men aiming blows in a close fight.

275. The use of a compound word can also be forceful; and common usage forms many forceful compounds.* Many such can be found in the speeches of the orators.

276. One should try to use words appropriate to the subject. If an action is violent and wicked, we say a man perpetrated it, or, according to the nature of the deed, that he committed, performed, or executed it.

277. A sudden rise in emotional tension is not only impressive but forceful, as where Demosthenes says: "It is not necessary to keep your hands in the folds of your cloak when you are speaking, Aeschines, but you should keep them there when on an embassy."

272. The same example from Demosthenes, *On the Crown* 136, was used in 80 to illustrate how a bold metaphor should be turned into a simile.

273. *On the Crown* 188. The rhythm of this sentence is discussed at length by "Longinus," *On the Sublime* 39.4.

274. The same sentence of Xenophon is rejected as unsuitable in impressive prose in 89. For Demetrius' attitude to the Homeric simile see notes on 80 and 89.

275. Demetrius gives two examples of forceful compounds in common use: χαμαιτύπη (knocked or "laid" on the ground), a common prostitute, and παραπλῆξ (oblique, or struck sideways, or mad, in its medical sense), the root of our "paraplegic." These are colloquialisms, almost slang, and as Greek words are easily combined, a good deal of slang consisted of compound words.

276. The translation can only illustrate the general point. The Greek words are διεβιάσατο for an action that is violent and wicked, ἐξέκοψε or ἐξεῖλεν for open and reckless violence, and ἐτρύπησε or διέφυγε for guile and secrecy.

277. The reference is *Embassy* 421 (255). Demosthenes has been contrasting the dignified bearing Aeschines has assumed with his disgraceful conduct and then suddenly turns on him with the words quoted in the text. He is, of course, accusing him of bribery. See App. I, A for ἐξαίρεσθαι.

278. And again in the passage: "When he was appropriating Euboea . . ." the *epanastasis* does not aim at grandeur but at forcefulness. And this happens when, in the middle of what we are saying, we are emotionally aroused and denounce somebody. The first example was a denunciation of Aeschines, here of Philip.

279. It is also forceful to ask your audience questions without giving the answer. "When Philip was appropriating Euboea, and made it a base against Attica, was he doing wrong, was he breaking the peace, or was he not?" He embarrasses his audience, and seems to prove them wrong, and they have no answer. But if one changes this to read: "Philip did wrong and broke the peace," it is like a piece of obvious information and does not put them in the wrong.

280. The figure called *epimonê*, dwelling on a point longer than is required to state the facts, may also contribute to forcefulness. Here is an example from Demosthenes: "A dread disease, men of Athens, has fallen upon Greece . . . ." Put differently, it would not have been forceful.

281. *Euphemism*, as it is called, can also be forceful, when bad things are given fair names, and impiety is made to sound pious. The Athenian who proposed that the golden Victories should be melted down, and the gold used for war purposes, did not say bluntly: "Let us melt down the Victories to prosecute the war." That would have sounded like a bad omen and an insult to the goddesses. He put it more euphemistically:

278. Epanastasis too is a rise in tone, tension, and force. This section and the following discuss the same passage of Demosthenes, *On the Crown* 248 (71), which Demetrius expects his readers to remember. The rise in emotional tension here lies in a sudden denunciation of Philip for breaking the peace often, and it is cast in the form of rhetorical questions. There are thus two factors involved, as Demetrius explains.

280. Demosthenes, *Embassy* 259 (424). Here again, one must have the whole passage in mind. It begins as follows: "A dread disease, men of Athens, has fallen upon Greece; it is hard to deal with, and will require much good fortune and much vigilance on your part. The best-known men in the cities, those thought worthy to lead in public affairs, are betraying their own freedom, unfortunate men, and bringing upon themselves a voluntary slavery which they euphemistically call friendship and fellowship and good relations with Philip. And the others, whatever men are in positions of authority in each city, who should punish those persons and put them to death immediately, are so far from adopting such a course of action that they admire them and envy them and would each be glad to be one of them."

Demosthenes then goes on to give examples of how fatal the supposed friendship of Philip has been to other cities; he reverts to the image of disease, and emphasizes how Philip everywhere has bribed prominent citizens and used them for his own purposes (260–267). This is indeed an excellent example of epimonê.

281. Quintilian gives the same example of euphemism in 9.2.92.

"We shall have the Victories to help us with the war." Put in this way it did not sound like destroying the Victories, but seeking their help.

282. There are, too, the forceful expressions of Demades. These are of a peculiar and strange kind; their force results from three things: expressive words, a kind of allêgoria, and hyperbole.

283. When he said, for example, "Alexander is not dead or the whole world would smell his corpse," the use of "smell" instead of "be aware of" is a hyperbole and at the same time has an element of allêgoria, while to say that the whole earth would be aware of it pointedly expresses Alexander's power. The phrase is startling as a combination of these three figures at the same time. What is startling is always forceful, for it inspires fear.

284. Here is another example of the same kind: "This decree was not drafted by me; the war itself drafted it, with Alexander's sword as its pen." And again: "The power of Macedon, with Alexander gone, is like a blinded Cyclops."

285. On another occasion he said: "Our city, no longer the warrior of Salamis, but a slippered old dame greedily gulping her gruel." The old woman implies weakness and exhaustion, and he expresses this feeble state hyperbolically; "gulping her gruel" also means that the city was spending its war resources on public feasts and banquets.

286. This must suffice about Demades' forcefulness; its use involves a certain risk, and it is hard to imitate; it has a poetic flavour, if indeed veiled meanings, hyperboles, and expressive words are poetical, but the poetic is here mixed with the comic.

Innuendo

287. What we call innuendo is employed by the speakers of our own day in a ridiculous manner, with a vulgar expressiveness which may be said to make the meaning obvious, but it is a true figure if used for two purposes: good taste and discretion.

---

282. For the meaning of ἔμφασις, that is, expressive or strong words in this and the following section see App. I, A, s.v.

287. This section has been misunderstood. Innuendo is used when you do not want to make your meaning clear, either because it would be in bad taste (as in the example from Plato in 288) or because it is hardly safe to speak openly (as in the case of despots, etc. 289–295). This is quite different from allêgoria because the motive is different. In allêgoria you do not mind your meaning being plain, the camouflage (100) in fact is intended to make it plainer, more frightening, and vivid than the simple statement would be (e.g. your grasshoppers will sing from the ground; and other examples at 99–102 and 151). But when using innuendo *you do not want or do not dare* to speak plainly.

288. To preserve appearances, as when Plato wants to censure Aristippus and Cleombrotus for living daintily in Aegina while Socrates was for many days imprisoned in Athens, and for not crossing the straits to their friend and teacher, although the distance was less than twenty-five miles. He does not blame them explicitly, for that would have been mere abuse, but he expresses his feelings tactfully as follows: Phaedo is asked who was with Socrates and enumerates those present. Then he is asked whether Aristippus and Cleombrotus were there too and he says: "No, for they were in Aegina." The point of all that precedes is made clear by the words "they were in Aegina." And the result is much more forceful in that the facts themselves, rather than the speaker, seem to point to the enormity of their conduct. Although it was presumably quite safe for Plato to attack Aristippus and his friends, yet he prefers to do so by innuendo.

289. Frequently, however, when we are speaking to a dictator or some other violent individual and we want to censure him, we are of necessity driven to do so by innuendo. So when Craterus of Macedon was insolently receiving Greek envoys while lying on a high golden couch and clad in royal purple, Demetrius of Phalerum censured him by using this figure: "We too received these envoys at one time, and Craterus there was among them." For by pointing to him with the word "there" (τοῦτον) all the insolence of Craterus is pointed to and censured by using the figure.

290. The same kind of device is seen in what Plato said to Dionysius when the latter was telling lies and going back on a promise he had

---

What then does Demetrius mean when he says that speakers in his day used this figure in a ridiculous manner (γελοίως, not, as Roberts renders it, "to a ridiculous extent") because they do so μετὰ ἐμφάσεως ἀγεννοῦς ἅμα καὶ οἷον ἀναμνηστικῆς? ἔμφασις means a clear indication, sign, or expression of something, and this can only mean that they make much too plain what their intention is, while ἀναμνηστικῆς means calling to mind. I therefore take him to mean that the use they make of innuendo as a figure is ridiculous because in fact they make their meaning too clear and spoil the effect, that is, they use far too plain and vulgar words, which immediately call their real meaning to mind and make it obvious. ἔμφασις does not mean innuendo, as Roberts takes it, for that is the figure itself. The use of ἀναμνηστικός as calling directly to mind may be compared with its use by Aristotle in his essay On Memory (449b 7 and 453a 5) where he draws a contrast between those, including animals, who have a retentive memory, and the ἀναμνηστικοί who can consciously recall things.

To express this figure, Demetrius uses the verb σχηματίζειν and the passive participle ἐσχηματισμένον, words which he does not use in any other connection. See Appendix I, A under σχῆμα and σχηματίζειν.

289. For the use made of this passage to prove or disprove the authorship of Demetrius of Phalerum see Introd. pp. 39–40.

made. "It was not I, Plato, who made any agreement with you, but, by the gods, you did so yourself." These words prove Dionysius a liar, and the form of speech has both dignity and discretion.

291. Men often speak equivocally. If one wishes to speak like that, and also one's censure not to sound like censure, then what Aeschines said about Telauges is a model to follow. Almost his whole account of the man leaves one puzzled as to whether he is expressing admiration for him or satirizing him. This kind of writing is ambiguous; although it is not irony, yet there are indications of irony.

292. Innuendo may also be used in another way, like this: men and women in positions of power dislike any reference to their faults. When we are advising them on a course of action, therefore, we shall not speak frankly. We should either blame others who have acted in a similar way, we may, for example, condemn the despotic severity of Phalaris when talking to Dionysius; or again we shall praise others, be it Gelon or Hiero, who have acted in the opposite way and say they were like fathers or teachers to their Sicilian subjects. As he hears these things, Dionysius is being admonished, but he is not being censured; moreover he will envy the praise bestowed on Gelon, and he will want to deserve such praise himself.

293. There are many such occasions in the company of despotic rulers. Philip, for example, had only one good eye, and any reference to a Cyclops angered him, indeed any reference to eyes. Hermias, ruler of Atarneus, though in other ways gentle, found it difficult to endure any reference to knives or surgical operations, because he was a eunuch. I mention these things to draw attention to the proper way to speak to princes, and that it very much requires the circumspect manner of speech which is called innuendo.

294. Moreover, great and powerful popular assemblies frequently need

291. The *Telauges* is said to be one of the works of Aeschines the Socratic. Aeschines is also mentioned in 205 and 297. For Telauges see on 170.

The text is uncertain at the beginning of this section. Radermacher athetizes. Roberts' εἰκαιοψόγους is a doubtful word. Perhaps we should read οἷς ἐοικέναι εἴ τις ἐθέλοι καὶ ψόγους εἰ καὶ οὐ ψόγους εἶναι [θέλοι τις]: that is, "if one wishes to resemble these (i.e. those who speak equivocally) and one wishes one's ψόγοι *also not to be* ψόγοι (= to sound like something else)." The repetition of θέλοι τις at the end is improbable but makes sense and was probably added in the margin to clarify the meaning. This differs from the Ms reading εἰ καὶ ὁ ψόγους (as reported by Roberts) by only one letter, οὐ for ὁ, and I have adopted it in the translation. In any case, the general meaning is fairly clear. A ψόγος was the opposite of an encomium, that is, an attack on somebody, and was a recognized literary genre.

292. Throughout these sections, σχηματίζειν refers to the particular figure of innuendo.

to be addressed in the same manner as despots, as did the people of Athens when they were masters of Greece and nurtured such flatterers as Cleon and Cleophon. Flattery is ugly, but censure is dangerous; that manner is best which lies between the two, namely innuendo.

295. And sometimes we shall praise even the wrongdoer, not for what he did wrong, but for what he did right. You will tell a bad-tempered man that you heard him praised for the gentleness he displayed yesterday when so and so was in the wrong and that he is an example to his fellow-citizens. For everybody likes to be a model to himself, and wants to be praised more and more, indeed to be praised continually.

Different Modes of Speech

296. Just as from the same wax one man will make a dog, another an ox, a third a horse, so the same subject-matter can be expressed in the pointed and accusatory manner of Aristippus: "Men leave property to their children, but they do not leave along with it the knowledge of how to use the legacy," and this is the Aristippean manner; or it can be put as a suggestion, as Xenophon mostly does: "One should not leave only property to one's children, but also the knowledge of how to use it."

297. Then there is the peculiar manner called Socratic, which seems to have been emulated especially by Aeschines and Plato. Here the above advice becomes a question, something like this: "Well, my boy, how much money did your father leave you? Quite a lot, more than you can easily account for?—Quite a lot, Socrates—Then surely he also left you the knowledge of how to use it?" The boy is in difficulties before he realizes it; he is made aware of his ignorance, and set on the path of education. All these different manners are suitably in character, and certainly not the proverbial Scythian manner of speech.

298. This type of writing was very successful at the time it was first discovered; people were struck by its vivid imitation of actual conversation and its high-minded exhortations.

So much for the various forms of expression into which a subject can be moulded, and for innuendos.

Forcible Arrangement

299. Smoothness in the arrangement of words, as especially affected by the school of Isocrates, who avoid all hiatus, is not very suitable in the forceful style. A hiatus often increases forcefulness,* its avoidance

297. For the proverb about Scythian speech see 216.

299. The hiatus has been fully discussed as often contributing to the grand style in 68–74. See notes there.

Demetrius gives an example of hiatus from Demosthenes, *On the Crown* 18: τοῦ

deprives the passage of force, for the echoing sound of the clashing vowels contributes to its forcefulness.

300. Indeed what is unpremeditated and spontaneous itself makes a more forceful impression, especially when we show our anger at a wrong we have suffered. The care which a smooth and melodious arrangement betrays belongs not to the expression of anger but to jest or display.

301. Just as we mentioned that the figure of omitted connectives contributes to forcefulness, so does an altogether loose word-arrangement. A proof of this is found in Hipponax. When he wants to attack his enemies he breaks his rhythm, makes it halting instead of straightforward, less rhythmical, and this suits the forcefulness of his attack. Rhythm which is smooth to the ear is more appropriate to eulogy than to censure. So much for hiatus.

The Vice of Coarseness

302. There is, as we would expect, a faulty style neighbouring on the forceful, and this we call the coarse. There is coarseness of subject-matter where an author openly speaks of things ugly and unmentionable, as when the man who was accusing Timandra of prostitution filled the courtroom with descriptions of her basin, her instruments, her rush-mat, and many other such unseemly details.

303. The arrangement of words appears coarse when it is jerky;* also when the clauses are quite unconnected, like fragments of speech. Continuous long periods, too, which make a reader pant for breath not only surfeit but repel him.

γὰρ Φωκικοῦ συστάντος πολέμου, οὐ δι' ἐμέ, οὐ γὰρ ἐπολιτευόμην ἔγωγέ πω τότε (The Phocian war was not due to me, for I was not yet in public life) and he rewrites it to show how the omission of every hiatus weakens the tension: τοῦ πολέμου γὰρ οὐ δι' ἐμὲ τοῦ Φωκικοῦ συστάντος, οὐ γὰρ ἐπολιτευόμην ἔγωγέ πω τότε. He is quite right, though of course other factors also come in when the word-order is changed, for example, he also avoids some consonantal clashes. It is because hiatus is common in Greek, at least between similar long sounds, that so much emphasis was given to its avoidance by Isocrates, with the result that its use in Demosthenes is usually deliberate. We may perhaps render the effect in a general way by translating the sentence of Demosthenes: "For the outbreak of the war in Phocia I bear no responsibility, indeed I was not in public life," and re-write: "When the Phocian war began I bore no responsibility for it. I was not yet in public life."

302. Reading ὀλίσβους (instruments) with Radermacher, not ὀβόλους with Roberts.

303. The Greek for jerky is διεσπασμένη, and we had διασπασμός in a discussion of hiatus. We were there told that excessive hiatus "interrupts our flow with jerks and starts." The jerkiness mentioned here need not refer exclusively, or indeed mainly, to hiatus, but generally to both sound and rhythm.

The text of the omitted illustration is extremely uncertain. Roberts' reading οὑτωσὶ

304. The choice of words can make disagreeable even subjects which are pleasing in themselves, as when Clitarchus says of a kind of bee: "it feeds on the countryside, and rushes into hollow oaks." You would think he was talking about a wild bull or the Erymanthian boar instead of a bee. The passage is both coarse and frigid, and indeed these two faults are close neighbours.

δ' ἔχον τὸ καὶ τό, κτεῖναι (so and so being the case, kill . . .) does not make good sense. Radermacher's ὁ δ' εἰπὼν οὑτωσί· αἰσχρὸν τὸ ἔκγονον κτεῖναι (the man who spoke thus: it is shameful to slay one's child) does not seem particularly jerky though it has a number of gutturals. In any case it is highly conjectural. As so often, a few words are meant to remind the reader of a well-known passage, and, as we do not have the context, the effect would be lost on us in any case.

304. It is natural for the two vices to be close neighbours since their corresponding successful styles, the impressive and the forceful, also have much in common.

APPENDIXES

THE LANGUAGE OF DEMETRIUS

BOTH Radermacher and Roberts put very great emphasis upon the "late" nature of the language of our treatise. Dahl built his whole case upon it, and these linguistic arguments may fairly be said to have influenced most modern scholars in accepting a date not earlier than the first century A.D.

Roberts lists 53 words (pp. 56–58) as belonging "to the post-Classical age, none of them being found earlier than Alexandrian, and some not earlier than Graeco-Roman times." This obscures the fact that even the traditional authorship is compatible with an early Alexandrian date. He adds 16 words used in a "post-Classical sense," and 13 which are "especially Attic." And in his notes he further condemns others as probably or certainly "late."² There are also 16 ἅπαξ λεγόμενα, words which occur nowhere else.

I need not repeat here the general considerations already put forward on pp. 46–50 above, but they should be kept in mind, and the detailed examination of words and expressions which follows is meant to supplement them. We need not expect a strictly Attic style, rather a mixture, while certain Atticisms, like the use of the dual, might well occur, not least if the author were himself of Athenian origin, and especially if he was somewhat given to mild affectations. The "fragments" of Demetrius of Phalerum give us no help here; they are termed fragments by courtesy only; they are references in other authors to what he said, there is hardly a direct quotation among them, and certainly none that gives any indication of style. Words that occur nowhere else, unless their forms are of a late nature, are no indication of date either; sixteen of them is not a large number in a technical treatise of a period not otherwise represented in our remaining texts. Such words occur in most authors.

A

We shall deal first with technical terms, some of which are in themselves of considerable interest.

(N.B. Wherever, throughout this Appendix, words are said to be used by certain authors without exact references being given, these will be found in Liddell-Scott-Jones. It seems superfluous to repeat such easily available references, except where the illustration is of special interest.)

ἀλληγορία: We are told that this word is not used before Philodemus and Cicero, the Classical term being ὑπόνοια which Plutarch tells us (*De Aud. Poet.* 19e) was replaced by ἀλληγορία in his day.

But Plutarch is speaking of the "allegorical interpretation of Homeric myths"—such as the love affair of Ares and Aphrodite in *Odyssey* 8. The process is certainly old, and Plato calls it ὑπόνοια (*Rep.* 2.378d). This is the usual meaning of the modern term "allegory" though the word is still defined by the *OED* in more general terms, as saying one thing and meaning another. However, the sustained allegory which Plutarch has in mind is quite different from a statement such as "Your grasshoppers will sing from the ground," that is, "I shall devastate your land." It is in this latter sense, and in this sense only, that Demetrius uses the term to indicate the figure of speech which Aristotle describes (*Rhet.* 3.11.6) as τὸ μὴ ὅ φησι λέγειν, "to mean what one does not say." The word ἀλληγορία means precisely that etymologically, that is, to say one thing and mean another. In Demetrius it means nothing more (99–102, 151). It is very unlikely that Aristotle's figure remained without a name for two centuries and ἀλληγορία was probably first used with this simpler meaning.

The author of *Ad Herennium* (4.34.46) does not use the term, but his *permutatio* carries a very similar meaning, and refers only to specific phrases which mean something else than they say. In Philodemus' *Rhetorica*, ἀλληγορία is mentioned as a trope, and linked with metaphor, without further explanation (Sudhaus 1, pp. 164, 174, 181). Cicero, in *Ad Atticum* 2.20.3, seems to have this simpler figure of speech in mind when he says that, because of the dangerous political situation, ἀλληγορίαις obscurabo. This is still the "veiled meaning" of Demetrius; so also in *De Oratore* 3.41.166, Cicero mentions the Aristotelian figure without naming it. It is defined as *ut aliud dicatur, aliud intelligendum sit* and distinguished from the metaphor because it involves more than one word. In *Orator* 27.94 the term allêgoria is used for a series of metaphors (= *alia oratio*). Here the meaning seems to widen.

So in Dionysius of Halicarnassus who uses the word when criticizing Plato's diction (*Demosthenes* 5 = *To Pompey* 2); he lists as faults excessive epithets, inappropriate metonymies, poor metaphors, "long and frequent ἀλληγορίαι without measure or timeliness," and excessively poetic forms, but here too, as a matter of *diction*, it still seems to be the limited figure of speech rather than the sustained allegory. Quintilian discusses ἀλληγορία in very close relation to metaphor; at 9.1.5 it is classed as a trope together with metaphor, metonymy, catachresis, and others. At 8.6.44 it is still classed with the other tropes; he translates it by *inversio* and defines it in the usual way (cp. *Ad Herennium* above) as: *aut aliud verbis aliud sensu ostendit, aut etiam interim contrarium*, but when he gives as examples Horace's ode on the Ship of State (1.14) and Virgil's ninth Eclogue, we have the sustained allegory, though the simpler meaning is by no means excluded as is seen from the oratorical examples he gives. Moreover, he comes back to the simple figure at the end where he gives *pedem conferre, iugulum petere*, and *sanguinem mittere* as trite examples of allêgoria, and actually quotes the "Dionysius at Corinth" phrase which we find in Demetrius (9 and 241 but not as an example of it).

Demetrius is clearer because he does not try to include so much. It would seem that the term allêgoria was coined to cover what we may call "veiled meaning"; that this is closely akin to ὑπόνοια is obvious and indeed Demetrius himself uses ὑπονοούμενον to describe the meaning that is implied but not expressed. Yet it may not have replaced ὑπόνοια as the word to designate the sustained allegory till later. It is, as we have seen, first used (in extant texts) in this sense by Quintilian, Plutarch's contemporary. At any rate, that meaning does not occur in Demetrius.

ἀνθυπαλλαγή: together with the verb ἀνθυπαλλάσσειν (59–60), meaning to use another case instead of the natural one. The word is not found in earlier writers, and in this sense, apparently, only in Apollonius Dyscolus (second century A.D.).

ἀστεϊσμός (128–130): This word, together with the verb ἀστεΐζομαι (149) means witticism in later critics. Aristotle, however, uses the adjective ἀστεῖον in *Rhet.* 3.10 in a much broader sense; witticisms are included in the examples he gives, but the examples on the whole show clearly that by ἀστεῖον he means "happy" or "successful" phrases, whether witty or not. The meaning of the noun in Demetrius is at times uncertain; he, too, seems to use the word in the wider sense, including elegant as well as witty phrases. At 128, after distinguishing two kinds of elegance, he says that the second kind (οἱ τοιοῦτοι ἀστεϊσμοί) is no different from jibes. This would seem to imply that the first kind of ἀστεϊσμοί is different so that the word is probably used as equivalent to the generic term χάριτες (= γλαφυρόν). So at 130, the grim joke about Οὗτις, we are told that Homer makes the Cyclops terrible, ἐκ τούτου τοῦ ἀστεϊσμοῦ. Either the specific meaning of witticism or the generic meaning of "happy phrase" is possible here.

But the more general meaning seems clear at 149: "Two hounds were

chained in the front court, and I can tell even their names—but what are
their names to me?" And Demetrius comments that by changing his
mind and not naming the dogs, ἠστεῖσατο. Roberts, it is true, translates
"jest," but this is not a witticism. It is an example of μεταβολή, like the
quotation from Sappho in the previous section, an example of cleverness
and elegance, that is, of γλαφυρόν generally.

It follows that Demetrius seems to use ἀστεϊσμός and ἀστεΐζομαι in
much the same sense as Aristotle uses ἀστεῖα, rather than in the later
sense of witticism and so the adjective ἀστεῖος is used in the quite general
sense of "attractive" in 114.

δεινότης (240-301): In Demetrius, means the forceful, passionately
intense manner which he, alone among critics, isolates as a separate
"style," and he uses δείνωσις as a synonym (130).

We first meet δείνωσις as a technical term in Plato's *Phaedrus*, 272a,
where it is coupled with ἐλεινολογία as two ways of arousing the emotions
of an audience; the latter "to arouse pity," while δείνωσις means "to
make things appear terrible." Aristotle uses the word four times in the
Rhetoric. At 2.21.10 we are told that it is fitting to speak of a particular
offence in general terms in passionate complaint or ἐν δεινώσει, that is,
when trying to make the crime appear dreadful, increasing the emotional
reaction to it. Among the various ways of impressing a judge, at 2.24.4
Aristotle notes τὸ δεινώσει κατασκευάζειν, that is to support your own argument and to destroy your opponent's by making the crime appear terrible
and intensifying the emotional reaction. δείνωσις can also be used to
arouse indignation, that is, the feeling that this is a dreadful thing.

This same meaning of δείνωσις is found in Quintilian who gives a good
definition of it as (6.2.24): *rebus indignis, asperis, invidiosis addens vim oratio*, that is, "to intensify things shameful, cruel or hateful," and he remarks
that Demosthenes possessed the capacity to do this to a high degree.
Elsewhere too he uses it to mean "to make intense," 8.3.88: *in exaggeranda
indignitate* (which is probably the origin of the inexact translation in our
dictionaries as "exaggeration"). It is the exaggeration of *feelings* or
emotions, which Quintilian also calls *intendere crimen* (9.2.104). This is
a natural development from δεινός in the sense "terrible" or "fearful" and
it is the capacity to make things appear so. This is the sense of Demetrius'
δεινότης or δείνωσις.

The adjective δεινός, however, also means clever in our Classical texts,
as in the phrase δεινὸς λέγειν, a phrase so common that both the adjective
and the noun δεινότης (cleverness or skill) came to be applied to rhetorical
cleverness without further qualification. It is in this sense that Demosthenes could speak of his own δεινότης, that is, rhetorical skill (*Crown* 276)

and Thucydides says that Antiphon was suspect to the crowd because of his δεινότης (8.68.1).

In rhetoric, therefore, the word δεινότης had two meanings, (a) passionate force or intensity and (b) rhetorical skill generally. Plato and Aristotle use δείνωσις in the former meaning, and it was probably the current technical term, being formed from δεινόω. Demetrius uses both forms in this sense. It was of course inevitable for this passionate intensity to be quite early recognized as especially characteristic of Demosthenes.

But when, by the time of Cicero and Dionysius, Demosthenes was recognized as the supreme literary artist, the critics seem to have wanted to make the best of both meanings, perhaps unconsciously. In his *Demosthenes*, Dionysius is *not* primarily concerned with the quality of forcefulness; his aim is to prove the orator supreme in all styles of diction and word-arrangement. He does use δεινότης in the special sense of forcefulness at least twice (chs. 10 and 13; H. Usener and L. Radermacher's edition [Leipzig, 1899], p. 149, line 11, and p. 157, line 10) but more often in the general sense. Elsewhere too Dionysius uses the term now in the general, now in the restricted sense, and in the special sense of forcefulness he applies it also to Thucydides and Isaeus. In the second century A.D., Hermogenes clearly defines δεινότης as the capacity to use *all* qualities of style well, and protests against those who restrict it to those qualities which accompany the grand style (περὶ ἰδεῶν 2.9, Walz 3.354 and cp. 360). Demetrius' usage is different from either.

In his interesting discussion, Δεινότης, *ein antiker Stilbegriff* (Leipzig 1934), L. Voit clearly differentiates the two meanings of the term (3–6), and gives a good account of the meaning in Demetrius (15–30), but he does not clarify the meanings in Dionysius, and tends to identify δεινότης with πάθος and the grand style.

Here again our author seems to be free from later confusions, and to use this technical term, especially in relation to Demosthenes, in an earlier rather than a later sense.

διήγημα: in the sense of διήγησις, narrative, or almost in this sense, for in 8, 137, 241, and 270 the word signifies the thing said at least as much as the way of saying it, and even in 201. This is a perfectly natural formation even if it does not occur in extant texts of the Classical period.

ἔμφασις, ἐμφατικός: the words derive from ἐμφαίνω, "to make clear or manifest." ἔμφασις is used by Aristotle of an image or reflection in a mirror, in water, or even in dreams, and he seems to have been the first to use it.

We find it in Dionysius in the sense of expression or indication, as when he says that there are careless passages in Thucydides which give not the slightest *indication* of his usual forcefulness (*Thucydides* ch. 16,

U-R 349.2: οὐδὲ τὴν ἐλαχίστην ἔμφασιν . . . τῆς δεινότητος ἐκείνης). In Philodemus (the context is uncertain) it is joined with σαφήνεια, lucidity, and
the adverb is used in close connection with both σαφῶς and ἐναργῶς,
vividly. (See Vooys' Lexicon.)

The word ἔμφασις came to be used, however, as a technical term
denoting a specific *virtus* or quality of style. Quintilian defines it (8.3.83)
as implying a deeper meaning than the words express, either meaning
more than one says or something one does not say, that is, using pregnant
words, for example "to be a *man*," and the like. This meaning is also
found in Trypho (1st century B.C., Walz 8, p. 746, λέξις δι' ὑπονοίας
αὐξάνουσα τὸ δηλούμενον, and he gives an example also used by Quintilian)
and in later writers such as Tiberius (Walz 8, p. 543). In Trypho it is a
trope, in Tiberius a figure. See further Quintilian 9.2.3 and 9.2.64 where
it is also a figure.

There is no trace of such a meaning in Demetrius; indeed he does not
seem to use the word in any very technical sense. As he uses ἐμφαίνω
in the sense of "to make clear" or "to express," so he uses the noun to
mean indication or expression, and the adjective is applied to words that
are expressive or clearly indicate something. We are told (51) that a
weaker word should always precede a more *expressive* or vivid one:
ἰσχυρότερον, ἐμφατικώτερον, and ἐναργέστερον there describe much the
same idea. At 57 we are told that the connectives καὶ νύ κε somehow
express or indicate the same as words of pity (ἔμφασίν τινα ἔχον οἰκτροῦ
ὀνόματος) and at 171 that a man's jokes are somehow an *expression* or
indication of his character (τοῦ ἤθους τις ἔμφασις). Homer uses grim jests
for the sake of forcefulness or *expressiveness* (130), while the peculiar
force of Demades is due to three things: expressive words (ἐκ τῶν
ἐμφάσεων), allēgoria, and hyperbole (282). Throughout, ἔμφασις and its
derivatives are linked with the idea of clarity (cp. Philodemus above)
except that in 291 it has the kindred meaning of "indication" (as in
Dionysius) where we are told that a certain kind of equivocation, though
not the same as irony, yet clearly indicates irony (εἰρωνείας ἔμφασιν
ἔχει). At 287 (see note *ad loc.*) contemporary speakers are said to use
innuendo in a ridiculous manner because they use it μετὰ ἐμφάσεως
ἀγεννοῦς, that is, with vulgarly clear *indication* or *expressiveness* of the
implied meaning.

Again, Demetrius uses ἔμφασις without reference to a later meaning, in
what seems closer to the Classical manner.

ἐπανάστασις: in Classical texts means "rising up" or "rising up against"
(rebellion), and in medical writings it means a "swelling." Demetrius
(278) uses it of a rise in the emotional tone which follows from excitement

in the speaker, *not* merely "rise in tone" (Roberts, Dahl, *LSJ*). See under ἐξαίρειν. The word does not seem to be used elsewhere in this sense, or as a technical term.

ἐνθύμημα: Demetrius uses the word in the strictly Aristotelian sense of a rhetorical syllogism based on probability only (*Rhet.* 1.2.8–9), and he seems to labour an obvious point when he insists on the difference between it and a period (30–33).

The word was used in three senses: (a) the general sense of thought or reasoning which, though more frequent in later critics, is quite Classical, (b) the Aristotelian technical sense of rhetorical syllogism, (c) a conclusion drawn from a contradiction. This last sense seems to occur later— in Cicero *Topica* 55 and Quintilian (8.5.9 and 5.10.1–3 where he gives all three senses). It seems to be referred to in Demetrius (cp. διάνοιά τις ἐκ μάχης λεγομένη at 30 with Quintilian's *quod pugna constat* in 5.9.2). It can, however, be traced back to Aristotle himself, who distinguishes two kinds of enthymemes (*Rhet.* 2.22.15); that which proves something from premises agreed to by an opponent (= ἐν ἀκολουθίας σχήματι), and the other which disproves an opponent's position (τὸ δὲ ἐλεγκτικὸν τὸ τὰ ἀναλογούμενα συνάγειν). Then one subdivision of the first type is described as ἐκ τῶν ἐναντίων (2.23.1). This is the obvious source of the *e contrariis* and probably of Demetrius' ἐκ μάχης.

Enthymeme then is used by Demetrius in a strictly Aristotelian sense. Later writers often have other meanings.

ἐξαίρειν: The Classical meaning is to raise, magnify, exalt, and it is so used in 122 and 123. As a rhetorical term it has the same meaning: to elevate the style, or describe in elevated style. In 234 we are told that letters to potentates should be somewhat ἐξηρμέναι, that is, dignified, elevated, and τὸ ἐν τῇ ἑρμηνείᾳ ἐξηρμένον (119) which means an elevated or exalted style. While this meaning does not occur (apparently) in earlier texts, it is a perfectly natural adaptation of the Classical meaning.

At 277, however, ἐξαίρεσθαι does not refer to elevation of style, nor does it refer to "elaborate language" (Roberts), for there is nothing elevated or elaborate about Demosthenes saying to Aeschines that he should keep his hands in the folds of his robe not when making a speech but when going on an embassy. It is not the language or style but the emotional tension which rises, and the word is here used in the Classical sense of "getting excited," not in a technical sense at all. (For references see *LSJ s.v.* III. 2). This rise in emotional tone is then called ἐπανάστασις (278) and ἐξαρθέντες is applied to the speakers (Roberts here correctly translates as exaltation); it describes the process involved very well.

ἑρμηνεία: We are told (Roberts p. 55; cp. Hammer 5–8, Dahl 78–79) that: "The very title-word ἑρμηνεία seems itself to imply a considerably later date than that of Aristotle and Theophrastus, with both of whom ... the accepted term for style is λέξις, while with Aristotle ἑρμηνεία is a logical and grammatical rather than a literary term." It is true that Theophrastus wrote a book called περὶ λέξεως, but as we know practically nothing about it, and have no idea whether he used the term ἑρμηνεία, or in what sense he may have used it, we had better leave him out of account. The notion that our word was to Aristotle "a logical and grammatical term" is based on a passage in the commentary of Ammonius (*ca.* 500 A.D.), wherein he tells us that a work of Aristotle περὶ ἑρμηνείας did not deal, like that of Demetrius, with style, but with the logical and grammatical implications of the proposition (*In Arist. De Interpretatione*, especially pp. 4–5 in vol. 4, Berlin Edition). Ammonius evidently felt Aristotle's title needed some explanation, and he says that Aristotle adopted it because the statement (as contrasted with prayer, wish, etc.) is the only kind of logos which *expresses* (ἑρμηνεῦον) knowledge which is in the mind. This implies that the term was not generally so used, as Ammonius was well aware and as is indeed the case. Like λέξις, it usually refers to the expression as against the content, and is quite Classical, as well as Aristotelian, in this sense.

Diogenes of Apollonia (*fl.* 440 B.C.) said that at the beginning of a discourse one should make one's main point clear, and that *its expression* should be simple and dignified (τὴν δὲ ἑρμηνείαν ἁπλῆν καὶ σέμνην, Diels 2. p. 59 fr. 1). Xenophon says that among the blessings of men are reason and *the power of expression* (ἑρμηνεία) by which we communicate with one another. Plato, in *Theaetetus* 209a, says that the definition is the statement or expression of the difference—ἡ τῆς διαφορότητος ἑρμηνεία. In Aristotle's *De Anima* 2.8 (420b 18) the word means "speech," as in Xenophon; it is also one of the functions of the tongue in the *De Respiratione* (476a 19). We may compare *Poetics* 6.18 (1450b 12–15) where diction is defined as ἡ δι' ὀνομασίας ἑρμηνεία, "expression through words," and in *Topics* 139b, σαφὴς ἑρμηνεία means "clear expression"; the word is currently used in this last meaning in the *Rhetorica ad Alexandrum* (see Appendix II), including both diction and word-arrangement, as it does in later critics like Dionysius.

As for the verb ἑρμηνεύειν, which in Demetrius means "to write" or "express" (46, 120, 121) in a quite general sense, it is also quite Classical. Thucydides says about Pericles (2.60) that he was able to know what was needed and to express it, καὶ ἑρμηνεύειν ταῦτα, and in Plato's *Laws* (966b) the guardian must know the truth and be able to *express it in words*, λόγῳ τε ἱκανὸς ἑρμηνεύειν.

Roberts' further suggestion (*CR* 15.254) that Demetrius may have used a different title to distinguish his work from that of Theophrastus may well be true, but is less likely three hundred years later. He also suggests that the word had the advantage of a verb to go with it. Or the title may have been due, as with other changes in terminology, to a desire for greater precision. In Aristotle's *Rhetoric* λέξις often applies to diction only, at other times it refers to word-arrangement, and sometimes to style in a general way, including both. Our author uses ἑρμηνεία as the generic term, and almost everywhere restricts λέξις to diction (see Introd. p. 33 and note 39). Whatever the reason, the title of our work was a perfectly natural one at any time that it may have been written.

κακόζηλος, κακοζηλία: A new technical term which Demetrius uses to denote attempted elegance which miscarries and becomes affectation or preciosity (186–189). He tells us it was the common name for this (186: τῷ κοινῷ ὀνόματι) but he also implies that the term was of recent origin (239: ὡς νῦν ὀνομάζομεν). Liers pointed out that one Neanthes, in the early third century b.c., is said to have written περὶ κακοζηλίας ῥητορικῆς, but the evidence for this has been questioned (Dahl, pp. 87–88).

The word does not appear in Cicero or Dionysius, and when it re-appears in our texts, it carries a different sense. The elder Seneca uses it to refer to harsh or bitter expressions or phrases (*Controv.* 9.1 (24). 15; 9.2 (25). 28; and *Suas.* 7.11). By the time of Quintilian, who discusses it fairly fully, it applies to any extravagance of language, though not of content (8.3.56–58) and he mentions that immoderate hyperbole is the surest way to κακοζηλία. It is also treated by Hermogenes (περὶ εὑρέσεως 4.12) and there means extravagance of both idea and style. The author of *On the Sublime* (3.4) notes it as one result of overelaborating a puny idea and Diomedes (451) in the late fourth century a.d. defines it as *nimio cultu aut nimio tumore corrupta sententia.* No reference from the first century a.d. on seems to give it the specific sense of preciosity, or would-be elegance which we find in our treatise.

Here again the general sense in which the word is used in the first century a.d. and after is not found in Demetrius.

κακοφωνία: (219, 255): harsh sounds, cacophony. The noun does not occur before, but Aristotle has the adjective κακόφωνος (*De Audibilibus* 802b 23) where he says that the flute is clearer if it is wet. The noun is a perfectly natural formation.

ξηροκακοζηλία: is explicitly said to be a recently invented technical term, and defined as (239) a combination of two faults: affectation in subject matter and aridity in word-arrangement. This word we are told, "must surely belong to an advanced stage in the study of style." True, but as such study had been going on for 150 years at least, even the early Alexandrians were quite capable of inventing even such an ugly word as this. It did not survive, for we find it in no other critic or rhetorician.

παραπληρωματικός: in 55, of connective particles used as mere fillers. The verb is used by Aristotle (*Mech.* 848b 28) to mean "filling in" a geometrical figure and Euclid uses the noun παραπλήρωμα in the same sense. The noun is also used by Dionysius to indicate a mere "filler."

περιαγωγή: of the rounding of the period in 19, 45, and 202, and the participle περιηγμένη in 19 to describe the "historical" period which is not "brought around" like the rhetorical. Though not so used by Aristotle, the verb περιάγειν is perfectly suited to describe the process of rounding off a period, and the use of the noun follows naturally. The meaning is clear and this may have become a technical term at any time. It is but rarely found in later critics.

πρόσωπον: used of a character or *persona* in drama (195), epic (130) and narrative (134), or of a personage to whom a letter is addressed (234); also of an author not speaking in his own person but through personification or prosôpopoiia (266). The Classical meaning is face or countenance; Aristotle uses the word in the *Poetics* for the mask used in the theatre and hence it came to mean *dramatis persona*. We know that the word was current in this sense by about 200 B.C. It is not surprising to find it a couple of generations earlier.

σημειώδης: at 208 we are told that the plain style will avoid σημειώδη σχήματα. This is translated as striking figures (Roberts: "peculiar figures") and this sense, we are told, is post-Classical. The form does not occur before Aristotle who, however, does use it twice (in extant texts). In *De Divin. in Somniis* 462b 15 he says nearly all men believe dreams to be *significant*, that is, indicative of the future and in *Meteor.* 373a 30 he says that halos round the stars are less significant (οὐ σημειώδεις δ' ὁμοίως) than those round the moon, and a similar sense of the word is found in Theophrastus, *De Ventis* 35.

One should not be dogmatic about the general meaning of a word of which we have so few examples. It seems to carry the idea of significant, of something more than appears, containing as it were a sign of something else. It is later applied by Dionysius to the significant or pregnant diction of Thucydides (*Letters to Pompey* 5) as compared with the simple diction of Lysias (*Isocrates* 2). This is a very natural development, if indeed it was a development. In our passage σημειώδη σχήματα means, probably, figures packed with meaning. Allusiveness or innuendo would be such a figure (287–295), and figures of this kind should be avoided in the plain style. Not just striking figures, but striking in this particular way— which is very close to the Aristotelian usage.

συναλοιφή: elision which runs words together (70), and so the verb συναλείφειν. The word is common in later criticism; it is used by Aristotle in the sense of coalescing, and also by Theophrastus. In *Rhet.* 2.6.8, it is used in the sense of to minimize, make little of. The usage in Demetrius is much more natural.

συναφεία: used at 63 of repeated connectives, the opposite of disjointed phrases, and in 182 of words so linked together as to disguise the rhythm. The meaning is to join or link together. The adjective συναφής, united, and the noun συναφή are used several times by Aristotle and Theophrastus.

σχῆμα: as "figure of speech." This meaning first occurs in the *Rhet. ad Alex.* (see App. II). *LSJ* quote Plato, *Ion* 536c, but what Plato means there is that those possessed by a god (κορυβαντιῶντες) find plenty of words and *stances* (in the dance) to sing songs to their gods (καὶ εἰς ἐκεῖνο τὸ μέλος καὶ σχημάτων καὶ ῥημάτων εὐποροῦσιν) but are quite insensitive to any other songs.

The word is of course extremely common in later writers—and is sufficiently established for us by its occurrences in the *Rhetorica*, even though Aristotle does not use it in this sense.

σχηματίζειν: the Classical meaning of to give a certain shape to was naturally transferred to rhetoric as "to construe" or "give a certain shape" to one's expressions or sentence or speech, and also "to use σχήματα or figures of speech."

This latter meaning is common in Dionysius but it does not occur in Demetrius. He uses the noun σχήματα in a general sense (298) where he is discussing the different ways in which the same thought can be expressed (suggestion, question in dialogue, etc.), but he seems to reserve the verb (292) for the particular figure τὸ καλούμενον ἐσχηματισμένον, that is, innuendo. This is a particular σχῆμα in which the thought is clothed, and he uses the verb only in reference to it. It is the figure which Quintilian later called ἔμφασις (*q.v.*). The word is not so restricted elsewhere.

(Both verb and noun are used in the *Ars* attributed to Dionysius of the χρῶμα (= *colour*) given to a speech or statement, a meaning of σχῆμα that some denied, and examples given in chs. 8 and 9, of "saying one thing and meaning another" at times come close to Demetrius' ἐσχηματισμένον but both the words are given a much wider meaning.)

Such are the new or striking technical terms to be noted in our treatise. The number of new terms is not impressive. In some of the more important cases Demetrius seems to use the word in an earlier rather than a later meaning, or a meaning found in later texts is absent in our treatise. We have seen this to be true of ἀλληγορία, ἀστεϊσμός, δεινότης, ἔμφασις, and κακοζηλία. This seems significant. Other definitely new terms are ἀνθυπαλλαγή, ξηροκακοζηλία, παραπληρωματικός, περιαγωγή, and πρόσωπον. Besides these, I can see nothing remarkable in the use of διήγημα, ἑρμηνεία, κακοφωνία, σημειώδης, συναλοιφή, συναφεία, or σχῆμα. Our author also uses ἐπανάστασις and σχηματίζειν in a sense not found elsewhere.

If we keep in mind the length of time the technical vocabulary of rhetoric had been developing and the paucity of our knowledge of it, there is nothing here that would lead us to conclude for a later date. On the other hand, both the absence of later meanings in the use of some technical terms and the total absence of some which were very common in Dionysius and later writers seem to make a late date improbable.

B

We shall now deal with words that are Classical in form but said to be used in a post-Classical sense:

ἀναγράφειν: at 223, where we are told that Artemon *published* the letters of Aristotle. The meaning may be post-Classical, but so was the process of publishing other people's works (to publish one's own was simply γράφειν). The Classical meaning is to record or publish on stone. It seems a very natural extension.

ἀπαγγελία: at 114 Theophrastus is said to have defined frigidity as τὸ ὑπερβάλλον τὴν οἰκείαν ἀπαγγελίαν, and this is probably a quotation. However our author may be quoting in his own words, but in any case the word does not seem to carry here the later meaning of style.

The Classical meaning is "report" or "statement," and, in a more technical sense, "narrative" (as against dramatization in Plato and Aristotle, as against other parts of a speech in *Rhet. ad Alex.*). Here it seems to have a meaning somewhere between the two, i.e. "the frigid is that which overshoots its natural expression," that is, the natural way of saying it. There is no reason to suppose Theophrastus did not use the word in this sense in his definition.

αὐτόθεν: at 122 we are told it means "in itself" (Dahl, "an und für sich"), or "at first" (Roberts 57), and that this is post-Classical. Actually, the meaning "at once" is quite well established and fits in very well: "We wish to exalt, for example, the Spartan ephor who had a man whipped for playing ball in an earnest, un-Spartan way. This strikes us *at once* as a trifling thing when we hear it but we can play upon its importance. . . ."

βάσανος: at 201 we are told that to begin a sentence with any case but the nominative or the accusative brings obscurity and βάσανον to both speaker and listener. The verb βασανίζειν means "to test" in Classical times, usually by torture, and the noun βάσανος is such test or torture. It is interesting to note that in Classical usage the emphasis is on testing or proving, and that in later usage only is the word used with emphasis on the *pain* of torture—and βάσανος is then used in the sense of pain or torture, which, it is suggested, is the meaning here. It probably does mean this—a mere change of emphasis—but it might also mean that such a sentence tests the reader's or speaker's ability. Probably the word implies both. Though Rhys Roberts condemns the word for meaning "torture" in his glossary, he actually translates it as "put on tenterhooks," which is no closer to one meaning than the other. In any case, the word might have been used with this later emphasis at any time. We might translate: "brings obscurity and is a trial to both speaker and hearer."

διαπαίζειν at 147: *"making game* of the Trojans."* The transitive use seems late, the Classical usage would require a preposition, εἰς or πρός.

δοκιμάζειν 15: "to approve," "to pass as fit" is completely Classical. Examples in *LSJ* from Plato, Xenophon, Lysias. The sense is the same and occurs also in *Rhet. ad Alex.* Nor can I see anything wrong with ἀποδοκιμάζειν as "to reject" (200).

ἐκτίθεσθαι 35: "we have *set down* the limit of a period," and 200: cp., for example, *Poetics* 1455b 1, that the poet must set out his story in outline. And see *Rhet. ad Alex.* 1437b 35. Other examples from Aristotle in *LSJ*.

ἐπιφέρειν 34, 51, etc.: in the sense of "to add." The Classical sense is usually "to bring" or "place" something and it is used in many contexts. It became a critical term, often meaning "to cite," sometimes, as here, "to add" something. While it is not used in this exact meaning or context by Classical writers, the sense is not very different. It is used in the same sense in *Rhet. ad Alex.* (App. II). And cp. Aristotle *Rhet.* 3.6.7, where it means to add an epithet.

εὐήκοος: "pleasant to the ear." Hippocrates used the word in the sense of "hearing well," and Aristotle in the sense of "obedient" and also of "audible." In 48 it is, naturally enough, used to indicate the opposite of δυσήκοος and the equivalent of λειότης, a quite natural sense. See also 258 and 301.

ἠχώδης: in 42 refers to the quality of the hexameter that unfits it for prose; it is too "sonorous," it resounds too much; similarly in 68. ἠχώ for a ringing sound is of course quite Classical. "Hippocrates" uses the form ἠχώδης (in neuter plural) for a "ringing" in the ears.

λογικός: in 1, ἑρμηνεία λογική, "prose writing"; at 42 and 117 οὐ λογικός means "not suitable for prose"; and at 41 the neuter is used for the prose character of a passage. The noun λόγος is frequently used by Aristotle to mean prose, but he uses the adjective λεκτικός in this sense (a word later used by Dionysius of style as against content). Is this another deliberate change in terminology? If so, it did not establish itself, for Dionysius (e.g. *Composition* 12 and 14) uses λογικός to mean rational. The word occurs, apparently, only once elsewhere, in Diogenes Laertius (5.85), for a prosewriter.

λοιπόν: The use in 36, where, after enumerating his four styles, Demetrius says that *for the rest* there are the styles mixed from these, is perfectly natural. With or without the article λοιπόν is frequently used adverbially by Classical writers. Roberts (p. 252) specifically objects to the meaning "next" or "now" in 240. We may not find an exact parallel, but this seems very close to, for example, Plato, *Gorgias* 458d: "It is surely shameful for me now (τὸ λοιπόν), after proclaiming that anyone may ask any question, not to be willing to do so (i.e. answer)," or the Aristotelian use of λοιπόν, for example *Topica* 6. 139b. 6.

παρέλκειν 58: ὡς γὰρ παρέλκει τὸ αἴ αἴ. Roberts translates: "as these exclamations are merely dragged in" and says that this meaning "to be redundant" is late. This is quite true, but it is not clear that this usage itself is not derived from the meaning "to draw aside," "to put off" or "distract" which may be the meaning here, that is, "as these exclamations distract attention so does every pointlessly inserted connective." In any case, the technical meaning "to be redundant" may go back to Chrysippus (280–207 B.C.) who wrote a book περὶ τῶν παρελκόντων λόγων.

Of this group of words, only αὐτόθεν, λογικός, and παρέλκειν may be used with a definitely non-Classical meaning, though even there the deviation from the Classical may not be as great as would appear at first sight. διαπαίζειν betrays a non-Classical construction. ἀπαγγελία is in any case a quotation from Theophrastus. In ἀναγράφειν and ἐπιφέρειν there is a natural extension of meaning. The rest seem unexceptionable.

C

We will now deal briefly with the remainder—words that are supposed to be definitely late—Roberts' first list, and some others from his notes, except for the few technical terms already discussed:

ἀδολεσχότερος 212: "prolix" or "verbose." ἀδολέσχης, together with the verb ἀδολεσχέω, and the noun ἀδολεσχία are all well attested. The form in -ος, however, of which we have here the comparative, is not found again until Roman times. We should perhaps note that Plato uses ἀδολεσχικός.

ἀνυποκριτός 194: ὑποκριτός, which Demetrius has just used, is well established, frequent in Aristotle for "suited to acting" or "dramatic" delivery. Demetrius now needs a negative of this and coins one, a perfectly normal formation, no more significant that if we wrote un-histrionic. It is not found again in this sense. The later meaning "sincere," "guileless" is irrelevant here.

ἀπλοϊκός 244: As Demetrius has just used ἀπλοῦς, he may be using this for the sake of variation, but it *is* a late form and was used later in the ethical sense of "simple" as here. It is, however, a natural derivative; compare the verb ἀπλοΐζομαι which would also be a very late form to us, except that it happens to be used once by Xenophon and precisely in this sense of simple frank behaviour! Both were probably colloquial.

ἀποτομία 292: "We shall condemn the *severity* of Phalaris when talking to Dionysius." The noun is formed regularly from the adjective ἀπότομος which is used by Herodotus and Plato in the sense of precipitous. The word is not found till Roman times and the metaphorical sense "severe" would be considered late were it not that Euripides uses the adjective once in that sense (*Alcestis* 983). The noun follows naturally.

ἀποφθεγματικός 9: adjective regularly formed from ἀπόφθεγμα, apophthegm or pithy saying. The noun is used by Xenophon and Aristotle: the adjective is found in Epicurus (342–271 B.C.).

ἀρκτικός 56: from ἄρχομαι, to begin: of a conjunction placed at the beginning of a clause. The form is "late," that is, not found again till the second century A.D., but it is not irregular.

ἀσημείωτος 202: Demetrius has been comparing well-constructed sentences to a road with many signs and stops (σημεῖα). He then coins this negative for an unmarked road from the verb σημειοῦν which is used by Theophrastus. This particular negative hardly occurs again.

ἀσφαλίζειν: in the sense of *to make* a metaphor *safe* at 85. At 193 we have ἠσφαλμένη λέξις, that is, language which it is "safe" to use, avoiding the risk of being accused of bad style. Our author is rather fond of this metaphor (cp. the use of the adjective ἀσφαλής in 19 and 41, and of the adverb ἀσφαλῶς in 78). Solmsen points out that the notion of "safe" language is not found in Aristotle, and he attributes the metaphor to a later Peripatetic (*Hermes* 66 [1931] 245–246). It is, however, a very natural one. Xenophon speaks (*Memor.* 4.6.15) of ἀσφάλεια λόγου, that is, a safe way of carrying on an argument, and the *Rhetorica ad Alex.* (1446a 19) of the safest kind of proofs, for which compare *Phaedo* 85d. Its application to the language itself is surely perfectly natural and could have occurred at any time. The use of ἐπισφαλής at 27 for risky language belongs to the same order of ideas.

αὐλητρία 240: instead of αὐλητρίς, but this is clearly a quotation from Theopompus.

γνωμολογικός 9: used with ἀποφθεγματικός. The noun γνωμολογία and the verb γνωμολογεῖν are both used by Plato and Aristotle, so what could be more natural than this adjective? It is in any case used in *Rhet. ad Alex.* (App. II).

διαμόρφωσις 195: "the whole of the rest of the scene *has been shaped* throughout with the actor in view." μορφόω and μόρφωσις are used by Theophrastus, and Epicurus used μόρφωμα, as far as we know for the first time. The compound is emphatic: "shaped throughout."

διασπασμός 68: "haphazard clashes of vowels are like stops and *jerks*." διασπάω is Classical and frequent in the sense of breaking apart, tearing asunder. διάσπασις is found in Aristotle and Theophrastus. The simple σπασμός is found in Herodotus, Sophocles, Hippocrates, meaning spasm or convulsion. The compound is justified by the sense of "breaking up."

δυσήκοος 48: "hard on the ear," the opposite of εὐήκοος (see above). Compound words in δυσ- are very numerous, and almost every author has some of his own. These compounds are perhaps more numerous after the strictly Classical period but they are no indication of date. δυσκατόρθωτος (127), for example, is the same kind of formation as δυσκατέργαστος, which is found in Theophrastus. The same might be said of δύσρητος (302), δύσφθογγος (246), δυσφωνία (48, 105), and δύσφωνος (69, 70, 105). Some of these are never found again.

ἐναφανίζειν 39: "to obscure," "cause to disappear." ἀφανίζω, "to obscure," "do away with," is Classical and frequent. The compound is used to balance ἐγκρύπτω, itself perfectly Classical, and is used rightly. This is not a case of careless use of compounds such as is very frequent in late authors.

ἐξαιρέτως 125: ". . . but this kind of hyperbole is *especially* termed impossible," that is, above all others. The adjective in the sense of "chosen," "special," is of course Classical and frequent. The adverb, however, is not; it is for us a late word not found again till Plutarch.

ἐξαπλοῦν 254: τὸ ἐξαπλωθέν, that which is explained or unfolded. The simple verb ἀπλόω is also a "late" word.

ζηλοτυπεῖν 292: "to envy." Here used with the dative whereas it usually, *in both earlier and later writers*, takes the accusative. This may be careless, or poor Greek, but it is no indication of date. Roberts' suggestion that this may be on the analogy of the Latin *aemulari* seems fanciful.

θαυμασμός 291: "admiration." The word is not found till late, but, curiously enough, the verb θαυμάζω has no active noun to correspond to it in Classical Greek texts—and Demetrius may have been attracted by the jingle θαυμασμὸς εἴτε χλευασμός. Roberts points out (285) that a similar form—ἐξετασμός—is found once in Demosthenes (*On the Crown* 16) and nowhere else in Classical literature till Plutarch, a salutary reminder.

κατάβασις: in 248 we find the expression οἱ καταβάσεις τρέχοντες. Roberts suggests that "perhaps the meaning is 'a flight of steps,' cp. καταβάσιον in Roman and Byzantine Greek." But the meaning of downward way, slope, is clearly Classical, for example Herodotus 7.223, and "running down slopes," that is, downhill, gives a very good sense.

καταληκτικός: 38–39, of the "final" paeon. Demetrius is following Aristotle, but the word is his own. The verb καταλήγειν (4.154) is Classical; though we have no other example of it applied to a sentence until Roman times, it is a perfectly natural usage. The same is true of the noun κατάληξις in 19. These are semi-technical terms.

κατασμικρύνειν 44, 123: "to diminish," "minimize." This form is not found in our texts elsewhere till the first century B.C. The parallel form κατασμικρίζειν is used once by Aristotle in the same sense (*Eth. Nic.* 1163a 4) and never reappears. One form is as natural as the other.

κατερᾶν 302: This particular compound is not found again till late, but ἐράω (ἀπεράω in tmêsis) occurs in Aeschylus, meaning "to vomit." ἐξεράω is used several times in this sense in Aristophanes as well as in the Hippocratic corpus. The word is a strong one, deliberately used with full force: the accuser of Timandra "vomited" his obscenities all over the court. In the milder, usually later, sense of "to pour," συνεράω is found in Aristotle. This particular compound is as natural as the other, and quite suited to its context.

κινδυνώδης 80, *et seqq.*: "risky," the opposite of ἀσφαλής above. The usual Classical form is ἐπικίνδυνος, but κινδυνώδης is found twice in "Hippocrates," *Prognostics* 14 and *The Art of Medicine* 65. Both these treatises are probably fifth-century works, and certainly earlier than the third century B.C.

κρεανομία 285: Roberts admits (p. 257) that the word seems to have been used by Theopompus. κρεανομός and κρεανομεῖν are Classical, so why not the noun?

κυκλοειδής 11: the period is compared to a circular road. At 30, Demetrius uses the more common κυκλικός, which would probably also be pronounced late except for its use by Aristotle. κυκλιός is the common Classical form, but adjectives formed with -ειδης are very common.

λεκανίς 302: The word is quoted from "the accuser of Timanda." It may have been Hyperides, though this is questioned. In any case, Aristophanes uses λεκανή, λεκάνιον, λεκανίσκη and is also said to have used this particular form (fr. 805).

λιθοβολεῖν 115: of the Cyclops throwing the rock. The verb is not found again till late, but λιθόβολος is used by Thucydides and λιθοβολία by Hippocrates, so why not the verb?

λόγιος 38: "the grand style, which they now call λόγιον." As so often with derivatives from λόγος, there is some confusion owing to the different meanings of the root-word, that is, reason, speech, or prose. Hence λόγιος is found in three senses not clearly differentiated: it can mean "wise," "eloquent," or "writing prose." The last meaning is at least as early as Pindar (*Pyth.* 1.94). The meaning "wise" is as early as Herodotus and is still found in Plutarch. Sometimes there is further confusion with λόγιμος, famous. *LSJ* list Demetrius as the first to use the word in the sense of eloquent, but this is doubtful. Eloquent, or at least capable of expressing oneself, may well be the best meaning in some earlier passages, for example Herodotus 4.46, while in later passages where it is usually translated "eloquent," it may well mean wise, or carry both meanings at once.

μεταμορφοῦν 189: "to change the shape" of a thing. The form is not found earlier, but the cognates are Classical and the word natural enough. See on διαμόρφωσις above.

μονοσύλλαβος 7: "Every master is *monosyllabic* to his slave," that is, curt, laconic. The word, naturally, is a grammatical term, and it is thus not surprising that we only find it in the grammarians, for example Dionysius Thrax (late second century B.C.). But compound words from μονο- were easy to form at any period. It is no stranger than Aristotle's μονόκωλος of a simple period. And Demetrius uses his compound in a striking phrase.

ὁλοκληρία 3: "wholeness." The word is used by Chrysippus (late third century). The adjective ὁλόκληρος is quite common in Classical texts; the noun is natural at any period.

ὀνειδιστικῶς 280: "tauntingly." This adverb, and the adjective ὀνειδιστικός, from which it is formed, are both late. Common as the words ὄνειδος, and ὀνειδίζω were in Classical times, it is curious that no adjective from this root seems to appear in our texts except the Homeric ὀνείδειος, which seems to have gone out of use. Euripides once uses the poetic form ὀνειδιστῆρες in *Heracles* 218.

προαναβοᾶν 15: This double compound is used in its full sense of "shouting *aloud beforehand*."

προκαταρκτικός 38-39: of the "initial" paeon, as καταληκτικός is the final paeon. It is a more emphatic form than the simpler καταρκτικός, and means *right* at the beginning. The form is used by Chrysippus (280-207 B.C.). The verb from which it is formed would also be thought a late word used by the grammarians, except that it is used by Thucydides, at 1.25.4.

προλέλεκται 302: from προλέγειν, "to say before." The verb is used by Plato in this sense (*Rep.* 337a, *Euthyd.* 275e), and the perfect λέλεγμαι is quite Classical, if not strictly Attic in compounds. At 39 the participle προλεγομένη is used in the sense of "spoken first," that is, at the beginning of a clause. The meaning is natural in both cases.

ρυθμοειδής 221: "rhythmical," for the more Classical ρυθμικός. The form was never common, but in its context it is perhaps more exact: that the plain word-arrangement must not be rhythmical, indeed not be even "rhythm-like." See also on κυκλοειδής.

σπειρᾶν 8: "to coil up," that is, as animals gather themselves up before they spring, so there is a coiling up of words that has a special force. The word σπεῖρα for coil is quite Classical; Aristotle uses σπείραμα, as does Aeschylus. The verb σπειράω is not otherwise found before Nicander (second century B.C.). Demetrius uses the perfect participle in an excellent metaphor (probably with *Rep.* 336b in mind) and the existence of the verb can almost be assumed from the use of the nouns.

συγκάλυμμα 100: of using allègoria as a "cover." This particular noun does not occur in our Classical texts, but the verb συγκαλύπτω is used by Homer, Euripides, and Plato, and the parallel form συγκαλυμμός is found in Aristophanes, *Birds* 1496, in the same sense; both κάλυμμα and προκάλυμμα are also Classical. There is, moreover, a striking similarity of phrase with Aesch. *Prometheus* 523: συγκαλυπτέος (i.e. λόγος). In view of these clear parallels, that Demetrius used συγκάλυμμα and not συγκαλυμμός seems to have no significance.

συγκαταλήγω 2: another double compound used with strict accuracy; that is, sense and sentence *together* come to a *definite* end, quite as justified as συγκαταλαμβάνειν used by Thucydides and Xenophon. The form συγκαταλήγειν is not quoted by *LSJ* from any other author.

συμπεραιοῦν 2: "Sometimes the clause does not *complete* the sense *at the same time* (as itself)." There is no objection to the compound, but συμπεραίνω would certainly be more natural. The confusion between the two seems, however, to have occurred early, for example, Xenophon, *Hellenica* 2.4.39.

ὑπερπίπτειν 42: "An excess of long syllables *goes beyond* the limits of prose and rhythm." This metaphorical usage, we are told, does not elsewhere occur till the fourth century A.D. (which would prove almost too much!). However, the metaphor is very easy, not very different from Theophrastus' quoted definition of frigidity (τὸ ὑπερβάλλον . . . τὴν ἀπαγγελίαν, 114). The verb itself is used by Aristotle and Hippocrates.

ὑποδάκνειν 260: of sayings that are laughed at but have a sting to them. The use of the simple δάκνειν (to bite) metaphorically for "to pique," "annoy" is Classical and common. The ὑπό in the compound is given its full value, that is, it has a bite or sting *underneath*. That we do not find it used before is irrelevant; it is not used again in precisely this sense either.

ὑποκατασκευάζειν 224: κατασκευάζειν became the regular word for "to elaborate," "work up," etc. in matters of style. This is a natural extension of meaning, and indeed it seems to have kept something of the meaning "to fabricate" or "trump up" (see *LSJ*, *s.v.*4). Here the compound is again used in a precise manner, with ὑπό being given its full value. Though a letter, as Artemon said, may be looked upon as one side of a conversation, yet it should be *unobtrusively* more studied in style.

φιλοφρόνησις 231–232: "courtesy," "good will," used in the discussion of letter-writing. As the verb φιλοφρονοῦμαι is quite Classical (Herodotus, Plato, Xenophon), the noun is natural enough even if not found again till later.

Of this last list of about 50 words, only half a dozen would excite any comment if they appeared in a Classical text, namely ἀδολεσχότερος, ἐξαιρέτως, ἐξαπλωθέν, λόγιος, and συμπεραιοῦν; perhaps we should add the unusual construction of ζηλοτυπεῖν and, more doubtfully, ἀποτομία and ὀνειδιστικῶς.

D

There remain to be considered a few examples of linguistic usages that seem characteristic of later Greek. We will consider these under separate heads:

Adverbs

The forms λανθανόντως (181) and λεληθότως (297) as adverbs formed from participles, are typical of later Greek. The forms do not occur elsewhere before Roman times. (λεληθότως does occur in the pseudo-Platonic *Axiochus* 365c, but that is itself a work of uncertain date.)

Now it is true that adverbs were more freely formed from participles after Greek had become the Koinê, the common language of the Eastern Mediterranean, but *some* adverbs were formed from participles in Classical times, for example προσηκόντως, εἰκότως, etc. συγκεχυμένως is found in the *Rhet. ad Alex.*, and even in Aristotle. More surprising, νουνεχόντως is found in Isocrates and ἐχόντως νοῦν in Plato (*Laws* 686e), two horrid forms which would certainly have been condemned if Demetrius had ventured to use them!

ἄλλως: the meaning of this often troublesome adverb is questioned by Roberts (p. 219) in 41 and 178. (The use in 48 and 289 where it means "otherwise," "in other respects" seems quite natural.)

In 41 we are told that a general paeonic effect was really what Aristotle had in mind, but that he went into detail about the two kinds of paeons at the beginning and end of a clause, ἄλλως, for the sake of exactness. Roberts' translation "merely" is quite adequate, but strictly speaking the adverb means "in vain," "unnecessarily," which is a Classical usage. The meaning is much the same in 178, where Demetrius says that the differences between Doric and Attic are discussed ἄλλως, that is, as a sideline or digression.

Prepositions

Roberts objects to the use of διά "to denote the material of which a thing is formed" as late. And he instances 176: ὄνομα τὸ διὰ φωνηέντων "a word which consists of vowels." This is undoubtedly an extension of the stricter use of διά with the genitive, but we should note that all the uses of this kind in the treatise apply to words, periods, and so forth and that the notion is rather that the word is spoken as expressed "by means of" vowels. All these cases, at 12, 15, 69, 176, are the same and the idea behind it is rather *means* of expression than material. Demetrius is not so much thinking of the material of which a word or style consists, but the words or sounds through which it is expressed. This is a transitional usage rather than the later usage itself. A similar difference lies behind the use of ἐν which Roberts says is sometimes used "with something of an instrumental force." When Demetrius says that of clauses ἐν πολλοῖς ὅροις ὁρίζοντα τὸν λόγον, the idea seems to be that they limit the discourse at certain points, and the image of the prose or poetry as a sequence of words, at certain points in which things happen, will fit every example of this so-called "instrumental" ἐν. At 103 we are told that there can be grandeur *in* repetitions; at 167 Sappho mocks the porter *at* (ἐν) the wedding, and then she speaks in most ordinary language, *in* prose words (ἐν πέζοις) rather than *in* poetry. One might compare Plato, *Laws* 660a: ἔν τε ῥυθμοῖς σχήματα καὶ ἐν ἀρμονίαις μέλη ποιοῦντα. . . .

These uses are careless perhaps, and compare unfavourably with the greater care of the fifth century, and even of the fourth—but they are transitional rather than late.

Roberts' comment on the use of the preposition in the expression ἐπ' ἀκριβείας in 222 is particularly enlightening (p. 249): "these adverbial expressions which, though found in Demosthenes and Aristotle, are much more frequent in later Greek." Yet they occur a number of times in those two authors. This illustrates that Greek usage was changing even in the best Classical writers of the fourth century, and even in Athens. How much further had the process gone two generations later, and in Alexandria? This is particularly relevant of the use of prepositions. Furthermore, the expression in 222 appears to be a quotation from Theophrastus.

Conjunctions

The use of ἥπερ instead of ἤ after a comparative is not strictly Attic, but frequent in Homer and Herodotus. This is but another example of the mixture of dialects.

καὶ δέ is used four times, in 17, 150, 168 and 214. Reference to J. D. Denniston, *The Greek Particles*[2] (Oxford 1954) 199–202, shows that this combination is quite Classical, and fairly common. Moreover it is used by Demetrius rather precisely, as the δέ emphasizes a further point.

Article

Roberts (219) notes a certain carelessness in the omission of the article at times. He notes ἀρχήν and τέλος where τὴν ἀρχήν and τὸ τέλος seem required. This is true, though even Classical writers are at times careless.

Constructions

As there are many strictly Attic forms mingled with others that are Ionic or at any rate non-Attic, we shall not be surprised to find occasional uses *of the dual* (36, 235, 237). Roberts (p. 58) notes the first of these particularly, because of its verb-form. It may be relevant that we have there a statement that the plain and the impressive are the *only two* styles that, as opposites, cannot mix and the dual forms strongly emphasize this. The dual gradually disappeared, after Aristotle, but a scholar in Alexandria in the early third century might well use it now and again, even if it was later to be revived by conscious and deliberate Atticists.

The same is true of the use of the *Optative*. This too gradually disappeared, but there is no reason to think it might not be frequently used in the second quarter of the third century B.C., and that the use of ἄν (which is occasionally omitted even in the MSS of our best authors, though generally inserted by modern editors) had by this time become less careful, as we know it did later. Certainly it is at times omitted by our author, though at other times he puts it in (cp. 226 and 301 for example). The omission is particularly frequent with the imperfect indicative in the apodosis of a conditional clause (60, 70, 139, 198, 288). Radermacher at least would agree that the use of the optative has little significance (p. xiii: *nam optativi auctoritas nulla est*).

So with the subjunctive after εἰ. There are a few instances of this in the MSS of our best prose authors, though these too are usually corrected by editors. There are more examples in poetry where the correction is more difficult (e.g. in Sophocles, *Oedipus Tyrannus* 198, 874; *Coloneus* 1443; *Antigone* 1443). This faulty construction occurs twice, namely at 76 and 269. It is also found once in the *Rhet. ad Alex.*

Once our author uses a plural verb with a neuter plural subject. As Roberts says (p. 252), this construction "is frequent in later Greek and *even in Aristotle*" (my italics). One instance in our treatise is of little account.

Phrases

This leaves us with two phrases. The first, at 170, is ὡς τὸ πλέον meaning "generally" or "for the most part," for which the normal expression would be ὡς τὸ πολύ. The form, however, does not recur (Roberts p. 240), so is no evidence of time.

The second phrase is τοῦτ᾽ ἐστι (perhaps to be written in one word), as in 271: "figures of speech contribute to histrionic delivery and realism, *that is*, to forcefulness" (cp. 294, 301). This phrase, natural as it is, does not occur in Classical writers.

The adverbs, conjunctions, or constructions noted in this section do not appear to have much significance, except for the erratic use of ἄν, which is too frequently omitted for Classical writing and does seem to argue a process of degeneration; the somewhat careless use of prepositions confirms this impression, as does perhaps the omission of the article in one or two places, and τοῦτ᾽ ἐστι is, once noticed, uncomfortable, though very natural.

The general conclusions which may be drawn from the language of our treatise as a whole are discussed above. There is nothing which makes the early third century improbable; the technical vocabulary seems to favour this earlier date; a mixture of Attic and non-Attic being natural in the Museum at that time, and this particular mixture does not suit a very much later date, which, in my opinion, other reasons, noted elsewhere, make very unlikely.

THE *RHETORICA AD ALEXANDRUM* AND ITS LANGUAGE

THE *Rhetorica ad Alexandrum*, preserved for us among the works of Aristotle, has almost unanimously been considered spurious since the Renaissance. It has, however, been thought to be a fourth-century work typical of the amoral kind of treatises on rhetoric which Aristotle despised; it has very generally been accepted as the work of Anaximenes, an older contemporary, and is often thought to have been written before Aristotle's own *Rhetoric*.[1]

The discovery at the turn of the century of a Hibeh papyrus which contains a number of fragments from this *Rhetorica* pretty conclusively proves it to be a fourth-century work since the papyrus itself dates from the first half of the third.[2] Now this treatise contains a considerable number of words and expressions of much the same kind as we find condemned in Demetrius as "late." To these, scholars have been unusually indulgent and airily dismissed them as "interpolations," but they are solidly embedded in the text. This should make us more cautious in our approach to Demetrius, especially now that the fourth-century date of the *Rhetorica* is clearly established.

No doubt if we could accept the authorship of Anaximenes our case would be even stronger, but if we look at the evidence without prejudice, that authorship can only be pronounced doubtful, for the only real basis for it is a passage in Quintilian which occurs in a discussion of the main kinds of rhetoric. Quintilian says that, in common with most Greek

[1]See *Oxford Classical Dictionary* s.v. Anaximenes; L. Spengel, *Artium Scriptores* (Stuttgart 1828) 182–191; *Zeitschrift für Altertumswissenschaft* (1840) 1258–1267; L. Spengel and C. Hammer, *Rhetores Graeci* (Leipzig 1894) vol. 2, 1, 8–104; G. L. Spalding, *De Institutione Oratoria* (Leipzig 1844), note on Quintilian 3.4.9; E. A. Cope, *An Introduction to Aristotle's Rhetoric* (London 1867) 401–418, accepts the authorship of Anaximenes after successfully puncturing most of the arguments in its favour. See also H. Rackham's *Rhetorica ad Alexandrum* in Loeb Library (Cambridge, Mass. 1937, reprinted 1957) 258–262.

[2]Hibeh papyrus 26, published by Grenfell and Hunt in *The Hibeh Papyri* Part I (London 1906) 114–138.

authorities, he accepts the Aristotelian division into three kinds. He then says (3.4.9):

Anaximenes iudicialem et contionalem generales partes esse voluit, septem autem species: hortandi, dehortandi, laudandi, vituperandi, accusandi, defendendi, exquirendi, quod ἐξεταστικόν *dicit; quarum duae primae deliberativi, duae sequentes demonstrativi, tres ultimae iudicialis generis sunt partes.*

Quintilian here makes three statements:

(i) Anaximenes recognized *two* kinds of rhetoric, the forensic and the deliberative. Since the main subject under discussion is precisely the number of these kinds, Quintilian is not likely to be in error or careless. But this division is quite at variance with the *Rhetorica* where the main division is, as in Aristotle, into three, both at the very beginning (1421b 8) and again at 1432b 9.[3] Even if we emend these, as Spengel does, we are still faced with the fact that the first six "species" are discussed twice over in pairs, thus corresponding to the three kinds, with ἐξεταστικόν following alone, said to be comparatively rare by itself and usually combined with other kinds. The three pairs of course correspond to the three kinds.

(ii) Anaximenes has seven "species" of rhetoric. Now this division into seven is exactly what we find in the *Rhetorica, and nowhere else.* ἐξεταστικόν is not a species of rhetoric in any other author. This is the one strong argument for the authorship of Anaximenes.

(iii) Quintilian says that the seven species can be classified under the *three* main kinds, and includes ἐξεταστικόν under forensic. We are told

[3] It is true that the term ἐπιδεικτική is only used in the beginning, the second reference being to τὰ τρία εἴδη (the use of εἶδος for γένος is at most careless and no significance can be attached to it, as Cope saw). We should, however, note οὐκ ἀγῶνος ἀλλ' ἐπιδείξεως ἕνεκα at 1440b 13. A similar contrast is made at the beginning (1421a 14) between political and forensic speeches on the one hand and ἴδιαι ὁμιλίαι which does not, I believe, refer to "private intercourse" (Rackham) but to lectures and display speeches of Sophists which, contrasted with courtroom and assembly, are "private gatherings," see also 1421b 18. Similarly we find (1445b 28) καὶ ἐν τοῖς ἰδίοις καὶ ἐν τοῖς κοινοῖς ἀγῶσιν κἂν ταῖς πρὸς τοὺς ἄλλους ὁμιλίαις. There the ἴδιοι ἀγῶνες are probably private disputes in court, κοινοὶ ἀγῶνες public debates, both being ἀγῶνες as compared with the ὁμιλίαι of the Sophists. I believe that an unprejudiced reader will find the threefold division to be clearly in the author's mind throughout. The only reference to *two* genera is at the end of the introductory letter to Alexander. As this is unanimously considered a forgery, it can carry no weight, and the argument that no forger would be so stupid applies equally to anyone who left this glaring inconsistency within a few lines. But actually the reference is only to "political and forensic" as having been dealt with in other treatises. In any case, a forger might assume Alexander's main interests to be in political and forensic oratory!

that Quintilian here attributes the threefold division to Anaximenes and thus contradicts what he has just said so that we can forget his earlier statement. But this is not the case, for this last part of the sentence (*quarum . . . partes*) seems to be a comment of Quintilian himself (there is no *dicit* here, or any equivalent expression), that is, the whole statement that the seven species can be classed under the three kinds, putting ἐξεταστικόν under forensic. This the *Rhetorica* emphatically does *not* do: there the forensic includes accusation and defence, the seventh species, we are told, being occasionally found by itself or mingled "with the other species."[4] If we consider this a mere comment by Quintilian, it is irrelevant to the question of authorship.

From this whole passage we can only deduce (a) that Anaximenes recognized *two* main *genera*[5] of rhetoric which is *not* what we have in the *Rhetorica*; and (b) that Anaximenes recognized seven named species of rhetoric which are exactly what we *do* find in the *Rhetorica*. Unless we tamper with our evidence, there is no reconciling the two and the authorship of Anaximenes is at least doubtful.

Of course, the *Rhetorica* may have been written by another fourth-century rhetorician (there were many) who combined the threefold division of Aristotle with the seven species of Anaximenes, not too successfully. And indeed it may still have been written before the *Rhetoric* for the three-fold division need not have originated with Aristotle.

[4]See 1445a 30. In only one place in the *Rhetorica* does ἐξεταστικόν *seem* to be included under δικανικόν. This is where, after dealing at some length with the structure (i.e. the four parts) of deliberative (chs. 29–34, Rackham) and display speeches (ch. 35) the author says (1441b 30): λοιπὸν δ' ἐστιν ἡμῖν εἶδος τό τε κατηγορικὸν καὶ τὸ ἐξεταστικόν. What he *means* is obvious enough: there remain τὸ κατηγορικόν (including ἀπολογητικόν) *and* ἐξεταστικόν, and he duly goes on to deal with the first pair at length in this chapter, and with ἐξεταστικόν in the following. The words quoted are followed by ταῦτα πάλιν ὡς ἐν δικανικῷ γένει συνθήσομεν where ταῦτα seems to refer to κατηγορικόν *and* ἐξεταστικόν. But this is precisely what he does *not* do, for there is no further mention of ἐξεταστικόν in this chapter and it is dealt with quite separately from δικανικόν. If the text is sound this is very careless writing, though ταῦτα might refer not to the words immediately preceding but to the parts of a speech which he has been discussing for some time. We may also suppose that τὸ ἀπολογητικόν has dropped out, as Spengel does. At any rate, τὸ ἐξεταστικόν is *not* in fact included under forensic oratory either in this chapter or anywhere else. (See also Cope, p. 453.)

[5]Quintilian's statement that Anaximenes recognized two *genera* is sometimes supported by reference to Dionysius of Halicarnassus, *Isaeus* 19, where he mentions among the orators he has not dealt with "Anaximenes of Lampsacus who wanted to be a perfect practitioner (τετράγωνόν τινα) of every kind of discourse, for he himself wrote histories, systematic treatises on the poets; he published *Arts* (of rhetoric), and treated of deliberative and forensic debates." This implies that Anaximenes' *Arts* dealt with forensic and deliberative theory, but that his own practice obviously included the epideictic.

Quintilian certainly states that other authorities followed Aristotle in this, and he *implies* that Aristotle originated the three-fold division, but there may have been others. Certainly, forensic and deliberative were clearly differentiated before, and the display oratory of the Sophists was at least a century old. All three are found in Isocrates and it would not take a genius to enumerate them as three kinds.

All that is conjecture, but we can hang on to the established fact that the *Rhetorica* is a fourth-century work, that it is unique of its kind, and learn to be cautious about "late" expressions by examining the peculiarities of its language. With this end in view I append an alphabetical list of doubtful "new" and "late" expressions which occur in that treatise, some of them very frequently. Cope noted some of them in his day, some have no doubt escaped me, but, as will be seen, there are quite a number.

αἴτημα: the word is used by Plato and Aristotle in the sense of demand or postulate, but is used here only in the technical sense of demands made by the speaker upon his audience (1433b 17, 1436a 21).

ἀμφίδοξος: Theophrastus has ἐν ἀμφιδόξῳ for "doubtful," otherwise late. Here used of a *questionable* witness.

ἀνελεήμων: a late word (though natural enough as a negative of ἐλεήμων which precedes it, 1442a 14).

ἀντί: in a curious construction, almost equivalent to a final clause in 1446a 8: ἀντὶ τοῦ ταχεῖαν . . . τὴν διήγησιν λέγειν, that is, "in order to make the narration rapid."

ἀντιπροκαταλαμβάνειν 1433b 2. One of those elaborate compounds typical of later Greek: "to rebut an anticipatory statement." Apparently used here only.

ἀπαγγελία: 1438a 8, etc. Used here, with ἀπαγγέλλω, for διήγησις and διηγεῖσθαι, the narrative, though διήγησις is found also, for example 1446a 10 (see on ἀντί above). Not used elsewhere in this technical sense.

ἀπηρτημένος: at 1430b 8 means "irrelevant." No other such usage found, though Aristotle uses the verb in the sense of "detach."

ἀποδοκιμάζειν: "to reject," at 1438a 25 and 1446a 8, of an audience rejecting a speech. Cp. Demetrius 200.

ἀπολογητικός: 1421b 10, 1426b 23, *et seqq.* of rhetoric "of defence." A new technical term.

ἀπολογισμός: 1439b 14, 1444b 31. A new technical term which seems to mean an enumeration of the points in one's favour.

ἀποτρεπτικός: 1421b 9 *et passim*. A new term not used again till Lucian. The rhetoric "of dissuasion."

ἀστεῖος: used, as by Demetrius and Aristotle, of happy or felicitous expressions generally, for example 1434b 27, not, as later, of witticisms.

ἀστειολογία: a late word, apparently not used again till Marcus Aurelius.

βραχυλογεῖν: 1434b 10, 1441a 18. Obviously a late word, not used again till Plutarch, except by Demetrius.

γνωμολογικός: 1439a 5, a late word, not used again except in Demetrius.

διαλογισμός: 1433b 35. The word is used by Demosthenes of balancing accounts, but here it is a figure (σχῆμα) and seems to mean, in the recapitulation, the enumeration of points which tell against one's opponent, as opposed to ἀπολογισμός (above). So the verb διαλογίζομαι. Elsewhere (1439b 14) it seems to mean only enumeration.

δικαιολογία: used once by Demades. Otherwise late except here. It may mean justification, which is its proper meaning at 1438a 25, but at 1432b 34 it is contrasted with δημηγορία and refers simply to "a speech in court," an extension of meaning quite un-Classical.

δράματα: the best established reading at 1438b 15, where it is used as equivalent to πράγματα, a quite un-Classical usage.

ἐγκωμιαστικός: a late word, and used only here of a kind of rhetoric.

εἰρωνεία: correctly defined at 1434a 17 "saying something while pretending not to say it or calling things by the opposite name," but the first example is defined as προσποίησις παραλείψεως, and this figure is nowhere else called εἰρωνεία.

ἐλάττωσις: the word is Classical, but not in the sense of self-depreciation which it has at 1436b 34 and 1442a 17.

ἐνθύμημα: at 1430a 24 the word is defined as contradictions; it bears this sense nowhere else. Elsewhere, for example 1438b 35, it seems to have the Aristotelian meaning, and also at 1434a 36. The meaning contradiction is quite unique.

ἐνθυμηματιώδης: a late form, used here only, at 1439a 5.

ἐξεταστικός: 1421b 11 et passim. The word is Classical but is nowhere else used in the technical sense of rhetoric of investigation.

ἐπιβεβαίωσις: 1438b 29, clearly a late form, a technical term, "further confirmation."

ἐπιφέρειν: "to apply," "introduce," used as in Demetrius, for example 1423a 18, 1434b 24.

ἐπιχείρημα: at 1426b 37 seems to be used in the late sense of "argument."

ἐπάγγελσις: 1426b 27 = "statement." Apparently not used elsewhere.

ἑρμηνεία: At 1428a 10 it concludes a somewhat confused list which includes *prokatalêpsis, aitêma, palillogia* (*q.v.*) and also length of a speech, moderate length, and brachylogy. As there is no explanation, the meaning remains uncertain but it probably means style or language. Rackham's Loeb translation here has "interpretation."

At 1435a 3: ὅλως δὲ καλλίστην ποιήσεις τὴν ἑρμηνείαν probably means that you may make your "style" (or expression) as beautiful as possible —and the explanation follows after a discussion of τὸ εἰς δύο λέγειν which the author says must come first. He then (1435a 32) goes on to discuss style. (Here Rackham translates "statement.")

At 1436 we have a list somewhat similar to that at 1428a 10 referred to above which concludes with καὶ τῆς ἑρμηνείας τὴν σύνθεσιν (ἅπασαν ἴσμεν). This probably means that we know how to put our language together (i.e. word-arrangement or style generally), but not "the whole subject of composing a statement" as Rackham again translates.

The word ἑρμηνεία then seems to have the general meaning of language or style; λέξις as used by Aristotle could replace it in each case and make sense. It cannot mean σύνθεσις τῶν ὀνομάτων as Dahl (p. 79) says it does in the *Rhet. ad Alex.* See also ἑρμηνεία in Appendix I, A.

ἑρμηνεύειν: Seems used in a general sense also, as τὸ εἰς δύο ἑρμηνεύειν is equivalent to τὸ εἰς δύο λέγειν (1435a 5–7), a somewhat obscure figure which seems to exhaust the relations between two agents and two objects.

καθυποπτεύειν: τὰ καθυποπτευθέντα at 1426b 28 as "suspicions." Is called by Cope an "extraordinary word" (*Introd. to Aristotle's Rhet.* 409). The word is apparently found here only.

κακολογικός: vituperative, the opposite of ἐγκωμιαστικός, as at 1440b 5. Not found elsewhere.

κατηγορικός: The word is used for "affirmative" by Aristotle, but not in the sense found here (1421b 10, 1426b 2 ff., *et seqq.*) of "accusatory" rhetoric. A late usage.

μεταφέρειν: used at 1426a 24 as equivalent to ἐπιφέρειν!

νουνεχῶς: at 1436b 33, a late form.

ὁμοιότροπος: and the adverb ὁμοιοτρόπως are constantly used instead of ὅμοιος and ὁμοίως. This is contrary to Classical usage—1424a 10, 1423b 13 and 33, *et passim.*

παλιλλογία: together with παλιλλογεῖν, used in the sense of recapitulation, 1433b 29 *et passim.* This is contrary to Classical usage.

παράλειψις: used for a figure which mentions while pretending not to mention, 1438b 6. Also found in Demetrius 263.

παράληψις: The usual sense is "receiving," but θεία παράληψις is used to mean "invoking the gods," at 1432a 34.

ἐκ παρομοιώσεως: used in Aristotle for assonance in consecutive clauses. Here it simply means comparison (1430b 10). Not Classical.

πραγματολογεῖν: a late word. At 1438b 20 it seems to mean "making a factual statement."

πέρας: a strange and un-Classical usage at 1439a 34, in the expression τὴν προτροπὴν πέρατι ὅρισαι which seems to mean "to round off an exhortation," "bring it to an end."

προγυμνάσματα: definitely a late word for rhetorical exercises.

προεκτίθεναι: At 1436b 1: "to make a preliminary exposition," definitely a late word.

προκατάληψις: 1432b 11 ff. *et passim*, "to anticipate an opponent's arguments." Definitely a late word and defined as by Alexander in his περὶ σχημάτων.

πρόρρησις: post-Classical in the sense of preliminary statement at 1438b 24. Cp. Philodemus *Rhet.* 1.31 Sudhaus.

ἐν τῷ σπανίῳ: Late form of expression for σπανίως at 1429b 33.

συγκαταλέγειν: used only at 1434a 38, as a compound of λέγειν, simply meaning "to introduce."

συγκεχυμενῶς: a typical late adverb formed from participle; once used by Aristotle but not elsewhere in Classical texts.

συμπαραλαμβάνειν: a double compound used without special force, in the manner of later Greek, with the simple meaning of "to adopt," "bring in" at 1428a 37, *et seqq.*

συναπτός: used once by Aristophanes, *Eccl.* 508 of reins "drawn together." Used at 1438b 18 and 35 of things linked together into a series or connected whole, a technical meaning not found elsewhere.

σύνθεσις: used at 1434b 35 of the collocation of particular words. The three συνθέσεις: a word ending with a vowel followed by another beginning with one (i.e. hiatus or σύγκρουσις), similarly vowel and consonant, consonant and consonant. This restricted meaning is strange, while at 1435a 37 σύνθεσις seems to be used in the usual sense of "word-arrangement."

σχῆμα: definitely used for figure of speech at 1438b 6, 1444b 34, 1449b 14. This use is post-Classical.

σωματοειδής: The Classical meaning is "corporeal." At 1438b 25 it is used in the late meaning of "organic" (not found again till Polybius), while at 1442b 31 ἐφ' ἑαυτῶν σωματοειδεῖς means "as separate sections."

σωματοειδῶς: Not found in Classical texts, used at 1436a 30 as "organically."

ταπείνωσις: a new technical term, the opposite of αὔξησις, that is, "disparagement," 1425b 40, 1426a 13 and b 20, 1428a 15. Apparently only used here in this sense. Dionysius and Quintilian use it of a low style (cp. Aristotle's use of ταπεινός in *Rhet.* 3.2.1, 1404b 3), similarly ταπεινόω in 1426b 18, *et seqq.*

τεκμήριον: curiously restricted to negative proofs in 1430a 14. This meaning is not Classical, nor is it found elsewhere.

τρόπος: The three τρόποι ὀνομάτων almost "kinds of words," that is, simple, compound, and metaphorical, a curious use of the word.

ὑπερβατῶς: a late form which usually refers to hyperbaton, here used of inverted order of words or of content, 1438a 28 and 35.

ὑπερβιβάζειν: a late word used of transposing subject matter at 1435a 3.

ψεκτικός: a late word, here "vituperative" rhetoric, 1421b 10, 1425b 38, and so on.

This considerable number of suspicious words and expressions, if found in a work of unknown date, would almost certainly have been used as evidence of a "later" date.[6] As the *Rhetorica*, however, is definitely a fourth-century work, the above list should be kept in mind when we study the language of a work like Demetrius. Nor is our list complete. From Cope (409–412) we may add to it the use of ἰδέα for εἶδος, εἵνεκα for ἕνεκα, μήτε for οὔτε (twice at 1436b 19), ἀναλογητέον (the probable reading at 1443b 15), ὑπεναντίος for ἐναντίος at 1442a (three times) and an example of εἰ with the subjunctive.

[6]Indeed, F. Susemihl did so in his *Geschichte der griechischen Literatur in der Alexandrinerzeit* (Leipzig 1891–2) 2, 451–457.

INDEXES

ANCIENT NAMES